An introduction to
Television documentary
CONFRONTING REALITY

MANCHESTER
UNIVERSITY PRESS

Richard Kilborn and John Izod

An introduction to
television documentary
CONFRONTING REALITY

Manchester University Press

Manchester and New York

Distributed exclusively in the USA by St. Martin's Press

Copyright © Richard Kilborn and John Izod 1997

Published by Manchester University Press
Oxford Road, Manchester M13 9NR, UK
and Room 400, 175 Fifth Avenue, New York, NY 10010, USA

Distributed exclusively in the USA by
St. Martin's Press, Inc., 175 Fifth Avenue, New York,
NY 10010, USA

Distributed exclusively in Canada by
UBC Press, University of British Columbia, 6344 Memorial Road,
Vancouver, BC, Canada V6T 1Z2

British Library Cataloguing-in-Publication Data
A catalogue record for this book is available from the British Library

Library of Congress Cataloging-in-Publication Data
Kilborn, R. W.
    An introduction to television documentary : confronting reality / Richard Kilborn
and John Izod.
        p.   cm.
    Includes bibliographical references and index.
    ISBN 0-7190-4892-3 (cloth). — ISBN 0-7190-4893-1 (pbk.)
    1. Documentary television programs—Production and direction.
I. Izod, John, 1940– . II. Title.
PN1992.8.D6K55   1997
070.1'95—dc21   97-20312

ISBN   0 7190 4892 3 *hardback*
        0 7190 4893 1 *paperback*

First published 1997
01 00 99 98 97   10 9 8 7 6 5 4 3 2 1

Typeset by Special Edition Pre-press Services

Printed in Great Britain
by Bell and Bain Ltd, Glasgow

Contents

Acknowledgements   vii

Note on the availability of recordings   viii

Introduction   ix

Part I Documentary debates

1 *Mapping out the terrain*
  WHAT IS DOCUMENTARY?   3

2 *How real can you get?*
  REALISM AND DOCUMENTARY   27

Part II The documentary text

3 *Shaping the real*
  MODES OF DOCUMENTARY   57

4 *Tackling the text*
  DOCUMENTARY ANALYSES   88

Part III Fact, fiction and drama

5 *Telling a story*
  FACT, FICTION AND DOCUMENTARY   115

6 *Making a drama out of a crisis*
  THE DRAMA-DOCUMENTARY AND RELATED FORMS   135

Part IV Documentary production and reception

7 *'Just do it our way!'*
  INSTITUTIONAL CONTROL AND PRODUCTION ECONOMICS   165

8 *How do they do it?*
  ASPECTS OF DOCUMENTARY PRODUCTION   190

9 *Is there anyone out there?*
  AUDIENCES FOR DOCUMENTARY   215

Notes   241

Bibliography   247

Index   253

Acknowledgements

We would like to extend our thanks to all those who have helped and encouraged us in the writing of this book: to the documentary film and programme makers who patiently answered our requests for information, to those working for broadcasting organisations who agreed to be interviewed and to other academics working in the field of documentary. Our particular thanks go to: John Corner, Stuart Cosgrove, Roger Graef, Roger James, Ian McBride, Peter Moore, Stuart Prebble, John Triffitt and John Willis.

We are also grateful to our colleagues in the Department of Film and Media Studies at the University of Stirling for their support. A special thanks to Tim Thornicroft who read through early drafts of the book and provided valuable comments from the point of view of someone teaching documentary production. (Here we openly acknowledge that one of the best ways of learning about documentary is to be involved in the making of one!)

Finally, we would like to thank the several generations of media students at Stirling with whom we have indulged in lively discussion on documentary and its relationship to other forms of media output. It is to our students – past, present and future – that we dedicate this book.

Note on the availability of recordings

Of the documentaries referred to in this book, not all that many are currently available in the form of video cassettes or 16-mm prints for hire or for purchase. As broadcasters seek to maximise the commercial potential of their products, however, and the new 'retrieval' technologies continue to be developed, it is likely that students of documentary will be able to access more material than hitherto. For the time being, we recommend that readers check the availability of recordings with the following organisations or agencies:

- The British Film Institute (BFI) has a film and video library which hires out a range of film and television materials. The BFI also runs a viewing service whereby students and researchers may (for a small fee) view material held in the National Film and Television Archive. For details of both services contact: BFI, 21 Stephen St, London W1P 2LN. Tel. 0171 255 1444.

- Documentaries can also be accessed in one of thirty or more archives and film libraries in the UK. Details of these can be found in the *BFI Film and Television Handbook* published annually and available from the BFI at the address given above.

- The BBC now releases many of its programmes in the form of video cassettes for purchase. Documentaries currently available include *People's Century*. For more details contact: BBC Worldwide Publishing, Woodlands, 80 Wood Lane, London W12 0TT. Tel. 0181 576 2000.

- Channel 4 likewise has a sales department responsible for marketing some of the programmes it has screened. Details on titles are available from: Channel 4, 124 Horseferry Road, London SW1P 2TX. Tel. 0171 396 4444.

- Finally, a word about making off-air recordings for study or research purposes. British institutions with an Educational Recording Agency licence may record any broadcast programme, apart from Open University programmes, for later use for the educational purposes of that establishment. For more details contact: ERA, 74 New Oxford St, London WC1A 1EF. Tel. 0171 436 4883.

Introduction

If we measure the degree of interest in a subject by the number of books published in that area, the last decade of the twentieth century has certainly seen a resurgence of interest in documentary. A whole succession of book-length studies have appeared. Some of them offer major reassessments of the form and function of documentary (Nichols, 1991). Others combine a critical evaluation of the genre with perceptive critiques of how individual film makers have contributed to the documentary tradition (Winston, 1995; Corner, 1996). Others yet have attempted to approach matters from the documentarist's own point of view and have sought to throw detailed light on how films or programmes are actually produced (Rabiger, 1987; Rosenthal, 1990).

The present book combines certain features of all these approaches. Whilst we shall necessarily look back at some of the key moments in the history of the genre – to explain how documentary came to assume the forms that it did – we shall concentrate most of our attention on contemporary documentary practice. To a large extent this will entail giving an account of the ways in which documentary has had to adjust to the requirements of the television medium. Our main aim is, in short, to explore (in an accessible manner) some of the major issues relating to documentary in the 1990s.

Since television has had such a major influence on documentary developments in the second half of this century, we spend some time examining how television institutions determine the sort of documentaries that are produced. Among other things we shall look at the way documentaries are deployed in today's broadcasting schedules. A particular line of inquiry here will be to show the relationship between documentary and other forms of television programming. As a result of television's need to generate large and loyal audiences, we have witnessed a marked tendency in recent years to introduce a range of mixed-genre formats. This has involved combining elements of one genre with those of another in order to make what the broadcasters hope is an attractive new hybrid. There has, as one can imagine, been a lively debate as to whether these new hybrids can still be called 'documentary' (see Nichols, 1994). We take the view, however, that they contain a sufficient number of documentary elements to justify their inclusion in a book of this type.

As well as examining how documentaries are produced and the role they play in the contemporary broadcasting ecology, we shall consider the different ways in which they can be critically approached and assessed. Critics, understandably enough, have always been keen to divide documentary work up into different categories or sub-genres and to establish the characteristic features of these modes. What we attempt to do is to give a brief survey of the characteristics of each mode, while recognising that there is no such thing as a watertight category. Many documentaries, on closer inspection, turn out to display features that belong to more than one mode, as programme makers seek to shape their account according to the constraints of a tight budget, or to tell the story in the way that seems most appropriate to the chosen topic.

All in all, in this book our approach to the subject is slightly different from that of previous studies. It differs in two major respects. First, we have been concerned to show the full impact of television on documentary's development. Second, we have attempted to focus attention on the broadcaster–audience interface: how audiences make sense of the documentaries they watch, and how broadcasters conceive the audience for the various forms of documentary/factual entertainment they transmit.

The use of the term 'factual entertainment' gives us a clue to the pressures that today's documentarists confront when producing work for television. Gone are the days when documentaries could stake a claim to a place in the schedules on the strength of their worthy, public-service credentials. Nowadays they compete with all other forms of programming and are perceived by television executives as a vehicle for attracting a certain type of viewer at a particular time in the schedule. In the words of one broadcasting insider:

> It transpires that commercially driven schedules demand more documentaries, not fewer. They can be used to target strong drama

or entertainment on rival channels, attracting a complementary audience. They are used to net specific social groups for the advertisers. In a regulated industry they are necessary ballast in the freightage of any station which also needs to carry, for example, a quantity of cheap American imports, vulgar game shows or tabloid-style news. (Triffitt, 1996: 1)

Structure of the book

The book comprises nine chapters grouped into four major sections.

In the first part we attempt to map out the documentary terrain by exploring some of the issues which have always been at the centre of the documentary debate. In Chapter 1 we explore such issues as:

* What are the defining features of documentary and what are its principal forms and functions?
* What is the range of documentary and through what channels do documentaries reach their respective audiences?
* Which are the main institutional and historical contexts that have resulted in certain types of documentary activity (including national traditions)?
* What role has television played in shaping documentary to its own ends?

In Chapter 2 we deal with the important issue of 'documentary realism'. Among other things we shall be considering the claims made on documentary's behalf concerning its special relationship with the real world. We shall also explore the nature of the 'contract' between documentarist and audience with respect to the status of what is being shown (the promise of authenticity).

In the second part of the book we consider ways of approaching and understanding the text of documentaries. In Chapter 3 we examine the forms that documentaries take and how they address their audiences, and in Chapter 4 we offer critical readings of individual documentaries which represent each of the major modes.

In the third part we look at the extent to which fictional, narrative and dramatic techniques have been regularly employed in the documentary cause. Chapter 5 explores the use of standard story-telling devices by documentarists and reflects on the relationship between 'fact' and 'fiction' in documentary discourse. Chapter 6 takes a close look at forms of programming in which there has been a merging of documentary and dramatic components (most classically in those hybrid forms known as drama-documentaries).

The final chapters of the book (the fourth part) concentrate on issues surrounding production and reception. Chapter 7 focuses on the economics of production and the role that institutions have played in the shaping of documentary's history, particular attention being paid to the way in which documentarists have related to the broadcasters on whom they have become increasingly dependent for commissioning their work. With this in mind, we also examine recent developments in the European, and more particularly British, documentary to show what impact broadcasting deregulation and increasing commercialisation are having on work bearing the documentary label.

Chapter 8 shifts the focus from broadcaster to documentarist. One of our objectives in this chapter is to explore some of the key issues surrounding the production of documentary. The intention is to illuminate aspects of the production process from the early planning phase to final post-production. To these ends we make extensive use of comments by contemporary programme makers, who give their views on issues ranging from gaining access to people and places to such matters as the documentarist's moral responsibility to the individuals in whose lives he or she intervenes.

Finally, in Chapter 9 we consider documentary from the point of view of the audience. Here the focus of interest is twofold: in the first section – on relations between broadcaster and audience – we look at strategies which broadcasters have evolved to secure an audience for documentary programming (including the devising of appropriate promotional techniques); in the second half – on audience/ viewer response – we make some necessarily tentative remarks (the evidence is not plentiful) about how audiences respond to documentaries. This concludes with a brief section in which we consider the impact and effects that documentaries might have.

PART I

Documentary debates

1

Mapping out the terrain
WHAT IS DOCUMENTARY?

The nature of documentary

Having committed ourselves to writing a book about documentary, we decided to ask some of our students what they thought documentaries were, what they expected to gain from watching them and in what ways this category of programming differed from other types of television output. Here are some of their responses:

'I watch documentaries to widen my horizons. I feel I'm learning more about the world in which I live.'

'Documentaries are a welcome relief from the endless round of games and quiz shows which seem to dominate the schedules nowadays.'

'What I expect from a documentary is that it will tackle issues in much greater depth than a news or current affairs programme ever could.'

'Some of these programmes are really quite exciting. You can get very involved in the stories they tell.'

'Watching documentaries makes me want to go out and discover more about the issues raised. The programme itself often just scratches the surface.'

'In some of the programmes I feel I'm being led by the nose. To tell you the truth, in one recent documentary I wasn't even sure whether or not it was a spoof.'

'Too many of the documentaries I've watched recently have simply featured talking heads. I expect a little more visual information.'

All these responses pick up on one or more of the main features of documentary today and therefore provide a useful starting-point for an attempt to map out what we see as the principal contours of the documentary terrain. They clearly indicate that viewers approach documentary with different sets of expectations. They also show that audiences apply different frames of reference when assessing the gains or pleasures to be derived from watching documentaries.

Representing the world 'out there'
Whatever else viewers expect from a documentary, they consider that one of its most important tasks is to tell us something about the workings of the socio-historical world – the sights, sounds and events in the external world *before* they are transposed into a representational form. The task of the documentarist is not only to record reality but also to give the recorded material a form that allows the resultant film or programme to speak to its audience in a language that can be readily understood. In other words, the production of a documentary is not simply an act of chronicling; it is just as much an act of transformation. The documentarist collects, frames and edits the material in such a way as to change it from a mere record of actuality into a form which we can refer to as 'documentary discourse'.

But in spite of all the transformative work that has occurred, one should, as a viewer, always be able to discern a clear relationship between the sound and image representations which constitute the documentary and the sights and sounds of the real world 'out there'. Thus, for all the many attempts throughout the history of documentary to fake or reconstruct events, there remains an overriding expectation that the basic components will comprise those 'fragments of actuality' to which Vertov referred and which the film maker captures and moulds into the documentary artefact. It is this expectation which is the cornerstone of what is generally referred to as 'documentary realism' (see Chapter 2). It amounts to the existence of a kind of contractual agreement between film maker and audience whereby the raw material for the documentary will be gathered from the socio-historical world and the resultant product will therefore not emanate primarily from the creative imagination of an authoring agent (in spite of the claims of certain documentarists that they are just as much '*auteurs*' as some of their illustrious counterparts operating in fiction film). It is necessary to express this consideration, since – as we shall discover – there has always been a lively debate as to the fictional/factual status of documentaries. They are all, by definition, products of a shaping intelligence. Likewise, most, to a greater or lesser degree, make use of structuring devices that were developed in narrative fiction.

Interpreting the real

For some of the reasons outlined above, documentaries can never be any more than a representation or an interpretation of events and issues in the real world. In other words, for all their claims to present the world as it is and their attempts to engage the attention of their audiences by the force of their argument, documentaries can never attain the level of objectivity to which they sometimes aspire. Thus, whilst many viewers may be disposed to believe in the general truthfulness of the account (especially when it has the mark of some institutional authority), they are aware that the account offered is one that is seen from a particular perspective. Documentaries can sometimes be powerfully persuasive; on the other hand, they will hardly ever be the last word on an issue. In the words of one of our students: 'Watching documentaries makes me want to go out and discover more about the issues raised'.

The very fact that documentarists have always, of necessity, employed certain structuring devices in their work has also meant that they have inevitably become involved in acts of interpretation, however much they may sometimes wish to deny it. We shall be examining some of these interpretive strategies later in the book, but for the time being would ask readers to consider the use of one such device. We refer to what is commonly called the 'problem–solution structure'. This involves the organisation of the documentary presentation in such a way that a problem is first identified and its ramifications worked through (usually after a number of witnesses have been called to account) before a solution is finally offered. Although this narrative structure appears to have various 'common-sensical' attractions, one can easily see how the constant application of such an organising principle will frame the issue under discussion in a particularly powerful way. Audiences may, for instance, become predisposed to accept the solution being offered in the documentary's concluding section and not accept possible alternatives. They may also get used to the value set which suggests that where a problem is identified a solution will also be forthcoming (see Nichols, 1991: 18–19).

The function of documentary

In addition to addressing some aspect of the contemporary or historical world, documentarists are also perceived to be presenting an argument or making a case. Documentary film makers are not simply in the business of recording reality but will often be encouraging us, in some measure, to view these events from a particular perspective. In other words, evidence will tend to be presented in such a way as to increase the likelihood of the audience falling in line with the film maker's argument.[1]

In determining the uses to which documentary can properly be put, a great deal will hinge on the institutional or broadcasting context in which the film or programme in question is being produced. Whatever the context, however, there has frequently been some expectation that documentary should operate in some measure as a vehicle of cultural or educational enlightenment. Some documentarists – especially those working in film as opposed to television – have always been at pains to stress the social function of documentary. As one commentator has observed: 'The key function of documentary, as I see it, is to explore the hard, awkward questions more deeply and more critically than other branches of the media do (or can)' (Rosenthal, 1988: 6). The issue of documentary's relationship to the wider society or to public culture is one that continues to be the subject of lively debate. It has its roots in the sense of social and political responsibility that individual documentarists have towards the society in which they are operating. Thus for John Grierson – for many the founding father of the documentary movement – the primary function of documentary was to allow the citizen to become meaningfully involved in the general social process (Grierson, 1966: 141–55). Similarly, Michael Grigsby, one of the leading British documentarists of this generation, expresses the hope that his films will heighten viewers' social and political awareness:

> I feel that, particularly now, society and people are very fragmented, very isolated, and have in many cases no means of being heard or of expressing themselves about their everyday life or their emotional situation ... I think it is incumbent on us as broadcasters, film-makers, whatever we are, to be looking at our society and trying to find those resonances, trying to hear those voices, to give people space. (Grigsby, 1995: 8–9)

A serious pursuit?

Another expectation that one of our students had of documentaries was that they should provide a different stimulus from the 'endless round of game and quiz shows'. Documentaries have indeed often been regarded as a form of antidote to the more entertainment-orientated part of the television schedule. They may make greater demands on concentration, but they have traditionally been seen as a type of programming which is on a par with the various forms of broadcast journalism. In the eyes of television viewers, therefore, documentaries are defined as much according to their relationship with other forms of television output as by being measured against the notional template 'documentary'.[2]

In spite of more recent developments in which film makers have been required to produce work that is more accessible to the television audience, documentary has not entirely cast off its reputation of being a serious, worthy, but ultimately rather boring form of programming. As we shall see in a later chapter, this has led to the more traditional forms of documentary not being given a high priority in today's television schedules.[3]

We shall be looking in more detail at the formative influence of television on documentary in the course of this book. For the time being, however, suffice it to say that: first, the history of documentary, at least since the late 1940s, is very closely associated with the development of television – and nowhere more so than since the late 1980s; second, some of the most interesting developments in the *form* of documentaries have been directly attributable to television's constant generation of new types of programming in the relentless quest to maintain or increase audience share. One of the clearest illustrations of this is a marked tendency to produce hybridised forms, in which generic boundaries have been blurred in the effort to create an attractive new format (see Chapters 3 and 6).

Documentary in different media formats

Dictionary definitions of documentary tend to highlight the idea of any account, presentation or performance that mobilises visual or verbal evidence in chronicling an event or mounting an argument. These presentations can of course utilise different forms of media, including: the written chronicle or report; stage, screen and radio productions; oral history recordings; photographic displays; and CD-ROMs or similar multimedia modes. Although most people nowadays who hear or use the word 'documentary' have televisual or filmic artefacts in mind, it is important to remember that these other forms exist (Paget, 1990: 1–58). It is, moreover, sometimes quite instructive to consider the respective gains and losses which occur when broadly the same subject matter is treated in different media formats.

Consider, for instance, the response of the student who was irritated that the documentaries he had watched contained too many talking-heads. What he might have been criticising here was a failure on the documentarist's part to introduce enough visually arresting or illustrative material. He may also, by implication, have been suggesting that the topic could have been better exploited in a different medium. With the documentary in question, for instance, it might have been the case that a radio documentary could have done better justice to what the documentarist was actually trying to achieve. Radio is a medium that is mercifully free from any requirement to provide visuals (other than those generated in the listener's imagination). It also enables an intimate bond to be established between listener and the speaking voice and permits the former to focus in on what is being said without any visual interference. In other words, for certain documentary projects, radio may well be regarded as the more appropriate vehicle, particularly where individuals are recalling events of which there is no photographic or film record.

A fictional enterprise?

If we agree with the student who thought that you could really get involved in, or even carried away, by the stories which documentaries tell, does not this suggest that they should be approached like any other form of story-telling? The more one reflects on how documentaries are put together, the more one recognises that – time and time again – documentarists have resorted to what appear to be standard fictional techniques, both to give coherence to the story they are telling and to ensure that audiences are able to relate to the events being played out before them. Accordingly, many documentaries bear all the hallmarks of a gripping story or a well-wrought drama. Individual 'characters' assume the conventional roles of hero, villain and victim and are played off one against the other in ways with which we are all familiar from television drama or film. Plot is used as a device for creating interest and suspense. Events are recounted in such a way as to create the impression that all hinges on the resolution of a conflict between opposed forces or warring factions.

In many cases there are legitimate reasons for structuring documentaries in this way. The problems for documentary arise, however, when the narrative impulse becomes such a powerful force in the structuring of the film or programme that it virtually assumes a life of its own. The precise relationship between the world conjured up by the story and the world of historical or contemporary reality becomes blurred. The viewer is borne along on the tide of the narrative and, at the same time, is constantly reminded that what is actually at stake are 'real life' or 'real world' issues which may require a different form of attention from the kind that is usually reserved for the consumption of fictions. We shall be returning to the question of documentarists' use of fictional strategies in Chapter 5 but should like now, as a final point in this introductory section, to broach the issue of viewer response.

Making sense of documentary

One of the questions which critics and documentarists alike have found most difficult to answer is of what interpretative frameworks viewers apply when they watch programmes that bear the 'documentary' label. To what extent, for instance, can the response of the student who said he watched documentaries to 'widen his horizons' be considered representative of the generality of viewers? And equally important, what credence do audiences put upon documentary accounts? Do they still treat them as if they offered the proverbial 'window on the world' or have they now learned to adopt a more sceptical outlook?

For years the conventional wisdom about documentaries was that they commanded the critical attention of the audience because they were seen to tackle important issues in a serious and responsible way. Audiences also had confidence in the veracity of what was shown. It seemed to be demonstrably the case that evidence from 'real world' sources was being collected and presented in such a way as to preserve elements of its authenticity. In other words, the basic relationship of the material to the real world still shone through. (For more on this see Chapter 2.)

Since the 1960s or 1970s, however, the perception of how viewers relate to cultural artefacts, of whatever kind, has shifted. In an age dominated by what is sometimes referred to as the 'postmodernist condition', many of the old certainties have faded. We have become used to living in an information-rich environment, in which multiple media outlets compete for our attention and where computerised, digital technologies offer us an ever greater choice of what we consume (see Lyotard, 1984). Although opinions differ as to the extent to which the postmodernist condition has caused us to jettison some of the older ways of seeing the world, it is generally thought to have had an effect on how, in particular, we engage with material we choose to view or otherwise consume. This is partly due to the fact that the sheer abundance of available material makes us view it in far more relative terms. It also has to do with the greater knowledge that modern audiences have acquired about how programmes are put together – knowledge which has led to a generally more sceptical attitude amongst viewers. This has meant that audiences nowadays will be more inclined than formerly to engage with programmes in a playful and sometimes detached manner, delighting in the *experience* of watching rather than being too concerned with 'what it all means'.

All this has implications for televised documentary. Postmodernist thinking invites us progressively to abandon the belief that there can be any such thing as 'referential truth'. As one observer has commented, 'Postmodernist analysis delights ... in the emancipation of meanings from their bondage to mere lumpenreality' (O'Sullivan *et al.*, 1994b: 234). Documentary, on the other hand, has always (almost as one of its first principles) claimed an especially close relationship with what we have described as the 'socio-historical world'. Anything which might be seen to render this relationship more insecure – in this case postmodernism's 'anarchic' aspirations – might be seen as having a negative impact on the referential claims that have been made hitherto on documentary's behalf. (One can see a possible link here between the remarks above and the disconcertment of our student who was not at all certain whether one particular programme was authentic or just an elaborate tease.)

The status that documentaries enjoy with their viewers has been further complicated in recent years by developments that are more technological than cultural in origin. We refer to the rapid advances in digital technology that have made it possible to manipulate, transform and distort any recorded image in such a way as to make a nonsense of the notion of there being any firm indexical bond between signifier and signified. Some critics have seen these developments as altering (potentially at least) the whole manner in which viewers relate to documentaries (Winston, 1995: 259). No longer can the evidentiary aspects of the image be taken on trust. No longer do we have any guarantee that what is projected in a single image has been captured in one location at a specific moment in time. Digital techniques can now integrate elements from many different sources or introduce computer-generated images into scenes produced using more traditional modes of filming. Although these techniques have so far not been used to any great extent in documentary work, it is clearly only a matter of time before they are.[4]

Towards a definition of documentary

Having introduced some of the issues which have always been prominent in debates on documentary's form and function, we would like in the following section to explore in a little more detail the ways in which the term 'documentary' has been understood and how, in the course of time, it has acquired a wider range of associations.

The creative treatment of actuality

The term 'documentary' was apparently first coined in 1926 by the man usually considered to be one of the founding fathers of documentary, John Grierson. He used it when reviewing the film *Moana* made by the American film maker Robert Flaherty. ('Of course, *Moana*, being a visual account of events in the daily life of a Polynesian youth and his family, has documentary value', cited in Rosenthal, 1988: 21.) Although Grierson's roles as a documentarist in his own right and as a publicist concerned to promote the 'cause' of documentary have been the subject of critical review (see especially Winston, 1995), there can be no questioning the significant role he played both in terms not only of the interest he stimulated in defining and developing the fledgling form but also of the impetus he gave to other film makers to produce work which had a clearly defined social purpose (see Corner, 1996: 11–16).

Grierson's much-quoted definition of documentary – that it is 'the creative treatment of actuality' (Grierson, 1966: 13) – also provides a useful starting-point for discussing documentary artefacts. In particular, it highlights the process by which a documentarist welds various components (words, music, images and sound effects) into an artefact that can have both functional and aesthetic appeal. And although Grierson probably did not recognise it at the time, the definition also usefully points up one of the more problematical aspects of documentary. As we already identified in our preliminary discussion, there are two counterpoised tendencies in documentary: with one (the actuality component) the documentarist is claiming our attention on the strength of her or his ability to reproduce or represent events which have occurred in the external world; with the other (the creative component) a whole series of structuring and narrativising ploys have been brought to bear in order to heighten the impact of the film or programme on an audience. It is this relationship between the selection and filming/recording of actuality material and its transformation into a skilfully crafted artefact that lies at the heart of the whole documentary enterprise.

Problems of definition

Documentary – like any mode or genre of film making – has gone through a major developmental process since Grierson's pioneering days. Some of these developments have resulted, not surprisingly, in a significant increase in the number of characteristics which have been attributed to the 'documentary' artefact. As is so often the case in such matters, views on specific defining characteristics differ according to who is doing the defining. Producers of documentary will tend to take their cue from the broadcasting institutions who commission their work. Critics and reviewers on the other hand will be inclined to measure 'documentariness' in terms of a set of values and properties derived from a large body of (allegedly) documentary material, produced over several decades. And finally – as we have seen from the comments of our students – viewers themselves will have their own ideas on what documentaries should deliver. In the case of television viewers, for instance, the defining qualities of documentary are likely to be determined by being measured against other types of broadcast output (news and current affairs programming) or set in contrast to the 'endless round of games and quiz shows which seem to dominate the schedules nowadays'.

Some of these definitional problems have to do with the fact that the label 'documentary' is now attached to a much wider range of audio-visual material than when it began to be used in the pre-war era. 'Documentary' can nowadays just as easily be applied to a thirty-minute piece of investigative reportage on television as it can to a full-length feature film such as *Hoop Dreams* (USA, 1994), which had a theatrical release and employs the full resources of cinematic language. 'Documentary' has in short become a *portmanteau* word with multiple points of reference.

Something of term's multiplicity is reflected in the differential usage of the documentary label in contemporary broadcasting.

First, the most common use is as a noun referring to a specific film or programme: 'Last night's Channel 4 documentary brought a harrowing account of human rights' violations in East Timor.' Second, in addition to this very specific usage, however, there is a marked tendency to apply 'documentary' in a far looser sense to suggest a style or mode of film making that accords with certain conventions on how information and evidence are gathered and incorporated into a programme. When used in this way, the emphasis is on the distinction between fiction and non-fiction film making: 'The films in this series are clearly the products of a very fertile imagination. At the same time they frequently veer in the direction of documentary.' Finally – and possibly most tellingly – 'documentary' is being increasingly used in a purely adjectival sense: 'The film used some very innovative documentary techniques' or 'This was a well-researched documentary investigation'. Here the reference is either to a general tenor of factuality which pervades the piece in question or to the adoption of a certain style or approach. 'Documentary', when used adjectivally, can also carry with it a further set of associations: that the programme or film is serious and sober and, as such, is deserving of due audience attention!

In all the attempts to map out the documentary terrain one of the favoured strategies has been to operate with the notion of exclusion zones. The particular concern here has been to mark documentary off from all forms of fiction film-making activity. Some observers see the matter in relatively black-and-white terms. For them the principal task of documentary is to produce a suitably authenticated account of a real-life event. This is in stark contrast to what they see as the main defining feature of fiction film (in all its many guises): that it deploys a variety of narrative and presentational techniques in the telling of a story that has been made up for the specific purpose of providing dramatic entertainment. For all these reasons – so the argument goes – documentaries can be conveniently labelled as 'non-fiction'. As such, they are – so the argument concludes – definable in terms of their oppositional or complementary status *vis-à-vis* the fiction film. The attempt to pigeon-hole documentary in this way may have its superficial attractions in that it appears to establish a neat, satisfactory division. As a critical project, however, it is fundamentally flawed. It suggests a distinction in form and function between the two categories, which proves in the event to be untenable. To give only one example, many fiction films make the claim that they are chronicling important realities of the human condition, whilst others are explicitly based on historically documented events. By the same token, documentary films frequently make use of a variety of fictional and dramatic techniques. Certain well-known documentarists (Paul Watson is an example) have sometimes claimed that *all* documentaries are to some extent fictional constructs.

Documentary as a genre?
The difficulties in reaching a consensus over documentary's defining characteristics are mirrored in a similar disagreement over how to categorise it using the standard critical terms. There is, for instance, no generally accepted view as to whether 'documentary' refers to a genre, a style, a type of artefact or just a particular mode of film making. Some critics (Britton, 1992: 26) happily employ the designation 'genre', whilst others feel that using it is potentially misleading. As Dai Vaughan has shrewdly observed:

> If it has proved notoriously difficult to define documentary by reference to its constantly shifting stylistic practices, it is because the term 'documentary' properly describes not a style or a method or a genre of film-making but a mode of response to film material ... The documentary response is one in which the image is perceived as signifying what it appears to record; a documentary film is one which seeks, by whatever means, to elicit this response; and the documentary movement is the history of the strategies which have been adopted to this end. (Cited in Crawford and Turton, 1992: 101)

The point that Vaughan is making here – and it is a view we share – is that it will always be difficult to gain a wide measure of agreement as to what are the particular generic features of documentary. It is true that viewers of factually based programming may have certain general expectations of those works which are promoted as documentaries (Nichols, 1991: 18–23), but uncertainty still remains concerning the *criteria* that should be applied in determining which works to include or exclude. Should the touchstone be the aims or purposes of the programme makers in producing their accounts? Should it be certain intrinsic features of the works themselves – in particular, all that appears to link the account rendered with the world 'out there'? Or should one allow the audience itself to be the final arbiter in deciding where to draw the line, especially since – as our student responses show – viewers have a clear notion in their minds about what constitutes a documentary? (See also Winston in Rosenthal, 1988: 21–33.)

Critics have sought to extricate themselves from this termino-logical dilemma by breaking down the wide range of 'documentary' material into more convenient sub-genres. Thus, whilst the term 'documentary' has not outlived its usefulness as indicating certain general qualities or viewer expectations, we have in the last two or three decades witnessed the introduction of a set of new terms to distinguish between different types of work. These terms (e.g. natural history documentary, fly-on-the-wall documentary) have had the effect of establishing new, more particularised sub-genres, even though – it has to be said – some of these are still notoriously imprecise.

National and historical contexts

Views differ as to how far back one has to go to discover the roots of documentary, but by common consent the major impetus came in the 1920s when groups of film makers – in Britain, Germany, the Soviet Union and the USA – began to produce ideas and develop practices which in retrospect can be seen to have contributed signi-ficantly to the documentary tradition. (For a good overview see Barnouw, 1974, and Jacobs, 1979.) It is important to recognise the contribution of these early pioneers. First and foremost, they pro-moted a lively debate on the nature and function of documentary expression: what it might achieve and what means it could employ to pursue those ends.

When one reviews the contributions of the documentary pioneers, one is always struck by the way in which, for all the shortcomings of the technology available at that time, their work highlights some of the central issues which have continued to dominate documentary discourse and practice. The work of Robert Flaherty (still best remembered for his *Nanook of the North* (1922)) raises a whole series of questions about restaging events for the camera. Dziga Vertov's work on the other hand (especially his *The Man with the Movie Camera* (1929)), focuses attention on the purposes for which documentary film can be employed and what steps can be taken to encourage critical reflection on the part of the audience. By contrast, the work of the German film maker Walther Ruttman, especially his *Berlin: Symphony of a City* (1927), shows what poetic and aesthetic effects can be elicited by the careful structuring of actuality sequences, thus laying the foundations for what has come to be known as the poetic documentary (see Chapter 3). And last but not least, Grierson's own documentary *œuvre* (together with his many *ex cathedra* pronouncements) highlights the potential uses of film documentary for social comment.

Although documentary is highly indebted to the generation of film makers who began working in the 1920s, its origins can be traced to a still earlier period. In one respect, of course, they lie in what we might call the documentary impulse: humankind's deeply ingrained desire to keep a record of transactions and events that are considered in some way significant. The resulting documentation – in whatever form it is set down – provides a testimony to the event's occurrence. (Here again one needs to emphasise that every document has to be treated with some of the same qualifications as the documentary itself. All documents are produced at some individual's or some institution's behest and this must be taken into account when assessing any 'truth value' they may contain.)

The manner in which any act of documenting has been undertaken has also always depended on available technologies. Until the invention of photography humankind's capacity for chronicling events had been limited to verbal or written accounts and to various forms of pictorial representation. With the coming of photography the process by which scenes from the actual world could be captured on light-sensitive film opened up new possibilities for accurately documenting the real. Photography was immediately heralded as a medium which could achieve hitherto unprecedented authenticity in the reproduction of scenes from everyday life. Although initially regarded as a largely mechanical operation, photography soon began to be recognised, however, as a much less neutral medium than many had so fondly imagined. (Here we uncover the seeds of what has subsequently become one of the main topics in the documentary debate: on the one hand the claim that what we are witnessing is a faithful portrait of the real, on the other the equally compelling recognition that to obtain these pictures the film maker had to intervene and that particular viewer positions were constructed from which this 'witnessing' could take place.)

Nineteenth-century developments in photography paved the way for the introduction of moving-image technologies later in the century. And just as it was possible to discern a strong documentary element in photography, so too the same impulse is evident in early cinema. The early, short films of the Lumière brothers, for instance, which delighted French audiences in the 1890s, again home in on scenes from everyday life (Roud, 1980: 394–7, Barnouw, 1974: 3–24). For the crowds who flocked to see them, one of the attractions of these actuality entertainments was that they could recognise so much of themselves, or others like them, in these brief snippets of reality. Coupled with this was the pleasure of what we might term 'surrogate observation' – the experience of being cast in the role of witness to a series of real-life events. Audiences knew that these events were historical, but the recordings carried with them a freshness and vitality so as to make it appear that everything was being played out in the here and now.

Many of these early essays in film making, as well as simply recording everyday incidents, concentrated on capturing the humorous and whimsical aspects of life, frequently with a view to maximising the commercial potential of the product. (This is, incidentally, something one encounters to an increasing extent in contemporary documentary!) Gradually, however, during the first two decades of the twentieth century film makers began to broaden the range of their film-making activities. Recordings were made of public or national events in which public interest could be expected or presupposed. Film makers journeyed to distant lands to produce the first travelogues or ethnographic accounts. Educationally enlightening films describing simple scientific processes began to be made. In other words, even though film makers were still severely limited by the nature of the equipment then available, the embryonic possibilities of documentary were already being actively explored. Formats and approaches which were to prove to be mainstays in the later history of documentary were already being tried out long before the 'movement' itself actually got under way (see Barnouw, 1974: 29–30).

From the 1920s onwards, as we have seen, documentary or non-fiction film began to achieve much greater recognition. And just as with any other cultural artefact, its development was determined in no small measure by the socio-cultural and political environments in which individual directors and film-making groups operated. We shall be exploring this topic in more detail in Chapter 7, but should like to illustrate the point here by briefly comparing the work of two of the best-known pioneers, John Grierson and Dziga Vertov. Grierson's strongly held belief was that documentary could be used as an effective tool in the task of providing cultural or educational enlightenment (Grierson, 1966: 141–55). At the same time, the funding for the work which he and other members of the British documentary movement produced came principally from state and/or industrial sponsorship. Opinions differ on the extent to which these agents actually exercised a controlling influence on the work produced, but recent evidence suggests that the leverage effected was greater than Grierson himself was wont to admit. Similarly, Dziga Vertov's views on what documentary could achieve are closely connected with, and determined by, the ideas which underpinned the Soviet system in which he lived and worked. For instance, in his critical essays he is concerned to emphasise how (documentary) film can be used as an instrument of consciousness-raising and as an aid to critical reflections about society. At the same time, for all his bold innovations (see in particular his *The Man with the Movie Camera* (1929)), much of his other work remains beholden to a political system which required of Soviet artists that they fall in line with the doctrine of Socialist Realism (the requirement that art-work should provide invigorating accounts of Soviet actuality).

The role of television

Few would question the significant, some would say life-saving, role that television has played in the continuing development of documentary. In the second half of the twentieth century television has been the single most important formative influence in determining the types of documentary that are produced and the forms in which they appear. Moreover, just as tracing the development of film documentaries through the early decades of the century throws some revealing light on the growth of cinema as a mass medium, so a close study of television documentary provides some fascinating insights into the workings of television (both with respect to its institutional practices and to its role within the wider society). The kinds of issue we shall be considering in the course of our inquiry are:
(1) How the institutional constraints under which television operates impact on the documentary material commissioned or acquired for transmission (including decisions on what programmes will not be shown)
(2) How commissioned material is required to adhere to certain preferred house-styles or to slot into established programme formats
(3) How certain steps are normally taken to ensure that material is accessible to a large mass audience.

In assessing the various ways in which documentary has been shaped by television we should make clear at the outset that for some commentators television is considered to have been a particularly malign force (see Rosenthal, 1988: 215, Loizos, 1993: 115–16). How legitimate are these charges and, in particular, what evidence is there for suggesting that television has stymied some of documentary's more interesting developmental possibilities?

Certainly it cannot be denied that television has used documentary for its own ends. Film makers and programme producers have always been expected to format their work in such a way that it falls in line with standardised broadcasting requirements. Likewise, in recent times the growing forces of commercialism in broadcasting have led to an increase in the number of dramatically enhanced modes of presentation. And it is equally true that, in whatever broadcasting system they are working, programme makers have been well aware that what they might wish to articulate (especially with regard to the expression of political views) is conditioned by certain set limits. Nevertheless, and in spite of all this, television has continued to provide important opportunities for documentary film makers.[5] It has, for instance, been instrumental in encouraging the development of interesting new formats. Some, such as the innovative *Video Diaries* format (about which more in Chapters 3 and 4), have grown out of earlier access programme initiatives whereby 'ordinary' viewers are given the chance to contribute their own programmes with the minimum of institutional or editorial control. Others, such as the popular though often controversial drama-documentary form, have resulted from the amalgamation of what were once considered two distinct programming categories into a single hybridised form (see Chapter 6).

As already suggested, the development of television documentary is very closely connected with the more general history of the medium. Where television has been dominated by a small number of terrestrial public-service channels operating in tightly regulated conditions, documentaries have often been deployed as a means of reinforcing the public-service credentials of the channel. They have been regarded as a highly appropriate vehicle for underlining that channel's commitment to a form of programming that has a high informational and educative value. Documentaries have been included in the schedule because they have been felt to encourage a thoughtful, reflective response and to act, in some measure, as an antidote to the large swathes of entertainment programming that make little or no demand on the audience's intelligence. As television has increasingly been subject to forces of commercialism, however, factual broadcasting in general and documentary in particular have had to adjust to the demands of a rapidly changing medium. In the eyes of more pessimistically inclined critics, this (as far as documentary is concerned) has turned out to be not so much an adjustment as a fatal downward spiral.

The result has been that, for some commentators at least, the question now is how much longer documentary can survive in an increasingly hostile environment. Our own view is that these gloomy prophecies of documentary's imminent demise are altogether too doom-laden, and we hope to illustrate that there are many signs of vigorous life. Certainly, from the perspective of the late 1990s, all the evidence points to a state of affairs where documentaries are more than holding their own against the 'challenge' of other types of programming. As one BBC editor, writing in March 1996, has commented:

> Faced with the question in 1991 or 1992 [as to how documentaries would fare in the coming years] many British documentarists would have predicted a bleak future. Refranchising ITV and allowing Channel 4 to raise its own advertising revenue were bound to create a much more competitive broadcasting world. And traditionally it was sport, feature films, drama and light entertainment which were the winners in a ratings game. Documentaries were an ornament on the mantelpiece of broadcasting and the first to go ... The reality could not have turned out more different. There has been an out-pouring of documentaries on all the terrestrial channels and a flood of new factual material on the satellites and cable. Up till now, at least, the quality has been high – better perhaps than at any time in the past. (Triffitt, 1996: 1)

We shall be looking more closely at how documentaries are fashioned to maximise audience appeal in Chapter 9. For the moment, however, we should just like to note that the rapid changes that have transformed the television landscape in the 1990s have caused television executives and producers to radically rethink how documentaries could be deployed in the programme schedule. Moreover, in contrast to the earlier broadcasting age, which was primarily determined by public-service concerns, today's broad-casters are more interested in what contribution documentaries can make to the overall identity of a channel or how they can be used instrumentally to compete with the programming put out by a rival channel.[6]

It would, however, be wrong to assume that we are necessarily entering a new golden age of documentary. Documentarists them-selves take the view that they are now required to work under much tighter constraints than they ever did previously: to stand any chance of being broadcast the material has to fall in line with each channel's standard documentary formats. For many documentarists the requirement that all their work be tailored in this way is regarded as a major constraint on their artistic freedom. Certainly, in the case of the documentary series, these straitjacketing pressures do sometimes result in individual programmes having to display a uniformity of style which may not always be appropriate to the subject matter. On the other hand, the knowledge on the part of the documentarists that their work is going to have to conform to a range of standardised criteria can sometimes prove to have a beneficial disciplinary effect; it does not necessarily result in the sort of compromises into which some documentarists feel they are being forced (see Rosenthal, 1988: 38–9, 204).

Apart from the constraints imposed by broadcasters' stranding and branding policies, one also has to recognise that nowadays most documentarists operate under very different working conditions from those of their colleagues in an earlier generation. The bureaucratic and institutional structures of television have always meant that documentarists working for this medium are subject to tighter control and regulation than those working in film units whose products were destined for cinematic exhibition.[7] But as television has moved into a progressively more deregulated age, so the conditions under which documentarists operate have also changed (in Britain and elsewhere in Europe). Far fewer documentaries are now made 'in house' by specialist documentary units, and an increasing number are produced by independent companies working on a single-commission basis. Whilst these companies may be spared some of the bureaucratic excesses associated with being employed by a large organisation, the conditions under which they now work have introduced a new set of constraints.

Modes of address: filmic and televisual

If television as an institution has had a shaping influence on what types of documentary are made, it has also had a marked impact on documentary's functions and characteristic modes of address. In the pre-television era documentaries were mostly screened in cinemas as part of an evening programme of entertainment which would typically include an introductory newsreel and/or a documentary, followed after a short interval for refreshments by the screening of a full-length feature film (never, for fairly obvious reasons, in the reverse order!). Knowing that these would be the circumstances in which many viewers would consume their films, documentarists adopted what they saw as an appropriate mode of address. They recognised, for instance, that the majority of viewers went to the movies primarily for diversion and entertainment. Therefore, if documentaries were to stand any chance of being even halfway positively received, their makers would have to adopt at least some of the dramatising strategies employed by fiction film makers of the day.[8]

When television was in its infancy, there was an initial tendency to assume that broadcast documentary would, broadly speaking, follow in the footsteps of the film pioneers. In Britain, for instance, there was a belief that television documentary could continue the task of cultural and social enlightenment to which Grierson and his co-workers had committed themselves some two decades previously (Scannell, 1979: 106, Bell, 1986: 65–80).

Gradually, however, as the new medium developed its own preferred formats, small-screen documentary began to be pulled away from its cinematic origins and be influenced more and more by specifically televisual modes. Although it still had many points in common with cinema, television acquired a different set of priorities. In particular, it was committed to a more diverse range of programming. Documentary therefore found itself in the position of having to adapt to the new styles and modes of address, as well as having to adjust to a stricter regulatory regime. In other words, some film makers felt that in order to gain entry to the television market they could not afford to be too politically outspoken or to produce work which might be considered otherwise too challenging for television's mass audience.[9]

As documentaries gradually became a regular feature of television's bill of fare, not surprisingly, they acquired some of the features of other programming modes. News and current affairs were one area of broadcasting that had much in common with documentary, and, institutionally, there were many opportunities for fruitful interchange (even though in most cases each 'sector' jealously guarded its rights to a degree of departmental independence). Here lie the seeds for what has become a sub-genre of documentary, the 'extended reportage' (Corner, 1996: 2). The tendency to blur the boundaries between a 'purer' type of documentary (one closer to its cinematic origins) and other broadcast forms has continued to the present day.

When we compare the different modes of address of television and cinema we should always be aware that they are at heart different signifying systems and that each addresses its respective audience in quite distinct ways. This is nowhere better illustrated than in a comparison of the 'conditions of reception' of the two media. With cinema the combination of high-definition image, large screen and darkened auditorium has always been thought to promote a more concentrated viewing experience. The cinema audience is arguably more committed in the sense that cinema-goers have purchased a ticket or built the visit into their social schedule. With television, on the other hand, the conditions of reception are quite different. Viewing usually takes place in the domestic environment and is consequently open to many more distractions (see Ellis, 1982). Broadcasters will therefore, so it is claimed, always have to work that much harder to retain the attention of viewers.[10] They have accordingly had to devise a whole series of strategies, some of which we will be considering in more detail in the final chapter.

For all these reasons, those involved in producing documentaries for television have had to become proficient at playing according to the medium's rules. Producers have by and large learned how to produce work that is not heavily dependent on the stylistic effects that can be achieved through a large- or wide-screen format or through superior sound reproduction (see Jacobs, 1979: 455). By the same token, they have also learned how to harness the new technologies (especially lightweight cameras and digital editing machines) to produce strikingly innovative work, some of which has taken documentary in exciting new directions.

There are also signs that some of the documentary die-hards are beginning to shed their old prejudices about the status of television documentary. In the early days of television there were often considerable friction between those who were committed to the new medium and those who had learned their trade as film makers.

Many belonging to the former camp were made to feel that they were betraying the cause of 'classic' documentary. It was certainly the case that the primary historical values of documentary were determined by cinema. It is just as true, however, that television has played a major role in revitalising the genre and in challenging some of the old orthodoxies.

Thus, in the final years of this century the prospects for documentary, including the many mutants which television has spawned, look relatively bright. The digital revolution – whether in the form of the various aids it brings to documentary production or in the way it is opening up new transmission opportunities – will certainly be a major force in determining the future of documentary. Not only will the production of documentaries become much cheaper than hitherto, but the proliferation of channels and other media outlets will lead to new possibilities for marketing and consumption.

On the other hand, one cannot afford to be too sanguine about documentary's prospects in today's rapidly developing media environment. For all its proven ability to adapt to changing circumstances, the chill winds of commercialism which blow through today's television institutions do not always make for a particularly conducive environment for documentary. For this reason we may well see more and more documentarists turning to those alternative modes of delivery (CD-ROM and the Internet) to accommodate work which in a previous age would have been commissioned and screened by terrestrial broadcasters.[11]

How real can you get?

REALISM AND DOCUMENTARY

Photographic images: capturing the real world?

One of the most succinct accounts of the way documentary films relate to the real world was produced by a film editor, Dai Vaughan. He identified the crucial difference that separates the work of those using the photographic media from all the other art forms. If a writer should set out to document the life of a horse, he or she would need only a pencil and a piece of paper. The painter must use rather more elaborate equipment – canvas, paint and brushes – while the sculptor would require stone, mallet and chisels. What all these artists have in common with the individual working with a lens is that they are performing acts of mediation. And all are attempting to capture something of what they perceive to be the reality of the creature. The photographer, however, has to have not only his equipment – camera and film stock – but also a horse.[1] After the film has been exposed, we have in one sense two horses: the original beast that now returns to the meadow and the one signified in the language of photography and film – the image (Vaughan, 1983: 27).

André Bazin said of photography (and his words apply to all the lens-based media) that its power lies in 'a psychological fact, to wit, in completely satisfying our appetite for illusion by a mechanical reproduction in the making of which man plays no part' (Bazin, 1967: 12). Precisely because it depends upon mechanical, chemical or electronic processes, lens-based imagery commands our faith that what it shows is the model, the original object itself. The object (in our present example the horse itself) is simultaneously captured within the frame and freed from the conditions of time and space that govern it in life (Bazin, 1967: 12–14). This relationship was later named the *indexical bond* by Charles Peirce to refer to the fact that lens-based imagery is produced under such circumstances that it is 'physically forced to correspond point by point to nature' (cited in Wollen, 1972: 123–4).

How real can you get?

There is a complication with Vaughan's account of the horse – a problem of behaviour centring on the horse itself. Its normal behaviour may be to gallop across the meadow to greet its owner when he or she comes along. Faced with not only its owner but also a camera crew, however, it might well take fright and run away. The production crew and the owner would then have to resort to a number of tricks to get the horse to appear to act in its usual manner.

Aware of this, Vaughan distinguishes between the pro-filmic event (what actually happened in front of the lens) and the putative event (what would have happened had the camera not been there). As he points out, some events, such as the swaying of a tree in high winds, will not be affected by the camera's presence; but others (and the more intimate or clandestine forms of human conduct are particularly liable to adaptation for the lens) may be much altered (Vaughan, 1983: 41–2).

The documentary image and its fictional equivalent

In Bazin's sense, documentary can be said at first sight to bear out the original (if illusory) promise of photography. And this basic characteristic – its referentiality – marks it out from the feature film. It offers us, as Nichols says, access to *the* world, while fiction lets us enter *a* world (Nichols, 1991: 109–10).

To go back to the creature with which we started, we can now draw out one typical contrast between documentary and fiction, whether a television play or a feature film. In both the latter genres, although the crew may make use of a horse in the filming of their story, once they have captured its image they usually cease to have any interest in the animal itself. Instead, its image is made over into a character in the plot. In fictions characters are always created within a story world; however, that story world is not necessarily imitative of the real world. As Edward Branigan argues, we find out more about characters not so much by referring to the real world via the indexical bond as by reading along the line of the fiction. In doing so, we follow the convention that generations of readers and spectators have come to accept as the way a story is told. It is what the characters say and do within the story – and what is said and done to them – that usually shapes them more than anything else. They are products of an internal chain of cause and effect that joins up the elements of the plot without necessarily linking the story world to the real one (Branigan, 1992: 100–1). We shall look at these ideas in more detail in Chapter 5.

By contrast, according to the traditional view, which Vaughan expresses, documentarists keep faith with the living horse. What he refers to as the *documentary impulse* guides their labours. That impulse drives them to create an account of the horse that attempts to hold true to the animal's actual circumstances. The act of keeping faith with the horse is the basis of the documentarist's tacit contract with the audience. From this simple requirement arise both aesthetic questions (of finding the best ways of showing on screen that one is keeping faith with the original material) and ethical issues (relating to the way in which documentarists should behave towards the people and topics they deal with, not only before and during filming but also after transmission of their programmes). What rights does the horse, or for that matter a human being, have when accounts of their behaviour are broadcast to a large, distant audience that is not necessarily qualified to judge from first-hand experience whether the picture given is a fair reflection of the horse or person in question? We deal with these topics in Chapter 8.

The indexical bond
The fact that imagery recorded via a lens has an indexical bond to its source object in the real world gives the appearance of guaranteeing the historical accuracy of what documentary programmes represent. This is one of the main features endowing screen documentaries (like photographs) with their authority. Of course, the supposed guarantee does not stand up to close scrutiny for exactly

the reason Bazin advanced – namely, that the photographic image merely satisfies a psychological appetite for illusion under the appearance of actuality. The same bond works just as effectively with many types of fiction which may have no claim to historical accuracy at all except that they are true to the appearances of a given time and place by, for instance, accurately rendering costumes, props and locations.

It follows that we have to look beyond the indexical bond to understand how realism functions, and to do this we shall examine the constructed nature of documentary realism. In the process we shall, of course, consider the nature of the textual strategies which reveal the realist function at work, but shall begin by referring to the way producers' ambitions are reflected in their text. Then we can show how the text invites viewers to co-operate in constructing their sense of its realism. Having covered that ground, we shall be ready to discuss some of the several forms that realism has taken in the documentary.

Documentary discourse – the language of experts
Individuals are seldom able to produce documentaries that reflect purely their own ideas. Almost always they must keep in mind what the broadcasting authorities are likely to buy from them (see discussion in Chapters 7 and 9). Thus the institutional constraints under which documentarists work – some as employees of large organisations, others under a somewhat different set of values, functioning as independents supplying programmes to those large organisations – will limit and shape the kind of work that gets broadcast. These constraints will be analysed in Chapter 7, but we can see immediately that where there exist accepted ways of making documentaries (the BBC, for example, publishes guidelines for its producers to follow) there must also be unacceptable ways of doing so. Such constraints on documentary practice give rise over a period of time to certain ways of approaching topics and certain ways of talking about and representing them. There is, in other words, a whole series of conventionalised devices by means of which the effect of documentary realism is triggered (see O'Sullivan *et al.*, 1994b: 257–9). These conventions change through time in response to a range of

social, cultural and aesthetic pressures. As a consequence, the meanings of both the terms 'documentary' and 'realism' are historically determined and liable to undergo changes as social values and conditions change.

Having said this, one of the most common ways film makers approach documentary topics (long since turned into a convention) is through the consciously distanced stance of the objective, but expert, observer; this person is simultaneously present and distant. Various factors, including location shooting at the scene of events and the presenter's visible presence in the field, together with conventionalised forms for documentary of picture and sound recording and editing, vouch for the immediate actuality of the world being reported. These practices contribute to the objectivising tendency of documentary through which the text seeks to communicate the sense that it is delivering an authentic picture of reality (Nichols, 1991: 189). However, other factors hold this immediacy at arm's length. The presenter (assisted unseen by the post-production editing team) delivers a narration that welds together the evidence provided by the camera, microphone and his or her own researches. It may well be backed by further evidence, including documentation, archival material and the testimony of other experts. As the material is assembled, it may be structured into an argument driven by logic, or some rational thought pattern, which extends across the full running time of the programme. The net effect is that the realist stance causes the documentarist to keep an emotional distance both from the topic and from the people portrayed.

Such a distance is registered as being necessary if the (expert) observer is to preserve the conventionally accepted measure of dispassionate objectivity. A more intimate stance might involve emotional engagement on the documentarist's part, but this would be better suited to the role of a participant. That role is rare in contemporary British and American televised documentary, where realism is usually divorced from explicit propaganda and seldom involves a direct call to action. We should remember that documentarists have to abide by the broadcasting regulations governing bias, impartiality and objectivity. This is not to say that no element of subjectivity is expressed in their work, as can readily be seen in this simple contrast: news journalists adopt a rhetorical stance in their reports, which assures the viewer that they are primarily conveying facts and only to a limited degree putting a gloss on them. By comparison, documentarists express their subjectivity by offering their own interpretation of the topic. That is a key difference, since a well-developed interpretative element is all but essential to the documentary (see Chapter 1 and Nichols, 1991: 187–91).

Realism in documentary discourse

Nichols, who reckons that documentary realism is the style that has characterised documentary more than any other, has given a succinct account of its nature. He compares realism in fiction (which serves to make a plausible world seem real) with documentary realism (the function of which is to render persuasive an argument about the historical world). Documentary realism always has a historical dimension because it concerns something that has occurred or is occurring in the world that people inhabit (Nichols, 1991: 165, 177).

What are the elements that contribute to our idea of the realism of documentary? The important thing to note is that it is not just the fact that documentary refers to the real world that allows the viewer to distinguish it from other forms of television programming. As we have seen, the referential function considered on its own does not make it easy even to separate factual footage in documentaries from that used in those fictions which try to present their story world as if it were the real world. So something else is required if the viewer is to register a documentary as realistic.

The importance of framing and context

Whenever we are involved in any act of communication, we are always doing so within a particular mental framework. The frame within which we operate determines both the nature of the messages we send and the interpretation we put on incoming messages. In other words, according to the frame selected, we interpret the message via one of a number of different sets of realities. For example, we decode a televised news item about a murder very differently from a killing in a Western. The framing of the two coding systems cues us to understand the messages in quite different ways.

Of crucial importance in the determining of meaning is the context in which these acts of communication take place. Even a very basic message like 'Blackburn Rovers, 3; Arsenal, 1' means nothing unless one knows that it refers to scores in the English soccer league. The message can literally not be understood by an addressee who does not know its context. Documentary programmes always have some form of context. For example, most are signalled as such in advance scheduling and listing magazines, and their content is also often flagged as well. In addition, it is usual for the material of each separate programme to be related to that of others in the same series or weekly slot. Viewers are thus made ready for decoding the subject matter on the terms proposed by the producer or the broadcasting institution (see Chapter 9).

Truth and reference are not inherent properties in communication but aspects of our interactions with the world based on our experience. In other words, while the frame provided by the programme maker gives evident clues to the way in which the text is to be understood as engaging with reality, the frame of reference we actually apply in the act of decoding will vary according to the stock of memories and experiences each of us as individuals has accumulated over a period of time. Meanings that we ascribe to what we hear and see are just as much products of our perceptual apparatus as they are inherent objective properties of any communicated message. In recognising some and interpreting others among the whole set of visual cues presented by the film, we make sense of what we see by translating it to familiar terms (see Bondebjerg, 1994: 67, 73–4). One such set of familiar terms (one frame) is 'the social world'; another is 'documentary'.

It follows that when we consider realism in the documentary we have in mind not only the claim of a programme to deal with matters in the real world but also its resemblance to other texts. There are two aspects to this. First, all texts – whether books, posters, films or television programmes – can only be 'read' because to some degree they resemble others. This characteristic, known as intertextuality, derives from the fact that any given text must share with other texts some of the coding which readers have previously learnt from them if they are to be able to decode it. Second, and more immediately relevant to the discussion of documentary realism, is the phenomenon known as generic verisimilitude.

Generic verisimilitude

This shorthand term refers to a specific instance of intertextuality – namely, our tendency to refer to other texts from the same genre when we consider the realism of a film or a programme. The idea can be seen with great clarity when we put it in the context of fiction. In the case of a Western, people may describe the climactic action of one film as altogether more realistic than that of another. How do they know? In today's audience there will thankfully be few people indeed who (lawfully or otherwise) have shot and killed another human being. People measure the authenticity or realism of the event enacted not so much by personal experience of the real world as by how it measures up to what they remember from other fictional accounts. We can observe the same phenomenon at work in the uses people make of soap operas with which they are familiar. The realistic status which soaps appear to acquire in the minds of many of their viewers results largely from those individuals' recurrent exposure to a world with which they become increasingly familiar. There seem to be two consequences of such familiarity for some viewers: the first being that they are more likely to believe in such a world; the second that, in a psychological sense, the world of the soap becomes in time no less real than the world the viewer inhabits (Kilborn, 1992: 89–90).

Incidentally, the acceptance of a given style of generic verisimilitude as realistic may not last. It is important to remember that all attempts to create realism by adhering to a set of generic conventions are historically determined. For 1990s audiences, for instance, the realism acclaimed by 1960s viewers of police series such as *Dixon of Dock Green* or *Z Cars* seems not only dated but also absurdly contrived. New series which have supplanted them, such as *The Bill*, appear to move at an altogether more dynamic pace and to have a greater realism. But if this is one factor, another is our reliance on the set of values that have been inculcated throughout the twentieth century by the giant media industries – namely, that every advance in technology carries with it the claim that it brings the medium closer to the direct presentation of reality. A third factor is that the viewer belongs to a culture whose values (and representation of those values) are constantly changing. As we shall see, the acceptable characteristics of realism alter with those ideological changes.

Before turning to the conventions that persuade us as viewers of the realism of documentaries, we may remind ourselves that, because communication is a two-way process, film makers themselves will in effect have generic verisimilitude in mind when they give their material its shape. In taking their materials from the real historical world, they will endow them with a form that is likely to have derived in part from one of the familiar genres – for example, an existing documentary mode or narrative film (see Britton, 1992: 26). Once again, we find evidence that the effect of realism depends upon deeply marked textual conventions. The makers and viewers of documentary contribute a great deal respectively to the encoding and decoding practices which mark out the text as realistic.

Conventions of documentary realism

What are the conventions that signal the historical and social realism of the documentary mode? There are several, and it is not necessary for all to be present in a given programme for the viewer to think of it as being realistic. Some are more likely to be found in one mode than another (see Chapter 3), while others have been more commonly employed in one historical period than others.

Pro-filmic conventions

Some conventions used in realist documentary depend on enriching our sense of being there. These include such occurrences in front of the lens (i.e. pro-filmic events) as location shooting, following the action and having the presenter talk directly to the camera from the scene of events. Another device that is frequently used to encourage a sense of being there is the on-camera interview in which witnesses or participants directly relate their experiences. The overall impact of these devices is to heighten the effect of realism for the viewer. People, objects and actions in the real world are given priority. The film maker is seen to be working strictly within the confines of the historical world rather than an imaginary one where different laws and conventions obtain (see Nichols, 1991: 79). All these devices assure the viewer that this is the case and that the resulting programme is realistic.

In some circumstances a classic element of documentary – which is pro-filmic but does not, strictly speaking, occur in the scene of action – can add to the effect of realism. This is scripted narration, delivered in voice-over. When the viewer trusts the narrator, and the latter is giving an account of the way things were, voice-overs foster the illusion that we are being spoken to person-to-person. The sense of realism stems from the fact that we tend to attach credibility to someone commenting authoritatively or helpfully on events being played out before us (see Chapter 4).

These features might also be found in news footage, but (as previously hinted) in documentary they are usually given a treatment that is both more extensive and more reflective than would be the case in even an extended news bulletin.

Filmic conventions

Other conventions are matters of style and, as often as not, achieve their efficacy by their very difference from the equivalent stylistic elements in fiction films. Although many of them were originally brought about by the conditions of filming or recording in the field, they nonetheless remain conventions. For example, in documentary we accept as normal the flat image quality and ungainly shadows that 'natural' lighting (which may be all that is available to the production crew) can produce. By contrast, in a feature film we would look for images to be moulded and made expressive of meaning by controlled lighting. Again, the uneven movement of a hand-held or shoulder-mounted camera (often necessary to follow a subject whose movements may be unpredictable) is not merely acceptable in documentary, but has become so recognisable as a convention that where it is used as a technique in screen dramas it gives the scene in question an aura of documentary actuality (Goodwin, 1986: 22–3).

The style of editing assembly will probably avoid building the classical, privileged point of view. Instead, like various techniques of presentation and shooting mentioned above, it may favour giving the viewer the idea of being present at the scene depicted. In other words, we may be positioned as witnesses rather than as vicarious, would-be participants.

Style and meaning
Although the individual style of one documentarist will differ from that of another, the common thread through most documentary programmes is the employment of what in the broadest sense can be described as a realist style (this is true even of the work of many reflexive film makers who wish to resist it). Virtually every aspect of that style is designed to persuade us that the film makers were there, and that, in viewing the historical world through transparent and referential indexical images, we have shared their experience (Nichols, 1991: 181).

If this is the predominant function of style in documentary, it is mirrored in the way in which meaning tends to be constructed from images. In fiction, images frequently have a metaphoric value. They stand for some thing or some idea other than that to which they are indexically bonded. If we go back to the image of a horse, in fiction it is common for this creature to imply some form of power. It may be the qualities of leadership and strength of the Western hero who rides the finest horse; it may be the wealth of the man or woman mounted on a well-bred nag in a period drama; or it may be the awakening sexual power of a young heroine or hero in a screenplay about maturing to adulthood. In documentary, however, images usually function in a metonymic mode. Metonymy is the rhetorical convention in which the image represents a part of a larger whole and partakes of the same order of reality as that to which (in the case of lens-based imagery) it is indexically bonded (see Nichols, 1991: 28). Thus, this rhetorical device serves to reassure us that the visible indexical bond of the documentary image does indeed authenticate historical actuality. Here, the horse is less likely to stand for the hidden powers of its rider than for horses in general. For example, a documentary on how burnt-out racehorses are sent to the knacker's yard at the end of their working lives will usually take the slaughter of particular horses observed as being representative of a larger problem. The programme may well imply, or even state explicitly, that this is the fate of many working horses whose owners see no profit in keeping them alive. In short, metonymy is a significant part of the persuasive machinery of documentary realism (O'Sullivan *et al.*, 1994b: 179–80).

The viewer's perspective

The documentary impulse expressed by film makers translates on screen into what Vaughan calls the 'documentary imperative' (Vaughan, 1983: 28). This phrase, since programmes cannot tell their audiences what they must think of them, is not a happy one, but it does convey the general idea that documentaries cue the viewer into certain kinds of response. In the first place, as Vaughan shows, such films try, by employing a range of the aesthetic and rhetorical devices available to documentarists, to persuade the viewer that they have indeed kept faith with their sources – with the horse Vaughan spoke of (Vaughan, 1983). We have seen plenty of evidence to support his assertion. Viewers interpret certain programmes as realist documentaries when they respond to built-in signals which cue that response. We have already itemised a number of framing devices and textual conventions which have this function. Now we can go further and show how documentaries seek to bind viewers into their projects by engaging their subjective sensibilities.

Documentaries engage the subjectivity of viewers by arousing their interest in the vitality of the historical world. In this aspect too, documentary practice contrasts with the way that fictions often endeavour to enhance our subjective engagement in the psychological experiences of the main characters. Documentaries arouse a strong desire to take pleasure from knowing; they do not cue with anything like the same power as fiction films the desire to enjoy the sensuous pleasure of gazing (Nichols, 1991: 157, 178–80). (We say more about epistephilia, or the desire to know, in Chapter 9.)

Earlier we described how documentaries exploit devices that place their makers within the historical world they are representing. We can argue that the realism of that represented world is further enhanced by indications that it is co-extensive with, or at least touches on, the viewers' own world in some way. There will usually be a link between the world that viewers know from their own life experiences and the world that is revealed on screen. Such links enrich our sense of the realism of the world which the programme presents to us; like every other device in documentary, they are constructed (whether consciously or not) and they inevitably carry an ideological burden.

Predominant among the mechanisms for linking the viewers' world to that represented is a virtually universal practice which we can call *accommodation*. Because most programmes have to play to as large a sector of the viewing public as they can attract, they are consciously accommodated (or shaped to fit) the perceived values and interests of the target audience. Natural history programmes, for instance, highlight moments of action that add drama to what might otherwise be monotonous coverage of animals' lives. Their narration frequently anthropomorphises the creatures they describe: by constantly relating animal behaviour to that of the human species, the programmes make the creatures more readily understandable because they seem to resemble us. To take another equally striking example of accommodation, programmes about other countries usually represent their people in terms which take some account of the stereotyped way in which they are seen in the land where the programme is to be broadcast. This process does not have to be as crude as having Scots wear tartan or the French eat garlic, but stereotyping (which is, after all, a convenient means of shorthand reference) usually distorts in a way that is immediately noticeable, and irritating, to the people portrayed.

The style of a programme is also likely to involve viewers' subjectivity. This is frequently achieved by adopting various forms of repetition. We can see this if we invent an example. A poor fisherman goes down to the sea, works through the night, but comes home with only a small catch. He tells us that the fish he sells are the only means he has to support his family, but exploitative factory fishing by fleets from a distant country are exhausting local stocks. A month later we go out to sea with him again. This time the catch is even smaller. A further month on, it is not enough to feed his family.

Repetition of this kind does two things for the viewer. First, it strengthens the effect of reality by stressing the specificity of people, places and situations and allows the viewer to observe the changes in them which occur as time passes. Second, recurrence increases the exposure of viewers to the emotions being experienced in the world depicted, and this is likely to intensify their affective response to those emotions. As we have already said, it is characteristic of the subjectivity cued in the viewer by documentary to strengthen the sense of human engagement within the real, historical world (Nichols, 1991: 79–80, 157).

Because the viewer of documentary is cued by the text to adopt the attitude of one who wishes to know more about the historical world represented on the screen, the arousal of emotions is usually subordinated to this drive. (The main exception to this general rule is found in the poetic mode – see Chapter 3.) Viewers will typically be offered a subjective position which invites them (like the film maker) to keep a certain distance from the programme's content. Indeed, with certain films the viewer is explicitly given the role of observer. Thus, in most cases, the space prepared for the subjective experience of viewers actually contributes to their sense of the programme's objectivity. It does so precisely because it invites them – while they are feeling a measure of emotional disturbance brought about by the content (for example, compassion and anger in the case of our imaginary fisherman) – nonetheless to keep the distance appropriate to the objective observer from that material. A stance is thereby prepared for viewers which mimics that of the film maker. A significant part of our sense of a programme's realism derives from the feeling of complicity to which that gives rise. And when we add our own eagerness to accept the photographic image as the guarantor of its authenticity, we can see that documentary makers are helped in persuading us of their programmes' realism by our desires as viewers.

Realism and documentary aesthetics

Some of the factors described above, in certain combinations, have repercussions on the aesthetics of documentary realism. This is not to claim that there is one particular visual or aural style accepted as realist. As we shall see, various styles and modes of realism have prevailed at different times and for different broadcast organisations and documentary movements, But the desire to know more about the real world, which we found was typical of viewers' orientation towards documentary realism, tends to correlate with their experiencing a stronger interest in the world actually represented on screen than in the manner in which it is shown.

This overriding concern with the historical world is the main factor causing the relative lack of emphasis on aesthetics. But there are other contributory elements: one concerns viewers' automatic cognitive practice in reading the signs in documentaries (as opposed to fictions). As we saw above, viewers redeploy their frames of reference when they are making sense of their own social world: they apply those frames to the represented world of documentary to make sense of it. It seems probable that the less any aesthetic innovations intrude into the process by which the text cues the viewer to 'pull down' the appropriate experiential frames, the more clearly the documentary will be seen to fit lived experience. Conversely, where a film producer deliberately employs artistic innovation so that his aesthetics make the pro-filmic world seem strange, it is likely that any other claims that the resulting documentary might have to realism will be weakened.

We have mentioned the concern of film makers not only to demonstrate that they were there but also to show their ability to preserve their distance as a means of guaranteeing the work's objectivity. This too leads many of them to aesthetic restraint.

Despite this, documentaries have often been the site of notable aesthetic innovations. Sometimes these were the consequences of technological invention, such as the advent in various epochs of: the earliest sound tracks; lightweight, synchronised sound equipment for use in tandem with 16-mm cameras; high-speed film; and the camcorder. Other experiments sprang from the sheer exuberance of the film makers. Among the earliest in Britain were some (including the celebrated play with verse and sound montage in *Coalface* (1935) and *Night Mail* (1936)) conducted by members of the Documentary Movement. Yet Grierson, under whose leadership these films were made, was always adamant that his directors must be 'sensible enough to conceive of art as the by-product of a job of work done'. The pursuit of beauty or of 'art for art's sake' in the work of the documentarist was a sign of aesthetic decadence. The realist documentary (as opposed to what he called the romantic documentary, which merely celebrated the beauty of the world) must demonstrate its makers' sense of social responsibility by a laboriously achieved sympathy with the historical world it represented. To be sure, the inspirational effort that process demanded might produce its own poetry, and thus the subjectivity of the director might be expressed in his own aesthetic signature. But the important requirement of the realist documentary was to show the social world as it had not been seen before (Grierson, 1966: 41).

This small piece of history is worth recalling because Grierson's values still govern the production of, and critical response to, many documentaries. (A good example of this is the 1994 BBC series called *The Trial*, one episode of which is analysed in Chapter 4.) The major exceptions to aesthetic restraint are found in the experimentalism of poetic and reflexive documentaries. When we examine the different modes of documentary (in Chapter 3), we shall see that the poetic and reflexive documentaries are so named because they use a variety of stylistic and structural devices precisely to call into question documentary realism. They are the exceptions that prove the rule.

Documentary realism and ideology

We have already seen abundant evidence to show that realism, like documentary itself, is inevitably a construction. It has to be so because it is impossible to achieve a perfect match between events in the historical world and the text that represents them. What may seem to the individual film maker in the course of production to be a process of interpreting social reality becomes something more in the context of a culture's communicating with itself. The meanings that audiences derive from documentaries are absorbed into and informed by the wider televisual discourse. The latter in turn contributes to the multitude of discourses through which society continuously defines and redefines itself and, in so doing, becomes part of the process of constructing social reality (Cormack, 1992; Nichols, 1991: 10–11, 143, O'Sullivan *et al.*, 1994b: 139–43).

This occurs all the more potently with most documentaries because, in common with the vast majority of cultural artefacts, they conceal the ideologies which they embody. They do this by making the values they embrace appear to be inherent characteristics of the people and objects in front of the lens, as if they had no relation to the perspective from which the film makers looked at their subject. This illusion is boosted by the complicity of the audience in believing that the images it sees do not so much actively mediate a view of reality as stand in for it (Britton, 1992: 26). Only when values held by the viewer differ from those inherent in the programme do they become obvious. This can occur with the passage of time: it is impossible today to miss the condescending patronage of working men celebrated by the upper-middle class narrator in Flaherty's *Industrial Britain* (1931), or the chauvinism that resonates from many pre- and post-war newsreels. And when documentaries are screened outside the society for which they were made, the strangeness of their values is usually plain. For example, audiences in capitalist countries quickly recognise that Marxist documentaries are constructed differently from the type of documentaries they are most familiar with, and that they embody unfamiliar values.

Forms of realism

Just as all languages and discourses undergo a constant process of change as time passes, so do our ways of seeing and understanding. Changes in patterns of discourse are bound up with (among many other forms of documentary mediation) the forms of realism. We conclude this chapter, therefore, with a short account of the principal forms that realism has adopted in documentary.

Documentary film, as Vaughan has argued, exists both as a record and as a signifying system. It is a record in so far as events occurring in the historical world have been filmed (see also Corner, 1996). It is a signifying system in two respects. First, the camera crew select what to record from the events occurring around them, and by so doing endow with significance the time and space captured on film. Second, the editorial process involves the selection of footage from what was recorded, the assembly of the resulting fragments, and the dubbing of sound. All these processes convert the record into a text and change the codes of social behaviour into filmic codes which carry meanings that are to a considerable extent constructed by the filming and editing processes. The activity of viewers, to which we referred above, is complementary to that of the makers in that (if the documentarists have been sufficiently persuasive in the construction of their programme) they accept what they see and hear as an authentic account. In other words, looking as it were through the filmic language – and making appropriate compensations – they perceive in the images what they take to be a true record of what happened (Vaughan, 1993: 99, 101–2, 108).

O'Sullivan remarks that it is the perceived 'truth to life' that qualifies a work as realistic. But what 'truth to life' amounts to depends on what one is looking for. And this comes right down to the level of perception where, depending on their expectations and past experience, different people form different images of the same object. So the nature of realism – both as a practice and a critical concept – is the subject of never-ending contestation (O'Sullivan *et al.*, 1994b: 258; Andrew, 1984: 37–8). As a consequence, the principal forms of documentary realism negotiate the balance between record and signifying system in rather different ways.

Empiricist realism
Empiricist realism refers to those forms in which the indexical bond is given priority, the idea being that realism consists in making a copy of the original as accurately as possible. Here programme makers and viewers are encouraged to concentrate on the film as record, and its function as a signifying system of coded statements is de-emphasised. Empiricist realism, based on the ancient idea of mimesis (or imitation), resembles the late nineteenth-century aesthetic practice known as naturalism, which reached its height in the intensely detailed descriptions of people and places created by Emile Zola in his novels. Today empiricist realism describes the practice which remains dominant not only in documentary but in

all factual television. Much televised documentary depends on the presentation of visual images that are easily understood as 'copies' of source material in the real world. The camera is thought of as a scientific instrument which records the exterior of things and people. There is a tacit claim that in the process certain meanings will be discovered or revealed. It follows that the text is addressed to viewers in such a way that they are given to understand that its images are transparent. Narration and interviews combine to assure viewers that the images mean what they are and are what they mean – in other words, that they provide a window on the world.

Although the concept of the 'surface realism' of this kind of naturalism has never been unchallenged, it has remained dominant for very long periods because it incorporates a set of potent rhetorical devices and assumptions (see Winston, 1995: 130–7). First, as mentioned above, the camera is assumed to be an instrument that produces representations which tell the truth. Second, in interpreting what is seen, the narrator is perceived to be merely relaying to the viewer what is taken to be the truth inherent in the images. As a consequence, the real world is seen as providing natural, compelling evidence to back up the arguments advanced in those documentaries which work in the naturalist style. Documentary is not alone in frequently providing such reassurances, since they lie at the heart of most television news and current affairs programmes.

Social and historical realism
There exists a sub-set of empiricist realism in British and North American television documentary which deserves separate attention, not only because it is so common but also because it derives both form and impetus in a direct line of descent from well-established past practice. Here the focus is once again on film and videotape as instruments of record rather than as vehicles for a signifying system. However, social realism goes beyond empiricist realism to the extent that, in the words of Peter Loizos, 'it implies an openness to the totality of human experiences' (Loizos, 1993: 9). The mark of social realism is its interest in showing ordinary people in their usual *milieux* – working men and women are seen as appropriate subjects for the writer, painter and film maker.

In the history of cinema social realism has well-known roots in the work of the young Soviet revolutionaries of the 1920s, Sergei Eisenstein and Dziga Vertov principal among them. Grierson's work as a film maker was to some degree influenced by Eisenstein's aesthetics. But where the Russians' goal was explicitly the revolutionary refashioning of society, Grierson and his colleagues in the British Documentary Movement sought first to make the various orders of society better known to one another and, second, to facilitate reform rather than revolutionise. As Winston points out, a deeper influence can be found in nineteenth-century French realism, the goals and aesthetics of which closely matched those of the British film makers. When these documentarists argued that their films must be the voice of the people speaking from their homes and factories, from their city streets and slums, they were echoing the social concerns of painters such as Courbet and Millet. And Grierson's idea that individual artists should subsume their self-expression to the greater importance of the collective purpose also had its source in the aesthetic programme of the French realists. Poetry should spring from the revelation of the contemporary world of the heroic underprivileged rather than from the self-indulgent virtuosity of the artist or film maker (Winston, 1995: 26–9).

As we mentioned in Chapter 1, Grierson's unswerving belief was that, in their 'creative treatment of actuality', documentary films should record and reveal society to its members for the information and advantage of them all (Grierson, 1966: 13). These are fine ambitions, and there has been almost constant debate since the 1930s as to the extent to which the British Documentary Movement fulfilled them. Only one aspect of this debate is relevant to our immediate needs, and this might be described as the 'us and them' phenomenon. The weakness of Grierson's practice in relation to what his theory claimed as social realism was that it was always 'us' (the documentary elite, a tightly knit group of youngish, educated and middle-class professionals) filming 'them' (and 'they' were often working people, the poor and underprivileged, and seldom professionals such as 'us', the film makers). In the filming and editing processes, 'our' values inevitably frame 'them', sometimes even producing an implicit (unconscious) claim which functions to persuade the viewer that 'we' (a group now expanded to include the viewer) have a truer perspective on 'them' than they do themselves.

When a documentary centres itself on a system of values that is alien to that of the observed, the latter are made into 'the other', those who are outside the recognised norms simply because they are different. As we shall see when we discuss ethics in Chapter 8, this is a problem often faced by a group of documentarists moving into a community (with various preconceptions as to what they will find there) and framing their account accordingly. The problem is particularly acute in the case of the ethnographic film, where the gulf between incoming film maker and documentary subject is likely to be greatest. Winston argues that the British Documentary Movement failed fully to engage with left-wing politics, dealing instead in stereotypical images. In the early 1930s the worker had been portrayed in the movement's films as hero, and the impact of the Depression was merely to alter that image into another latent figure, that of the underprivileged as heroic victim (Winston, 1995: 30–40).

Television at the end of the twentieth century is no less prone to a comparable sentimentality, and this is particularly clear when it turns its cameras on both rich and poor in impoverished nations. The former are frequently shown as at best unthinking exploiters of the latter, who fill the old role of long-suffering victims. Often the representation of people in these stereotypical roles, together with the juxtaposition of the powerful and the powerless, takes the place of an analysis which might investigate the origins of, and suggest remedies for, these often glaring inequities. This is a common, though by no means inevitable, weakness of social realism.

Psychological realism

There is inevitably a psychological dimension to realism (see Belsey, 1980: 67–84). As viewers, we tend to attribute greater realism to those segments or sequences that project a psychologically credible account of human actions and emotions (see Andrew, 1984: 19–36). In other words, viewers explain what they are hearing and seeing in terms of what they already know about behaviour patterns on the large and small screens. As we shall see, the encoding or language-like function of film is as much implicated in this form of realism as its recording function.

Three aspects of psychological realism can be discerned, although in practice they are often blended. First, psychological realism can refer to the attempt to give a persuasive account of the inner life of an individual, or even of a group of people. This can be done in a straightforward fashion if people describe their own experiences and feelings. Our endless fascination with such matters is the reason why journalists in news broadcasts can get away with asking interviewees that favourite question, 'How did it feel?' It does not have to be the person in front of the lens who gives an account of her or his inner experience, however. A narrator can do so too. We shall say more about documentary subjectivity in the next chapter.

Second, and frequently associated with the same goal, psychological realism can refer to an attempt to represent the world as if it were being seen from an individual's point of view. Indeed, film makers can do something as basic as using a distorting lens to convey to viewers the idea that they are being given the point of view of an individual under intense psychological pressure. Distortions and imbalances in the sound track, as well as distinctive and unusual editing patterns, can have the same effect. Although distortions to this end are seldom as blatant as they can be in screened fiction, they do occur. Their effect is dependent upon the degree of divergence from what we have come to accept as standard documentary practice. Here the encoding, or language-like, aspect of documentary is of (at least) equal importance to the recording aspect. For example, Fred Wiseman's films of institutional life make extensive use of long focal lenses, which flatten and fatten faces, while their sound tracks give a loud and active presence to ambient noise. These devices add greatly to the oppressive feeling of the institutions that the films are surveying.

Third, the term psychological realism is used to refer to the various forms of empathy that can be formed between viewers and the social actors to whom they are introduced as the documentary unfurls. This is designed to give viewers the (heart-warming or chilling) sensation that the subjects of the programme have the same human characteristics they themselves do. Empathy, our own identification with the figures on the screen, is a powerful means not only of engaging our attention, but also of getting us to conspire with the film makers in surrendering our disbelief – that is, in giving our vote to what we swiftly allow ourselves to believe is the realism of the scenes on the screen (Nichols, 1991: 171).

The exploitation of this form of psychological realism is massively important in many forms of screen drama precisely because it aids the suspension of disbelief. It is, for instance, one of the many factors that make soap operas seem realistic to many of their fans (Kilborn, 1992: 88–90). The Hollywood studios long since evolved a manner of film making (sometimes known as zero-degree style) in which the film is constructed so as to give the illusion of a transparent surface allowing direct access to the reality of the lives and feelings of the characters which the narrative presents. The feature film uses motivated editing and the overlay of uninterrupted sound effects and music to give the impression of unbroken experience of a continuing action. Documentary can emulate it, but has also developed its own devices to encourage the suspension of disbelief. An example is the illusion that an interviewee talking to an unseen questioner behind the camera is alone, and that it is normal for a person to speak his or her innermost thoughts out loud (see O'Sullivan *et al.*, 1994a: 106). Commentary is a very powerful device for binding together what would otherwise be seen as disparate images from diverse sources, and it suits the needs of documentary, which is more frequently concerned with issues than actions (Izod, 1984: 113–18, Nichols, 1991: 172–4). For this reason, documentary often takes its structure from the advancing of an argument rather than the development of a story, as is usual in the case of fiction (see Chapter 5). Nonetheless, the goal of giving the illusion of direct access to the world represented is much the same in both fiction and documentary.

Deconstructing realism
The popularity of empiricist and psychological forms of realism with writers and readers of fiction and the makers and audiences of feature films gave them a marked dominance over other forms. As we have seen, they also dominated documentary. However, from an

early date, these forms of address carried in the minds of some writers and film makers the taint of fabrication and fantasy, which came from their association with the production line of the world's most potent illusion-making factory – the Hollywood industry. In other words, empiricist and psychological realism began to seem like the machinery of illusion, not reality. In the way they drew attention away from the signifying element of screened programmes and concentrated on their function as records, these forms of realism seemed to such writers to be more apt to foster lies than truth. Marxists observed that it typifies the capitalist system to place emphasis on the commodity and to divert attention away from the processes of production. And thus, in the minds of Marxist media theorists, audiences for the screen products of a commercialised industry (as well as for commercial publications and theatre) resembled consumers (see Belsey, 1980: 126).

In reaction to this scenario, Bertolt Brecht, writing from a Marxist perspective in the 1930s (about theatre and the novel rather than film), sketched the outlines of what subsequently became an informal manifesto for many of those film and television programme makers who wished to resist the dominance of the established models of realism. For us, the significance of Brecht's work is that it provides a large part of the theoretical backdrop to a mode of documentary which looks at and questions not only the nature of the reality it represents, but also the way it does so – the reflexive mode (see Chapter 3).

For Brecht, a major limitation of photographic forms of realism (and by extension, empiricist realism) was that they revealed only the surface. He argued that a photograph of the Krupp arms factory would show nothing of the underlying reality – of the manufacturing processes, the exploitation of the workers, or its ties to the Nazi regime. In fact, reality was often political, social or economic, just as in this instance. That is, it centred on and was framed by the relations between people. But the machinery of psychological realism lulled the spectator into the assumption that everything shown was familiar and both politically and socially safe. For Brecht, the proper work of the realist in a capitalist economy was not to show how the world appeared but rather to reveal the social reality underlying those appearances. He advocated the use of what he termed the *'Verfremdungseffekt'* (the alienation effect). By this he meant that things should be made strange in such a way as to break the psychological bond of identification between spectator and subject. Audiences would thus be encouraged to view what was being enacted with more critical eyes. Spectators should remain external or distanced rather than being drawn in and should be able to gain knowledge rather than vicarious experience of their society (Wollen, 1982: 185, 201–2, Brecht, 1938, in Bloch *et al.*, 1980: 68–85). Nonetheless, realism must be popular – both intelligible and useable by the broad masses; it must take up and enrich their point of view and correct it where it might be in error. And for it to be popular it must change with the times. In other words, realism was not to be achieved through prescribed forms, but the writer or director should use

> every means, old and new, tried and untried, derived from art and derived from other sources, to render reality to men in a form they can master ... Reality changes; in order to represent it, modes of representation must also change. (Brecht, 1938, in Bloch *et al.*, 1980: 81–2)

We said earlier that the most potent arena of realism is inside the spectator's head. Aware of this, Brecht believed that the realist text should turn spectators into actors in the sense that it should be their business to complete the meaning of the text. They would need to do this if they were faced with a sequence of contradictions running through it which they had to criticise in order to make sense of what they were seeing. However, classic transparent realism would not stimulate the spectator to this kind of activity; something else was needed. He referred to it as epic theatre.

Like Brecht, his successors (some of them Marxist, others simply interested in challenging accepted cultural clichés) also questioned the supposed transparency of the image and sought, correctly, to show that it is always value-laden. Also like Brecht, the film makers among them devised a number of formal strategies to undercut the established forms of empiricist and psychological realism. Often they made their films not only so that were they aesthetically strange to their audiences (whether looking or sounding different, or being constructed according to unusual patterns) but in such a way as to draw attention to their own material nature. Equally important, they made the world they showed seem strange also. In that way they questioned dominant values that might otherwise have been taken for granted and undercut established models of realism. In all too many cases, however, they forgot Brecht's insistence that to be effective realist work must be popular in his extended sense of the word.

This kind of work finally entered the realms of television documentary in the form of the reflexive documentary, which, as a class of film, has all the elements described above. It draws attention away from the function of documentary as record and throws it on to its function as a signifying system – not only that, but a signifying system that is often puzzling to the viewer. Generally, its claims to realism rest on the way such a film queries the basis on which our apprehension of the real stands. We shall discover a good deal more about the reflexive film, along with other forms of documentary programming, in the next chapter.

'Seeing as': multiplying the real

We cannot end this chapter without taking our discussion of the processes of framing and perception, and the construction of images and worlds further. Up to this point we have dealt with realism as if the problems with which it confronted us centred exclusively on mediation of the real via the screen, while the nature of the real world itself was not problematic. That this is not the case can be seen on closer examination of the way our perceptions work.

We have already referred to the way that, on the basis of past experience, our expectation at any given moment of what we are likely to see on the screen directs our eyes and mind in forming the images that we actually perceive. Andrew says of this process that our eyes work differently in different circumstances and that they form images which vary in accordance with the expectations that direct them. When we face the screen, our eyes give form to the variations in brilliance, colour and density of the light coming from its two-dimensional surface and see these as images of objects, people and places. The constructive process of 'seeing as' is integral to our experience of both television and cinema: we have already remarked that each person's experiences shape his or her expectations and, hence, how he or she visualises the patterns on the screen (Andrew, 1984: 37–8). Perception is decidedly an active business.

However, the process of 'seeing as' is an essential part of our giving form not just to the screen world, but to the world or worlds around us, as E. H. Gombrich, Nelson Goodman and others have argued. We infer from the stimuli that our eyes receive what various patterns of light mean for us – this shape a human being, that one a chair, and so forth. But if we infer all images in this way, it then follows that we also infer the worlds we perceive. In that case, even when we stand shoulder to shoulder on the same spot, the world I perceive around me is likely, on the basis of experience and expectation, to differ from yours. In other words, there is no single, primary world upon which we all agree and to which we give various kinds of representation. Rather there are multiple worlds – and we give them various kinds of representation (Andrew, 1984: 38, citing Gombrich and Goodman).

This is not as strange as it at first sounds. In the fiction film, we are used to the idea of certain directors creating a distinctive world, like that, say, of Charlie Chaplin. And we can distinguish that from the worlds created by D. W. Griffith. Equally, in our lives among our fellow beings, we are used to inferring a variety of worlds. They impact to greater or lesser degree upon our lives – for most people they centre around the worlds of work and of home, but they might also take in, through our interest in television, the worlds of politics or sports. For a professional politician on the other hand, the world of politics would dominate, and all others might be tangential to it. As Andrew says, 'Whatever encompasses our attention is a world we have constructed to live within. Whatever organises our sense of that world or of some portion of it is a version; and versions we call representations.' (Andrew, 1984: 40).

As far as realism in the documentary is concerned, the recognition that we infer the world we perceive sharply reduces the value of claims that realism guarantees a text's imitation of the real world.

This has to follow when the idea of a single real world is brought into doubt. Rather, the concept of inference highlights the way in which claims that documentaries have a realist function conceal a potent ideological activity. That activity is not so much actually to copy the real world as to organise consensus among viewers that the representations displayed on screen do in fact show the one and only real world. The irony of the realist enterprise is that while it seeks to persuade viewers that a given text refers to the one and only real world (and even at the very moment when they may be disposed to accept that persuasion), they are in fact busy inferring from it multiple and various worlds.

Like it or not, then, the documentary is an instrument of propaganda for ways of 'seeing as', for guiding or encouraging audiences into accepting the views being propounded. This will be true whether those ways of 'seeing as' were originally conceived by an individual film maker or whether they represent inferences about the world advanced at the behest of an organisation – be it a commercial corporation, a broadcasting institution or a government.

In the next chapter we shall, among other things, show how the realist enterprise is handled in various forms of documentary.

PART II

The documentary text

Shaping the real

MODES OF DOCUMENTARY

When we look back across the history of documentary we can trace the emergence of a number of different modes of film and television production. They are a convenient means of distinguishing one kind of documentary from another because, at its purest, each has its own distinctive form and addresses the viewer in a manner different from the others. At first sight the modes are rather like genres precisely because they too depend for their continued currency on a broad set of conventions which are repeated time and again, in the process being varied and developed. However, when we look more closely, the likeness is not perfect. Whereas in fiction the various genres usually represent different types of imaginary world, the documentary modes represent the actual historical world in different ways. Thus, were they all to be deployed to represent the same event, each would claim to show things the other modes could not. Although all the modes were current on television in the 1990s, they rivalled one another in a way that fictional genres never have, as programme makers sought to challenge established means of making documentaries and were motivated to create new modes by their conviction that the old methods were inadequate for present needs (Nichols, 1991: 23).

It must be said at once that the boundaries between the modes are far from rigid, and it is not always possible to make a clear distinction between the different types. Many documentaries exhibit elements that belong to more than one mode. Indeed, since all the modes of address are now available for use, they are sometimes deliberately mixed by producers – as for example in today's television reality programming – into what can be described as a hybrid form, which may use 'voice-of-God' narration, camcorder actuality footage, studio interviews and dramatised re-enactments in a single three-minute item. (See Chapter 6 for more on hybrid documentaries.)

The expository documentary

The expository documentary is the form of documentary construction that is usually considered to be the oldest because it was first demonstrated by Robert Flaherty in *Nanook of the North* (1922). During the 1930s it was developed to the point where it became the aesthetic norm for films made by the British Documentary Movement under John Grierson and by documentarists working under Pare Lorentz for the US Department of Agriculture.

Narration in the expository mode

The expository mode addresses its audience directly, and more often than not does so through a narrator (or title cards in the case of silent films such as *Nanook* or Grierson's *Drifters* (1929)). The narrator interprets what we see, in effect telling us what we should think of the visual evidence before our eyes. Because the limited sound-recording technology of the 1930s made it easier to dub in an unseen speaker, narration of this type became known as the 'voice-of-God' mode. Television production technologists overcame those restrictions on sound a long time ago, and it is now almost as easy to record the narrator on screen as off. Yet the term remains in use because it describes so well the implicit claim of narrators in this mode to speak with authority. Because of its authority the voice becomes an anchor to which all the material in the documentary is tied. As our textual analysis of *Sad, Bad and Mad* will indicate, this device is still much in use (see Chapter 4).

Typically, a documentary made in the expository mode will expound on a topic, more often than not with the narrator's script acting as the main means via which information is selected, shaped and passed on to the viewer. The script is no less than the primary organiser of meaning, and lays out the argument or story which the images themselves sometimes do no more than confirm, like illustrations in a book. Indeed, the images are edited in strict accordance with the dictates of the script.

In the process of expressing the film's primary, ostensible meanings, the script usually colours the subject material with secondary connotations which derive from the values that were shaping the thoughts of the programme makers, whether they were conscious of them or not. Having said this, it is rare for the makers of an expository documentary to reflect in the film itself upon the values which shape its material. Rather, the commentary is presented as being objective and proven by the evidence that it and the accompanying images provide.

In accordance with its concern to prove a case, or at least persuade, the expository documentary frequently employs as narrator someone who represents (or is readily identifiable with) the target audience. Often in European and American television this will be a white, middle-aged, middle-class individual. Also commonly, and for the same reason, the documentary made in the expository mode usually seeks to communicate to the audience a single perspective only on its topic. It does this, in terms of its address to the viewer, by assuming that the audience comprises 'us' – people who share the values of the narrator. This is one of the aspects of the process (to which we referred in Chapter 2) of accommodating unfamiliar material to the perceived values of the target audience. Frequently, the subject material of a documentary is a representation of 'them' – people who are different from and strange to 'us', whether by nationality, race, class, income, gender or age.

Why should commentary have such a telling impact? In part through the strong force of convention. We have got used to the idea that the voice which speaks directly to us (as images pass across the screen and complement what it says) is a knowing voice. We trust it and take its authority as part of the unspoken contract between ourselves and the documentarists. In addition, we seem psychologically to be disposed to find persuasive the disembodied voice which addresses us while our attention is seized by the images playing, as it were, in the foreground. Both explanations make the term 'voice-of-God' peculiarly apt.

The power of expository narration is apparent even when it is coupled with actuality sequences rather than restaged material. Nichols has shown this in connection with footage of the Los Angeles Police beating the black motorist Rodney King. On one level the mute images recorded by a witness documented what happened; but their seemingly definitive meaning was radically altered in the original trial of the four police officers charged with the beating. This was brought about by the defence lawyers, who took upon themselves the role of narrators and furnished the court with, in effect, their own running commentary on the video. Their rewrite of the script seems to have persuaded the jury to take what others saw as raw brutality to be evidence of panic-struck self-defence (Nichols, 1993: 189–90).

In sum, the authority of narration is such that it anchors the meanings of expository documentaries. With only rare exceptions it eliminates whatever ambiguity might be inherent in the pictorial imagery. Indeed, it usually presents information in a rhetorical style designed to impress the listener with the thought that the commentator is offering the only reasonable way of looking at the topic under consideration.

Arranging things for the camera

It is not uncommon for the makers of expository documentaries to cover events after their occurrence. In such cases they restage or reconstruct the original action. The film maker says to the people concerned: 'Just do exactly what you did then.' When sound is dubbed on the resulting footage, the narration encourages the viewer to believe that the original action is what is shown on screen.

Although re-enactment has always been a source of controversy in the analysis of whether a given film is authentic or not, the practice was originally an unavoidable way of proceeding when camera and sound equipment was so cumbersome that it could not readily be taken to the scene of a one-off action. And, of course, many events of interest to the documentarist (the regular happenings of a person's working day, for example) are not unique occasions at all, but recur routinely. In this case the film maker says to the people in front of the camera: 'Just do exactly what you normally do.' What the crew records is then presented by the narrator as typical, which, as we shall see when we consider an episode of *Sad, Bad and Mad* (in Chapter 4), is a common way in which meaning may be constructed in the expository mode.

This is not the only mode in which re-enactment occurs. However, it was one of the characteristics of the expository mode against which those who introduced the observational forms reacted. It is not found in the latter. On the other hand, re-enactment is by definition a basic part of drama-documentary, and it also occurs in reality programming. We shall deal with those modes at length in Chapter 6, but there is a difference which we ought to note here. Re-enactment in the drama-documentary consists in the open and explicit restaging of an event, usually with actors playing the roles of real people. In contrast, re-enactment in the expository mode is seldom acknowledged, and in general the people who form its subjects play themselves as if they had been caught in the original act.

Stereotypes and reconstructions

Re-enactment encourages a kind of manipulation of actuality when a visual point is intensified. To take an example from *Road Racers* (BBC, 1984), a documentary about amateur motorcycle racers in Northern Ireland, one of the riders would go to his work in the garage of the village where he lived not on a motorcycle but on a push-bike. To heighten the contrast between the 200 mph speed of his weekend mount and his transport during the week the director asked him to put aside the smart ten-speed touring bike he actually used and ride an old green sit-up-and-beg machine. This made it easier to convey the impression of the young man as coming from a village where time stands still.

This can be understood as an example of the use of stereotypes to facilitate communication of an idea (whether visually or literally) while simultaneously depleting it of its particularity. Because it permits re-enactments, the expository mode is at risk of over-dependence on stereotypes. So too are the drama-documentary and reality programming. The ever-present temptation for documentarists is subtly to alter the actuality with which they are dealing in order to marry it the more sweetly with the preconceptions of their target audience. As we said in Chapter 2, the advantages of doing so include the fact that it makes it easier for the audience to understand what is being communicated. The disadvantages of working to stereotypes clearly include the risk, if not of falsifying outright the specific event filmed, then of betraying its particularity.

There is an associated consequence of featuring restaged material, a distinctive feature of the expository mode at which we have already hinted: namely, that it readily permits generalisation. Deploying stereotypes makes it possible to represent an individual or an event as typical of a class of people or activities (see Chapter 8). For example, we follow Fred Harris, a shop-floor worker, through a day in the factory. We are given to understand that it is much like any other day in his working life. Furthermore, it represents the typical working day of countless people in similar grinding manual jobs. This can of course be rendered explicitly, since it is a simple matter for the narrator's analysis to refer to the specific case illustrated as an example of tendencies also discovered elsewhere. But it can also be expressed by implicit indications, in which case the veracity of the particular incident witnessed on the screen (and authenticated by the commentary) seems to guarantee the wider general truth.

Editing in the expository mode

There is another no less compelling reason for the re-enactment of events which ensures that it still occurs in most films made in the expository mode. This has to do with its rhetoric or means of communication. On a single-camera shoot some restaging is often called for so that footage can be shot to cover parts of the action more than once. Without the extra takes the editor might find it difficult to cut between different angles on the same event (for example, moving from a wide shot to a tight close-up). It is worth specifying because it allows us to recognise how images in the expository mode are to some degree subject to the kinds of editorial convention made familiar to audiences through the feature film. Thus this kind of documentary to some degree 'piggy backs' on the visual rhetoric of the feature, a topic that is examined in greater detail in Chapter 5.

Expository film makers like to shoot in this way not only to add visual interest but also to make it possible to control the articulation of meaning. For example, cutting between close-ups of an individual, such as our imaginary worker Fred Harris, and wider shots of his machine room might complement the script. It could help the narrator in the process both of picking him out as an individual and showing that his circumstances are typical of those of his colleagues on the shop floor.

However, it is important not to over-stress the resemblance of the editing style in the expository mode to that of feature films, for the assembly of images tends to follow a somewhat different logic. In the expository documentary images are often employed as illustrations that authenticate the narration. Bill Nichols says, 'Editing in the expository mode generally serves to establish and maintain rhetorical continuity more than spacial or temporal continuity' (Nichols, 1991: 35). Thus, in the logic that governs the assembly of the images the authority of the argument led by the commentator tends to predominate over the organisation of space or the flow of time. This is a not uncommon characteristic of the televised documentary for the reason that we have already given: television programmes seek to hold their audiences in spite of domestic distractions and to keep them in touch with what is going on via the sound track.

Uses of the expository documentary

The dominance in the expository documentary of the authoritative narrator who utters supposedly uncontroversial knowledge throws an emphasis upon mimetic, or surface, realism, as Ian Lockerbie observes (Lockerbie, 1991: 226). Indeed, there has always been a tendency, continued to this day, for the mimetic to predominate over the aesthetic. That has been the case in Britain ever since the Griersonian documentary made the expository mode its mainstay, and even though many of the best works in this mode have been artistic milestones in the history of film and television. It is a functionality characterised by the transparency typical of a simple, empiricist Realism akin to nineteenth-century Naturalism, which (as we saw in Chapter 2) equates the real with 'visible actuality'. In so doing it concentrates on the surface of things and seeks to focus on the message while drawing as little attention as possible to the formal structures through which that message is mediated.

For example, the typical natural history documentary (such as the many presented by David Attenborough) actually makes use of extraordinarily versatile techniques to produce the finished effect; it is rare, however, for the narrative to deviate from the format of the simplest chronological plot line. Everything (including the hoists that swing the camera high above the jungle floor, stop-motion cinematography that speeds a plant's life-cycle through a fabulous and hectic moment, and computer-matted images that allow us to fly above the earth in the company of birds) comes second to the telling of the life story of the creature in question (see Chapter 8).

Lockerbie adds that the formal qualities of the expository documentary, notwithstanding its origin in the cinema and development through non-theatrical film exhibition, made it easy for it to enter into television practice. It converged naturally, he observes, with television's own styles of visual journalism and investigative enquiry. For they too foregrounded the lucid presentation of facts, delivered as if with omniscience and objectivity (Lockerbie, 1991: 226, and see Chapter 1). The expository documentary also married neatly with a medium which, as we have said, relied on the dominance of the sound track. These factors as much as anything else account for the continuing vitality of this mode to this day.

The observational documentary

After the Second World War the British Documentary Movement lost its sense of purpose. This was, among other factors, because the needs of both government and corporate sponsors had changed. Attlee's Labour government had little use for Griersonian propaganda, since state policies now included the social, educational and housing reforms the Movement had been arguing for. And for the most part, corporate sponsors wanted more direct and punchier advertising films than the indirect public relations products the movement had been delivering. In addition, the economy of the theatrical release of films was altering on both sides of the Atlantic, and there was little space for serious documentaries in the cinemas. So it was the popular acceptance of television, with its massive and growing audiences, that revived the fortunes of the documentary.

In offering documentary a new base television broadcasters also changed the form. This is not to imply that the expository mode disappeared: as we have just said, it flourishes to this day. However, we have already referred to television's different form of address (see Chapter 1). As a medium that delivers its programmes directly to the living-room, it actually fosters a desire for intimacy. Translated to the screen, this means getting close in on people's lives. The nature of the medium complemented the wishes of a number of documentarists of the late 1950s and early 1960s. They were growing increasingly unhappy with the distance at which the expository mode held its subjects, corralled, as it were, behind the guarding voice-of-God of the commentator. This new generation of film makers did not want to put their subjects through what they regarded as the charade of re-enacting roles. They wanted direct access to their actions and their words, not in a studio environment but in the places where they lived and worked.

To this end, Robert Drew and a number of associates in the USA began to devise both the aesthetics and the technology to enable them to make a new kind of film (Jacobs, 1979: 406–19). In the meantime, Jean Rouch and Edgar Morin were developing their thoughts on roughly parallel lines in France. These two first variants of what turned out to be the observational mode developed considerable potential to meet some of the needs of television programmers.

The technology of observational documentary

Although the category of the observational documentary as it was in its early years may be conveniently subdivided into two parts – the North American direct cinema and the French *cinéma vérité* (which evolved into the interactive documentary) – the two forms have in common that they exploited the new technology in the 1960s.

The advent of the 1,000-ft magazine fitted to a battery-powered, lightweight 16-mm camera facilitated the hand-held (hence mobile) long take much favoured in both kinds of film in the 1960s. The zoom lens made it possible to follow the action while constantly reframing it to record the most informative image. Meanwhile, the development of ever-faster film stocks meant that documentarists could shoot in most environments with nothing more than available light sources. All three devices made it possible for observational cinema to break the mould of earlier documentaries. In particular, where they had favoured group shots to reflect social groupings, the new forms emphasised the close-up of an individual moving freely in his or her own *milieu,* expressing his or her personal ideas, or listening to another person speaking (Arthur, 1993: 121).

The key technological explanation for this aesthetic shift of emphasis is found in an equally important electronic development – lightweight sound equipment that recorded a synchronous audio signal on quarter-inch tape. With this equipment the film maker could now, for the first time and with relative simplicity, both record participants speaking in shot as they went about their business and edit the tape, either in parallel with the images or independently of them. When rifle microphones were introduced to the recordist's pack, they improved the ability to select and privilege some sounds (usually the voice of a targeted speaker) over others. It was no longer necessary to bring a massive sound truck to capture the words of people standing stiffly in front of fixed microphones, as Edgar Anstey had first done with *Housing Problems* in 1935. Now film makers and interviewees could converse fluently as the latter went about their business. And while the difficulties of live recording meant that the quality of both sound and pictures shot in the field would often be rough (as it still sometimes is), this in itself added to the aesthetic of immediacy upon which observational cinema depends.

Observational documentary by its nature tends to require a high shooting ratio as the camera may have to be run for long periods when the crew cannot be sure that what they are recording will be of interest. So the later development of video technology made it possible to work in this mode less expensively since video tape costs much less than processed film stock.

Direct cinema

In a general consideration of observational documentary we need to examine what the programme makers claimed the new mode could do to help them gain greater authenticity and get closer to their subjects. Since their claims were often extravagant, we must distinguish them from the new rhetorical 'language' which they were constructing.

Perhaps the key difference in performance terms between the direct cinema mode and the expository style that preceded it was the refusal to allow re-enactments. Not only did the film makers who used direct cinema never say to the people in front of the camera: 'Just do what you usually do', they most emphatically refused to ask them to do anything at all. However, in their wilder assertions the new generation of documentarists claimed that the new form had something like the authority of scientific evidence, capturing what went on in uninterrupted takes without interference from the film crew. But notwithstanding such overenthusiastic exaggeration, the new style did indeed require the crew to be in on events rather than reconstruct them. The dramatisation of social history becomes the drama of the recording process as the camera follows the targeted person and produces a form of portrait (Arthur, 1993: 121). Direct cinema attempts to afford the viewer the opportunity to look in on and overhear the lived experience of others, to gain a sense of the rhythms and speech patterns of everyday life (Nichols, 1991: 42).

One of the main ways that direct cinema is distinctive in the eyes of its makers is that it prefers the crew to be all but invisible. Since the end of the 1950s considerable emphasis has been placed by those working in this mode on a related aspect of technological development, the miniaturisation of equipment. This was linked to the slimming down of the production crew to minimum numbers. Both changes were intended to enhance the viewer's sense of gaining unmediated access to the world. Sometimes the idea works in the way it was meant to, but there are occasions when the desire for invisibility has unforeseen consequences: paradoxically, a single film maker can sometimes be more disconcerting to those in front of the lens than a full crew. Sometimes the supposedly invisible presence of the film maker produces an uncomfortable feeling for the viewer, most noticeably when a participant recognises the presence of the camera or talks to a crew member (Nichols, 1991: 43).

There are other potential handicaps to the direct mode. Some of its leading producers deprive themselves of speech because of their insistence that commentary is a distancing device which reduces authenticity. They sacrifice what we have already seen to be the structuring device that organises a carefully managed point of view on a topic and orients the viewer through it. The absence of narration accounts for the disorientation many viewers experience when faced with films like those of Leacock or Wiseman. They are dropped into the middle of an action; the behaviour of the participants may be difficult to account for; and there may be no obvious angle on the topic which viewers can use to guide their response (see Kilborn, 1995: 24–7).

The directors of direct cinema were aware of the problem and attempted to compensate for the lack of narration in their construction of a new screen language.

Construction of a new rhetoric

The changes allowed the original exponents of direct cinema to claim that they had radically reduced the film makers' control of events in front of the lens, and the echo of their confident assertions can occasionally be heard to this day in the words of their successors. Events were said now for the first time to be allowed to unfold with minimal interference from the film crew. Although they were true in so far as they went, these declarations did not give a sufficient account of a number of factors. First, the more control direct documentarists cede to the people in their films during the shoot, the more carefully they pre-plan. For example, the work of leading British television producer-director, Roger Graef, is said to be virtually done when the cameras roll – to the extent that Charles Stewart, his cameraman of the early 1980s, recalls that they only ran the camera when they thought something that would interest them was about to happen (Collins, 1986: 127–8).

There is more yet to pre-production than this, a most important aspect being the choice of subject. We have already mentioned that direct cinema often foregrounded the individual – but this was not just any individual. Often subjects considered suitable were famous (like John Kennedy fighting Hubert Humphrey for the Democratic presidential nomination in *Primary* (Robert Drew and Richard Leacock, 1960)). This element added to the drama for the audience, then unaccustomed to eavesdropping on celebrities. Alternatively, subjects were chosen whose social role endowed them with an identity that was already established (teachers in Fred Wiseman's *High School* (1968); a bible salesman in Albert and David Maysles' *Salesman* (1969); and police officers in Roger Graef's thirteen-part series of 1982, *Police*). The point is that it was necessary for participants to have readily knowable identities to make up for the explanations of the missing voice-over narration.

In some films (*Primary* being a good example) an attempt is made to substitute the role of the absent narrator. In effect it is displaced on to journalists who are not affiliated to the film itself but are shown in press conferences asking questions for other programmes or magazines – a convenient means for the direct film maker to gain the advantage of hidden narration and interviewing while preserving the pretence of not interfering with life in front of the lens (Arthur, 1993: 122–3). Here is yet another device which offers the documentarist an indirect measure of control.

Typical of direct cinema is its distinctive rhythm. For instance, the sense of telling observation, of looking in on real lives, comes not only from the characteristic long takes and the recording of significant moments in the 'story' but also from the inclusion of periods of dead time. There are scenes in which nothing of narrative significance occurs but people simply get on with what we take to be their normal lives. The usual methods of eliding time within scenes – inserts and cutaways – are seldom used (Breitrose, 1986: 46). Since in the direct mode the rhythms of everyday life may be emphasised in this way, editing is often designed to sustain a sense of continuity in space and time rather than to support the logic of an argument (Nichols, 1991: 40). This is perhaps the main means by which the direct documentarist shapes the programme at the post-production stage. Establishing a sense of space and time in this way gives viewers the sense of being there. It compensates them for the loss of the position of ideal observer, which is often sacrificed as the people in front of the lens tow the camera operator around when they go about their business. It is not a new thought, but with direct cinema and fly-on the-wall programming viewers have to get used to seeing a lot of people's backs.

Ideology of direct cinema

Direct cinema and its successors give a sense of transparency which has been described as akin both to nineteenth-century Naturalism and to the empiricist Realism of the expository mode. It tends to encourage the viewer to accept that the real can be discovered through a detailed and scientific understanding of the way things appear on the surface, but it is more fluent in relaying that surface than the expository format. So this mode also allows the spectator to presume that the particular instance under scrutiny is typical of its class – that one high school, for instance, can stand for many others (Collins, 1986: 127-38).

Allen and Gomery show how the philosophical implications of direct cinema fitted the dominant political values of the Kennedy era. Such a documentary format was well suited to a time when American liberalism held that social problems were transparent. Society's ills could be relieved, it was thought, if they were understood; and they could be understood if they were first observed. The proper work of an enquiring press (including both journalists and documentarists) was the observation of social ills. It would enable the social institutions charged with dealing with these problems to rectify them through a rational programme of action. In other words, rather than wholesale radical restructuring, the optimal functioning of the socio-political system was seen to require no more than piecemeal improvement which any right-thinking person could put in place after making deductions from careful observation of the facts (Allen and Gomery, 1985: 232-4). As we shall see, this perspective is very different from that which animates many films made in the reflexive mode.

Cinéma vérité and interactive documentary

Making the distinction between direct cinema and *cinéma vérité* of the early 1960s, Erik Barnouw wrote:

> The direct cinema documentarist took his camera to a situation of tension and waited hopefully for a crisis; the Rouch version of *cinéma vérité* tried to precipitate one. The direct cinema artist aspired to invisibility; the Rouch *cinéma vérité* artist was often an avowed participant. The direct cinema artist played the role of uninvolved

bystander; the *cinéma vérité* artist espoused that of *provocateur*. (Barnouw, 1976: 254–5)

Where the rhetoric of direct cinema implies that the lives of the people observed by the camera are supposed to continue, as if they were oblivious to the fact that someone is making a film about them, in interactive documentary the presence of camera and crew is recognised. Those being filmed may talk direct to camera or acknowledge its presence in other ways. Alternatively, the film makers may themselves take advantage of the new synchronous sound systems to discuss topics with their interviewees, having the choice whether or not to appear on screen themselves. These opportunities were explored by Jean Rouch and Edgar Morin in *Chronique d'un été* (1961), this film usually being taken as the key innovator of the mode. They reversed the formal principles of the kind of anthropological film that Rouch had been making for some years. Instead of visiting an exotic culture untouched by western civilisation and attempting to make a scientific record of local customs and behaviours, they investigated 'the strange tribe that lived in Paris' (as Morin was to put it) to learn more about the state of France by putting themselves on screen to discuss live on film the issues of the day with a variety of people who were representative of wider society (Winston, 1995: 183–5).

Although, historically, *cinéma vérité* was the first instance of the mode, it evolved into just one version of interactive documentary, which appears today in a number of guises. Usually such programmes employ the on-camera interview as a means of recording the testimony of the interviewee. This makes their main procedures resemble those of the journalistic interview. Because interactive documentary emerged from such pre-existing television procedures, it has been readily normalised as a routine form of television practice. The on-camera interview gets round one of the disadvantages of the direct documentary in that it can only eavesdrop on what is said in front of the camera. In that mode, the viewer is denied access to anything the subjects may know but (possibly because they take it for granted) do not discuss. By contrast, the common thread running through the many forms the interactive mode may adopt is the encounter between film maker and subjects.

In this mode the film makers simply ask them (usually as witnesses) for the information to which they are privy. And of course they can respond directly to what the latter say.

Editing in the interactive mode
Editing in the interactive mode operates typically to maintain a logical continuity between individual viewpoints (Nichols, 1991: 45). However, this can be done in several ways, as the various possibilities mentioned above for this mode of documentary imply. The editing of pictures and voice tracks (whether separately or together) can be devised either to support or to undermine what participants say, since there is always the possibility that they are not telling the truth; or it can favour the words of some in preference to others. Alternatively, the presenter's words and the images which they validate can be deployed to give authority to the documentarist's point of view when it clashes with that of a witness. Doubts about the truth of what we are hearing can thus be used constructively, which is what Errol Morris did with the witnesses to a murder in *The Thin Blue Line* (USA, 1987), as we shall see.

Ideology in the interactive mode
It follows that in the finished programme the behaviour of film makers towards people on screen (whether in the way they interview, film, or edit what they have recorded) can vary widely: they may get so close as to share their subjects' circumstances or they may act as their mentors; they may seek to be impartial where there is conflict between speakers; or, at the other end of the scale, they may be hostile or try to provoke (Nichols, 1991: 44). At one extreme, with access or community programming for instance, control over the director and camera crew may be largely surrendered to a social group who instruct the film makers to make the programme in accordance with their intentions. At the other extreme, film makers not only retain total control but go so far as to act like unofficial prosecutors in a television 'trial'. The film makers' agenda may in such cases be so strong that they seek to control the meaning viewers take from what contributors say. Indeed, the interactive mode (precisely because, by putting witnesses on the screen

and letting them speak, it endows their words with authority) raises in particularly acute form ethical questions about the accuracy and objectivity of film makers (see Chapter 8).

Flies on the wall

Not least because television soon became the principal funder of documentary, producers began to reshape both the direct and the *vérité* documentary (as with every other pre-existing mode) in order to make them fit better the cultural and financial economies of television. As we have said, the documentary had to reach, entertain and hold larger audiences than before.

One response to this pressure has been that documentaries have for some years now been organised into series that are more likely to catch a viewer's attention (the nature of scheduling is examined in Chapter 9). They have this effect because the constituent programmes all centre on a single set of concerns or a particular way of seeing. This practice impacted on the television-based forms of observational programming which drew substantially on the techniques and stylistic mannerisms of their predecessors, direct cinema and *cinéma vérité*. Broadly speaking, two kinds of programme evolved – those which were preoccupied with institutions and others that were devoted to domestic lives.

The work of Roger Graef epitomises the former through such series as *Police* and *Decisions*. Programmes made by him typify a certain form of fly-on-the-wall production. They are characterised by the absence of staging and lights and by his agreeing to limit recording to matters covered by an agenda previously worked out with the institutions in which he is working. It is also typical of Graef's production methods that he refuses to intervene in the events that unfold before the camera; and in this respect (and the high shooting ratios such work requires) he is an obvious inheritor of the direct cinema tradition.

By contrast, most of the programmes produced by Paul Watson, including *The Family* (BBC, 1974) and *Sylvania Waters* (BBC, 1993) take domestic lives as their subject. In certain respects they owe a greater debt to the *cinéma vérité* tradition in that Watson's crew sometimes becomes a part of the action. Unlike Graef, Watson does not limit his filming to an agreed agenda. He is no stranger to controversy. There were suggestions by the family filmed for *Sylvania Waters* that he and his crew had selected scenes emphasising their rowdiness and racism and had omitted to present their more admirable qualities. Whatever the truth behind this particular allegation, in courting controversy this form of documentary responds to the insatiable preference of television schedulers that programmes should have drama and a pace that keep an audience engaged. This requirement makes infotainment a valuable product in the documentary market.

This could already be seen in the case of *The Family*, where a kind of feedback loop was established in that later episodes in the series were still being filmed after the earlier ones had been broadcast. Some members of the family group reacted to their sudden celebrity by playing the role of television personalities. The arrangement of a wedding, for instance, was dominated by discussions of how exciting (the bride's perspective) or wretched (the groom's) it would be to marry in the presence of the cameras. There is the implication of a form of staging in this.

Although fly-on-the-wall programmes made by producers with the kind of conscious social responsibility of a Roger Graef are much more restrained, they too are susceptible to the temptation of highlighting the extraordinary because it is more dramatic and more interesting to the casual viewer than the ordinary. And the handicap that afflicted direct cinema also limits fly-on-the-wall productions – namely, that they risk being superficial because the film maker cannot intervene or evaluate what his or her cameras record. This makes fly-on-the-wall a poor implement for setting events screened in their historical context, let alone for questioning social values.

Mixing modes
The hybridisation of television documentary goes even further, and we shall see more of this in Chapter 6. Paradoxical as it may seem, it is common in current television documentary practice for the observational and expository modes to be employed together. This too arises from television's need to grab and hold the viewer's attention. On the one hand, huge numbers of viewers enjoy eavesdropping on

the lives of others, be they doctors, lawyers, fire-fighters, single parents, or police. The direct testimony of both ordinary and extra-ordinary people fascinates; and the desire to experience at one remove what others have lived is a main attraction of the observa-tional modes. On the other hand, television cannot risk losing the interest of viewers by leaving them in the slightest doubt how to understand what they are watching. Hence the appeal of the expository mode, in which a narrator or presenter (who may also act as the interviewer) reinforces the central message of the programme to combat the distractions in the home. The hybridised documentary can get the best of both worlds, being able, for instance, to make use of both a commentary that provides a historical context to what is seen and direct access to the words and actions of the people in front of the lens (see Chapter 6).

The reflexive documentary

The reflexive mode is found where the manner in which the his-torical world is represented itself becomes one of the concerns of the programme. This is yet another mode which grew out of the dis-satisfaction of some programme makers with existing practice. They were reacting against the claims that observational documentary could achieve transparency. To them, the idea that television could show things as they would have been had the camera not been there seemed impossible. So reflexive documentaries make not only their subject matter but also their own formal qualities the object of questioning and doubt. In this mode, as in the others, documen-taries refer to the historical or social world, but while doing so they also investigate the ways in which they are showing and talking about it. Often they give more attention to the way they address the viewer than to the way they deal with the world.

Although we can look back to Dziga Vertov's *The Man with the Movie Camera* (1929) for an early example, the main development of the reflexive mode occurred in the later 1970s and the 1980s in Britain, Canada and the USA. As Lockerbie remarks, its growth is associated with a movement away from mimesis and towards formal innovation and experiment (Lockerbie, 1991: 228). *Chronique d'un été*, in which Morin and Rouch interact with their subjects on screen, was taken as a prototype (Breitrose, 1986: 47). And debates about reflexivity as the means of resisting the ideological domination of Hollywood movies were a feature of film theory in the journal *Cahiers du Cinéma* in the 1960s and in *Screen* during the following decade.

Documentarists working in the reflexive mode tend to target a minority audience, and they do so knowing that its ability to engage with innovative programmes has been enhanced in the 1980s and 1990s by two factors. The first is the sheer volume and variety of television programmes on air every day of the year. The second, as we have already indicated in Chapter 1, is that the television audience now has a much better understanding than it once did of how programmes are put together. Indeed, Corner suggests that the sophistication of viewers may actually work against the interests of reflexive documentarists in that reminding the audience that it is watching the processes of constructing a film may carry with it overtones of condescension (Corner, 1996: 25).

Rethinking the aesthetics of documentary

The contrast between reflexive and direct documentaries is clear, for the rhetorical presumption that usually governs the address of the latter mode is that (whatever was actually the case on the ground) the people in front of the lens are going about their normal lives as if the camera crew were not present. As if to prove it, if one of these people should look at or speak to the film makers, the illusion shatters momentarily and the spectator feels the jolt. Acknowledgement of the crew violates our sense that camera and microphone are supposedly neutral observers. It brings to our attention that a rhetoric is in play that denies its own existence and constructs a preferred perspective on the world that it persuasively invites the spectator to accept.

By contrast, programmes and films produced in the reflexive mode usually make the method of their construction intrude upon the viewer. Sometimes they make those methods obvious, but by no means invariably. They also frequently give rise to doubt in such a way as to discourage spectators from accepting that a single point of view is an adequate representation of the whole truth on any topic. A classic example is Errol Morris's *The Thin Blue Line* (1987), a hybrid film which participates in three modes: drama-documentary, interactive, and reflexive. Morris interviewed people involved in the successful prosecution of a man charged with the murder of a policeman in Dallas, Texas. His film screens the killing over and over again, restaged anew each time to fit the very different perceptions of, among others, the sole witness, the investigating police officers, the lawyers, the convicted man and another suspect. The plain incompatibility of their several versions of the event reveals the doubtfulness of the prosecution's case. The film was one of several factors that led to the case being reconsidered and the guilty verdict ultimately being overturned.

Like much reflexive documentary, the film's aesthetics and repetitious structure have what might be called a political dimension. Morris constructs his restagings in a deliberately artificial and glossy visual style, rather like that of contemporary *film noir*. In common with other reflexive documentarists, he employed actors to perform the roles of some of the people in the historical world. However, his work could hardly be more different from reality programming such as *Crimewatch UK* (BBC), which uses reconstructions to persuade viewers that what they are seeing is the way things might have happened (see Chapter 6). When Morris does film the actual participants, he presents them as talking-heads, but here too he disrupts convention. The lighting on the faces of some of his interviewees is dramatic; careful colour control is exercised in some shots, favouring blues and reds; the zoom, employed often in camera work to give emphasis to emotional moments, is never used; and the background to the talking-heads picks up geometric patterns that import into the heart of the film the postmodernist shapes of the Dallas skyline with which the piece opens. All these factors, in a somewhat Brechtian manner, make the resultant text strange to viewers by comparison with their usual expectations of documentary (see Chapter 2). The film's aesthetics have quasi-political implications too in implying that people's memory, perception and interpretation of events are distorted by the stereotypes (largely screen-based) that circulate in our culture. In common with much reflexive television and cinema,

The Thin Blue Line invites us to be wary of giving casual assent to stories (whether supposedly factual or fictional) made in accordance with dominant conventions and ideologies.

Interrogating the real in the reflexive mode

One consequence of this kind of deconstruction is the denial of realism, where that term is taken to refer to the unproblematic access to the world through traditional mimetic representation. As a result, the beliefs and values of not only those in front of the lens but also those behind it are made the subject of the film as it reveals the conflict between what may be a number of competing systems of belief. The viewer begins to question whether the images and sounds of the text could possibly represent the world adequately, since they are plainly a construction fashioned by the film makers. Thus, in the reflexive mode the encounter between viewer and film maker is emphasised, whereas the norm in the other forms of documentary is to concentrate attention on the film makers' encounter with the world (Nichols, 1991: 57–60).

For similar reasons, makers of reflexive film may enter the frame not as the participant observers familiar in the interactive mode but as *auteurs*. This ploy enables them to question the role of authorship in their own and, by extension, other documentaries (Nichols, 1991: 58). Not infrequently film makers using this mode actually represent themselves in such a way as to invite the viewer's ironic reflection on their ineptitude as professionals – the converse of the film maker as star. Nick Broomfield specialises in projecting the persona of an irritatingly persistent but amateurish investigator in, for example, *The Leader, his Driver, and the Driver's Wife* (1991), *The Selling of a Serial Killer* (1993), and *Tracking Down Maggie* (1994). In *Roger and Me* (Dog Eat Dog, 1989) Michael Moore plays the heroic, if bumbling, interventionist trying to intercede with Roger Smith, the Chief Executive of General Motors, on behalf of automobile workers in the plants that the company has shut down in Flint, Michigan (Corner, 1996: 155–70). The tactic can work well where the target is self-evidently a monster and the documentarist succeeds in getting him or her to turn at bay. Broomfield did this with the leader of the Afrikaner fascists in *The Leader....* However, if the viewer is not convinced that the target is a monster (which for many will be the case in Moore's *Roger and Me*) or if the film maker fails to get an interview with the subject (as in *Tracking Down Maggie*), the viewer is apt to think of him as both ineffectual and egotistic. That is not inevitable, however: for example, Moore's well-developed sense of irony is in *Roger and Me* not only turned on himself, it also colours his views on the ineffectual attempts by Flint's civic leaders to repair the economic damage to their town and makes his observations consistently mordant.

Some effects of self-questioning

In formal terms, the self-questioning approach leads naturally to complexity of structure. Lockerbie argues that texts often switch between different forms of representation: 'Snatches of song or dance, clips from other films, sequences of animation, and other film forms, are mixed in with documentary material' (Lockerbie, 1991: 228). Nichols identifies a number of formal devices which reflexive documentarists tend to employ to make their films strange and 'remove the encrustations of habit'. They include the deconstruction of familiar styles and coding conventions so that the viewer becomes aware of them. Parody, irony and satire are equally serviceable (Nichols, 1991: 67–75). Viewers' expectations of these documentaries therefore differ from their expectations of the other modes. They come to expect the unexpected, designed not so much to shock or surprise as to raise questions about the film's own status and that of documentary in general (Nichols, 1991: 62). In this respect they are experiencing a textual strategy not so different from Brecht's alienation technique. Precisely because these modes of address are unfamiliar in the context of documentary, film makers hope they will administer an enlivening shock. Their newly remade language can then be directed towards the social world to produce a politically engaged programme.

Political reflexivity

The discourse of certain documentaries may in certain social conditions present a challenge not only to the language, codes and conventions of established film-making practice but also to orthodox ideas (see also Chapter 7). When formal reflexivity complements political reflexivity, each can empower the other. This idea, voiced by Nichols, amplifies our remarks about the interpretative power of documentary in the opening chapter. He identifies feminist documentaries of the 1970s and 1980s as a set of films that exemplify this. It was a body of work which contributed to the enhancing of social awareness; and it arose both out of a desire to reshape the language of documentary and from pressures exerted by a widely based social movement (Nichols, 1991: 63–5, 69).

It is interesting to reflect that although it is now unfashionable to think of them other than as expository films with a paternalistic bias, many of the best-known documentaries produced under Grierson's aegis in the 1930s were politically reflexive in this sense. They deliberately challenged dominant practice not only in their experiments with form but also in establishing a discourse concerned with the working lives of ordinary people. The main difference from today's reflexivity is that Grierson and his colleagues did not set about questioning the nature of empirical reality. Nonetheless, today's writers usually judge the work of the British Documentary Movement to have functioned in support of the power of the state (see Winston, 1995: 17–96, Macpherson, 1980). Its role in producing documentaries that increased awareness of social problems (such as slum housing and appalling school buildings) tends nowadays to be de-emphasised. Such a change of interpretation raises the question whether the politically reflexive documentary of one epoch may, if its discourse becomes routine practice, be taken by historians of a later period to have been the conservative norm. It also reminds us that the reflexive documentary is by no means the only mode which can be used to heighten political awareness. Indeed, the reflexive tendency to regress from the social world to a concern with the mode's own mechanisms can inhibit its ability to deal frankly with a given topic.

Having said all this, those in charge of commissioning and scheduling documentaries tend to fight shy of reflexive programmes, mainly because they fear that viewers will not tune into them in large numbers. But they are also aware that the very conditions of television viewing are not conducive to over-critical reflection.

The first-person documentary

The origins of the first-person documentary lie in the individual's desire to record his or her own thoughts – originally, to put them on paper, more recently, perhaps, to record them on to audio tape. They also lie in the belief that these recordings of personal experience will be of interest to a general audience. Very few first-person screen documentaries were made on film because of the technical difficulties of making a finished, edited and dubbed product from the home. A great wave of them has been made possible by the high-quality camcorder, and they are products of the video age. The important technological developments for the market have included the fact that camcorders are relatively cheap to purchase and use domestic tape, which is far less expensive than developed film. They record synch sound readily (unlike Super-8 movie kits), and permit immediate playback. Because of the undeniable overlap between the home movie and the first-person documentary, it is tempting to say that the first-person documentary has existed ever since families with portable cameras began making home movies. Certainly the aesthetics of the latter have left their marks on the former. However, the home movie has a domestic audience to which its proud maker shows footage of people and places which that audience usually knows well because it is socially connected with them in some way. The documentary, on the other hand, always has an audience outside the domestic circle (although first-person programmes are often made with an awareness of the film maker's circle). Members of the wider audience seldom have any prior knowledge of the people on screen, and the first-person film brings new information to them.

Aesthetic choices in the first-person mode
Given that the home is often the dominant location of first-person films and that the film makers are not fully trained professionals, there are obvious overlaps with home-movie aesthetics, although once again there are differences. The principal of these is that the first-person film always has a theme and some sort of shape. Neither is essential to the home movie.

Nonetheless, we can readily see that camera angles are quite different from those which polished professional work has made familiar. Images are not composed with the same eye for a balanced 'speaking picture', and, as has already been suggested, narration is mainly left to the voice of the film maker. Filming is not always planned with a view to editing in cutaways and inserts, and as a consequence there is a great deal of quite mobile, somewhat inaccurate hand-held camera. Scenes tend to be built more within the camera than on the edit suite. All this can produce films made in unorthodox styles. If so, they face the challenge of taking the audience with them into strange territory. But they have the great advantage of breaking away from long-held conventions and showing us the social and historical world through fresh eyes while binding fantasy into their highly personal realism (Keighron, 1993: 24–5).

The principal device that licenses the entry of subjectivity into the documentary world is not a visual one at all but the return of narration after its banishment from direct film. When it is used in reflexive films, narration will often take the form of a personalised voice-over (Lockerbie, 1991: 228). In the first-person documentary, on the other hand, it may take the form of an inner monologue. Thus, in the case of the autobiographical film we have come full circle, since the voice-of-God spoken by an individual relaying his or her own thoughts has a virtually unimpeachable authority.

The licensing of subjectivity
The first-person documentary not only has the power but is almost under an obligation to feature one individual's idiosyncratic observations of society. Precisely because the format licenses subjectivity (we want to know how the film maker's view of the world differs from rather than confirms our own), subjectivity is one of its strengths. Even so, there is a set of gatekeepers between documentarist and public. The commissioners of programme series such as the BBC's *Video Diaries* exercise control in the selection of those comparatively few projects that go ahead from a large number of applications. It is usual (since this is access television) for them to choose projects proposed by people with opinions that are under-

represented on television, but they are under no obligation to do so. Thus, even though a format such as *Video Diaries* gives precedence to the personal world views of individuals, the control of what is actually transmitted on air remains with the broadcasting institutions. By the same token, the existence at the BBC of a Community Programming Unit has provided a vital fillip to the development of this form of personal documentary.

The first-person mode is able to do directly things which other documentaries have to labour at. It can reveal an individual's personality simultaneously from the inside (interior monologue) and the outside (the opinions of others, which may well be delivered pungently to camera by friends and family). The information which a film maker discovers by recording and reviewing his or her own thoughts and those of others can feed a process of self-discovery. Alternatively, the film maker may undertake a task or an adventure which has the same effect. One stage further on (as in Willa Woolston's *My Demons: The Legacy*, made for *Video Diaries* in 1992), the journey becomes both a recovery of autobiographical history and a self-administered therapy (see the analysis of this film in Chapter 4).

By definition, then, first-person films license subjectivity; and imagination often supersedes observation in them, so that they have the potential to reverse one of the founding dictates of the documentary movement – that it should respect the objectivity of the outside world, if necessary at the expense of subjectivity. This is not to deny that there must be something that is faithful to actuality in front of the lens. An autobiographical film will usually put on screen the images of the film maker's life in family, community and beyond. That may indeed be the limits of its ambition. But it can do other things: its business may be with the documentarist's fantasy life. In such an instance, first-person documentary does not always need to worry too much about Dai Vaughan's horse (see Chapter 2). It was 1983 when he wrote about the horse and the impossibility of making a documentary about a unicorn. At that time there was no evidence that televised documentary could engage with fantasy and illusion. That is no longer the case today.

Poetic documentary

The poetic documentary mode is distinguished by a number of elements, two of which are particularly striking. The first is that it departs from the familiar proposition that documentary should construct an argument about something – usually a topic that has a bearing on the historical world. Poetic documentaries tend to substitute showing and suggestion for argument. They can help to evoke a strong sense of being there (as opposed to focusing on a more conceptual mode of understanding). They may allow images and sound to dwell on the referent in the real world, but when they do so, as Nichols says, they will imply rather than explain (Nichols, 1994: 100). This is apparent in the example we examine in Chapter 4, Lucy Blakstad's *Lido* (BBC, 1996). Her crew collect many of the sights and sounds of the outdoor public baths that are her subject – those recorded sights and sounds are among her film's principal pleasures. But no arguments about the lido develop from them. Rather, like the images and sounds in Basil Wright's *The Song of Ceylon* (1935), they contribute to the sense of the location being a magical place.

The sense of the extraordinary which such films convey leads to the second element that characterises this mode. It consists of the fact that they give less attention to the referent in the historical world than to their effect on the viewer. Of course, that expressive and poetic elements should be found in programmes dominated by a realist agenda is not new; many of the most memorable documentaries are made so by a vigorous and striking style. This was as true of *Nanook of the North* in 1922 as of *The Thin Blue Line* in 1987. Poetic style has often been used to enliven the expository documentary and make it interesting to the eye and ear (Nichols, 1991: 35–6). Indeed, Grierson often claimed that some of the films made in the 1930s by the British movement had been the more effective for having a poetic style. In the 1980s and 1990s he has been castigated for having allowed the poetry to get in the way of social purpose – but then *Night Mail* (1936) remains vivid to the memory in a way that the doggedly functional *Children at School* (1938) does not (see Winston, 1995: 55).

What is new in the poetic mode is that these stylistic elements function as the principle that organises and dominates the film. The expressivity of the programme makes the viewer rather than the historical world their primary referent. Their emotional affect is designed to dominate the viewer's reaction to it; and in so far as such programmes draw attention to themselves rather than their referent, it may be to enhance a sense of shared experience on the part of viewers (see Nichols, 1994: 94, 102, 104). Some films may aim to raise issues in the collective consciousness. Others, like *The Song of Ceylon* and *Lido* have a dream-like surface which suggests an interest in the collective experience of the semi-conscious. It is as if the documentarist would like his figures to people the viewer's imagination.

There are two further hybrid formats which test the boundaries between documentary and related forms of television programming. They demonstrate once again the capacity of the television economy to shape the documentary to its needs. Although we deal with them in fuller detail elsewhere in this book, they are mentioned here because they are distinctive formats that have obvious connections with documentary.

Reality programming

We give a more complete account of reality programming in Chapter 6, and therefore simply summarise here some of the main features of this format.

Reality programming is the mode in which television packaging makes the most sophisticated intervention in actuality-based production as it seeks to highlight the sense of shared experience or lived reality. Such programmes use a wide range of television techniques to enhance the entertainment value of the material. Indeed, many are entirely devoted to prime-time entertainment (for example, *You've Been Framed* (ITV), a collection of home video clips of pratfalls assembled by the programme makers for their comic effect), and have no meaningful connection with documentary. But even where they do, the emphasis is on capturing the vibrancy of real-life events in short packages, each with its unmissable emotional climax. These 'hits' are linked into programme format by a celebrity presenter who often builds audience anticipation of each incident so as to focus that anticipation on the sequence of emotional impacts which arrive every three or four minutes. The entire package has to be easily digested and sufficiently attractive to encourage viewers to tune in week after week. It follows that each series has its own characteristic and tightly defined themes, and these are usually identified by the series title: *999* (BBC, UK), *Rescue 911* (CBS, USA), *Crimewatch UK* (BBC), *Cops* (Fox, USA) and *America's Most Wanted* (Fox, USA). Thus the preferred outcome is a tabloid style of programming that is strong on human interest but short on socio-political analysis (See Kilborn, 1994b).

Just as in the tabloid press, this kind of programming brings in its wake substantial ethical problems – relating in particular: first, to unwelcome intrusion into private lives in the gathering of information; second, to editorial distortion of what happened in the interests either of increasing the entertainment value of an item or of making it fit the thematic profile of the programme series; and third, to the desensitising effect upon viewers exposed to a cascade of five or six dramatic and emotive hits in each half-hour programme.

The drama-documentary

A large topic in its own right, drama-documentary is analysed at length in Chapter 6. It is particularly difficult to define, partly because its borders are as soft as those of any other hybrid form, but in addition because the term refers both to a mode which incorporates several types of drama-documentary and to certain production techniques. In brief, drama-documentary is found where the primary intention of the programme is to provide a documentary chronicling of events, but in which dramatic reconstructions have been employed whose function is to make the account more persuasive or to depict events (such as court cases in Britain, or the activities of terrorist conspirators) that could not be shown by other documentary means.

Because the drama-documentary inevitably makes use of the devices of fiction (though in a more restrained way than documentary-drama), key questions that always arise in considering such programmes concern the accuracy of the research on which the programme is based and whether the material was sensationalised to maximise audiences and meet the commercial imperative (Kilborn, 1994a).

The celebrated films of this type are usually one-off programmes whose subject matter aroused controversy, often because they dealt with issues that governments would rather not have stirred up – like *Cathy Come Home* (BBC, 1966) or, in more recent years, *Who Bombed Birmingham?* (ITV, 1990) and *Hillsborough* (ITV, 1996). However, drama-documentary has other functions which have become part of the standard rhetoric of factual television. As a technique that relies on the dramatic or quasi-fictional reconstruction of actual or hypothetical events, it supplies many of the dramatically heightened sequences in reality programmes. Examples include restaged scenes of the emergency services at work (*999* or *Rescue 911*), and hypothetical stagings of crimes (*Crimestoppers* and *Crimewatch UK*).

In one sense, drama-documentary brings us round to where we began this chapter in that, like the expository mode, it depends upon the reconstruction of events. The principal difference is one that critics of the mode often seem to forget: drama-documentary features reconstructions which are explicitly signalled as such. Through a variety of devices, including what may well be massive advance publicity, on-screen titles, explicit cues in the narration and credits for cast members, scriptwriters and researchers, the drama-documentary usually makes itself known to its audience. By contrast, the expository mode restages its events and seldom admits to it. Programmes that work effectively in either mode remind us that there is more to reality than surface appearance alone.

Tackling the text

DOCUMENTARY ANALYSES

The preceding chapter emphasised the idea that documentaries are artefacts constructed in a variety of ways. We want now to examine more closely how the individual components of the constructed text work together to create for viewers the experience of watching a documentary. Because the term 'documentary' covers several modes, the properties of individual texts will differ accordingly. There is no template description that will cover all the different types. Since the full range of possibilities is immense, we shall select for scrutiny typical examples to illustrate how the text functions in most of the modes. The exceptions are the drama-documentary and reality programming, which we cover in Chapter 6.

Despite what we have just said, the main components of documentary have remained fairly constant since the coming of sound. Most documentaries still rely on a mix of filmed sequences of actual or reconstructed events, archive material, commentary, interview material, diegetic sound and music.[1] Of no little significance in any textual analysis will be the addressing of those issues already broached in this book: What claims does the text make to provide a credible, realistic account? What structuring principles govern the editing process? What role does commentary (where there is any) play? And similarly, what function does music (where there is any) have?

Before we discuss specific documentaries, we consider the key role played by the editing process and also the importance in documentary of establishing the idea of a definable place and time. These functions are, of course, intimately connected.

Editing

It is not surprising, given that so much discussion about documentary centres on its capacity to represent the real, historical world, that for many people there follows a more or less unspoken assumption that the most crucial phases in its production are pre-production and production, or research and location shooting. But it is important not to underestimate the potential impact of post-production (see Chapters 8 and 9). Indeed, some documentaries, unlike story-boarded fiction, may actually be conceived and realised in the editing room; and all of them are shaped there, sometimes taking on forms and meanings which had not previously been in the minds of the producer or director. Even the creation of a plausible sense of time and place depends to a great extent on the editing.

> The way in which the camera is used, its many movements and angles of vision in relation to the object being photographed, the speed at which it reproduces actions and the very appearance of persons and things before it, are governed by the many ways in which editing is fulfilled. (Rotha, 1966: 79)

Today, the critical understanding of editing goes further and it is seen as an important factor in determining how we read a particular text and are positioned by it. Dai Vaughan is one of the most experienced of British documentary editors:

> What is required is an editing style that will invite a rhythmic response founded not on the rate of satisfaction of prior expectations but on the interest engaged by the shots – a style in which rhythm will be perceived as legitimating the action simply because the action itself will be the prime component of the rhythm. (Vaughan, 1988: 41)

In the analysis of documentary, therefore, we should pay attention to its rhythm, since tempo has a decisive impact on the way viewers are likely to interpret the text.

We should also seek out the criteria which appear to have been used to link image with image and one sequence of images with another; and also the way human speech, sound effects and music are mixed with one another and relate to the images. Consider, for instance, what happens when a short sequence is cut into an interview with a documentary subject and that segment appears to bear out what the subject is saying. Conversely, an image may be inserted which introduces a different perspective on what is being said and which may even contradict the spoken word. We shall refer to such instances in Ophuls's *November Days* (see below).

Comparison with one of the most frequently used patterns of editing in mainstream feature film is also instructive. In fictional modes the emphasis will typically be on driving the narrative forward and involving the spectator in the fictional world thus created. We are likely to be positioned to see parts of the action from the point of view of one or more characters and may be encouraged to empathise with them. Conversely, others may be made into abhorrent object-like figures whose perspective on the story we never adopt. Whilst the narrative line in many documentaries will be equally strong, it will usually, as we said in Chapter 3, be more concerned with establishing an argument or making a case than with pointing up dramatic action or embellishing characters.

Since most of us do not get the chance to watch a programme being edited, we are obliged to analyse finished text. This can be quite difficult. It is helpful to remember that the finished product represents no more than a fraction (in some cases a tiny fraction) of what was recorded. In observational modes the shooting ratio is 30 to 1 and higher. In first-person work, such as *Video Diaries*, it can reach 150 to 1 (Keighron, 1993: 24). Some of the material that is left out will simply have been technically inadequate, but a great deal will have been dropped because it does not fit the purposes of the director and editor. It can also help the analytical process to run the images without sound and, vice versa, to play back sound without watching the images. When they are dissociated, the principles underlying the construction of each and the marriage of both can be more readily observed because the text loses some of its seductive power.[2] And that illuminates the final point to be made about editing: that it is the prime factor (along, where relevant, with commentary) in integrating all the parts to make the whole text – which itself, to use a trusty but apposite cliché, turns out to be more than just the sum of the parts.

Creating a sense of place and time

As we have said in earlier chapters, documentary filming is almost by definition location-based. Nevertheless, documentarists will always be careful to ensure that the finished text contains a sufficient number of markers to give the audience the sense that 'this is the world we live in' or 'this is where the events chronicled in the account took place'. It is not uncommon for their chosen titles to refer either to when (see *November Days* below) or to where (see *Lido* below) they were shot. In other words, they usually work hard to create and reinforce a sense of the authentic (see Britton, 1992: 26, Nichols, 1991: 149–55, 181–5). Most documentarists will not be concerned to evoke a sense of mystery (as are some producers of fiction) but will wish to be open about where and when the events chronicled are occurring.

Place

Most documentaries will use one of the standard narrative devices to establish where things are happening. These include having the narrator stand in front of – or move through – the location in question or allowing the narrator's voice to be heard over shots of the location. Compare these techniques with those of fiction film. In the latter it is rare for there to be narration in the sense of a voice explicitly telling us what is happening: although there will usually be a series of establishing shots, these are designed to orient us as we enter a particular story space. With documentaries there is a different set of expositional techniques, and shots of a particular locale are presented with a different intention. Viewers recognise that these buildings, this landscape, this part of town, are to play a role in the following account, but not as a backcloth to some dramatic conflict which will unfold before us and into which we will be drawn, willingly suspending disbelief that such events could occur in such a place. In the typical Hitchcock movie, the Bates motel (in *Psycho*) or the corn field (in *North by North West*) become virtually synonymous with an inner state of being. They carry with them, by virtue of association, strong overtones of threat, horror and suspense. Often we experience them from a

character's point of view, which heightens the emotional tempera-
ture of a scene.

In documentary, shots of the real world will be taken by the audience to indicate that they have a role to play in a yet-to-be developed
argument. Thus our relationship with these locations is of a different order from the one we would have in fiction film. This is not to
say that locations in documentary are demoted to the status of a
backdrop: in many types of documentary they can become the focal
point of attention, as happens in natural history programmes, journalistic inquiries into living conditions or stories about environmen-
tal pollution. The manner of representing a particular place (the
vantage points from which it is covered, the editing style employed,
or the non-diegetic music dubbed on to underscore the visuals) does
provide clues to what that scene meant to the documentarist.
An example is Werner Herzog's terrifying vision of burning Kuwaiti
oil wells in his *Lessons of Darkness* (1992), where the images
complement spoken biblical texts and the music of Wagner's *Götter-
dämmerung* to supply a vision of a place like Hell. But there will
almost always be a greater measure of detachment or distance. It is
rare in documentary for locations to be objective correlatives of
moral or personal ideas.

Time
It is convenient to consider two aspects of this topic – first, the
rhythms according to which the passage of time is represented; and
second, the means by which documentarists indicate whether they
are dealing with past, present or future.

The passage of time in documentaries is a matter of record: it can
be and usually is noted. It is presented as measured and orderly. It
does not, as in fiction, bend with the fluctuations of the characters'
fortunes. A sense of the world passing in its daily rhythms is usually
communicated. Whereas in fiction film there are various ways of
dealing with temporal ellipsis, many of which conceal the way time
has been altered, in documentaries the passing of time, or the shifting between different time planes, is usually marked more explicitly.
This contrasts with the perception of time in many fictions, where it
stretches and shrinks under the impact of the emotions (which the

spectator is likely to be seduced into sharing) of one or more of the main characters. Often, indeed, in documentaries we are positioned as witnesses, which implicates us in vouching for the fact (because we believe what we are shown) that time is passing at its normal daily speed.

In fictions film makers may place their story in a particular historical setting, but this is often just part of a strategy to heighten the effect of realism. In documentaries there is usually a much more sustained effort to register precisely where we are in time. A host of devices is available to do this; perhaps the simplest operates where narrators are employed. Their use of the present, past or (rarely) future tenses and the detail of their scripts, even the characteristics of their delivery, are all reliable indicators. The people who are interviewed will also make plain whether they have in mind the present state of affairs, or something which might yet occur, or (often the strength of the elderly) things they recollect from the past.[3]

A particularly good example of how the passing of time is marked – and indeed how it can be turned into a structural feature of a documentary – is provided by the large-scale series, *People's Century* (BBC, 1996). Here the film makers made a regular practice of selecting from newsreel or archive coverage of events long since past an anonymous individual whom the camera happened to pick out at the time. They then traced and interviewed that person to put on tape the stream of his or her memories. The contrast between the present circumstances of these elderly people and the black-and-white wraiths of their youthful selves exploits the full potential of eye-witness accounts and makes a powerful device, first, for reminding us of the changes in not only individual but also national fortunes, and second, for allowing these witnesses to challenge received opinions of the significance of the events being covered.

Examples of documentary texts

In the remainder of this chapter we shall isolate some of the main features of documentaries that belong to the first five modes discussed in the preceding chapter. We shall study them in the context of that discussion and also look at how their components interact, with particular emphasis on the way sound and image work together. And we shall consider how the particular requirements of television discourse can be seen to have had a part in shaping these texts.

Sad, Bad and Mad: an expository documentary

Transmitted by the BBC in December 1994, *Sad, Bad and Mad* was the last of five programmes in a series called *The Trial.* The series broke new ground for television in that it was the first time that cameras had gained access to British courts of justice. As it happened, this breakthrough occurred in the Scottish courts, where a different legal system operates from across the border in England. The programme had several functions: it revealed a representative selection of the kind of routine cases that make up much of the week's workload of a procurator fiscal (the equivalent of a public prosecutor) in the Edinburgh courts; it formed part of a series depicting major aspects of the distinctive Scottish judicial system; and it was sold to the public for its voyeuristic appeal – for the chance to see real, if petty, criminals in the dock. And thus it aimed at a much wider audience than would have had direct experience of the judiciary.

Although its content was new, the structure and style of this documentary were based on familiar norms. Indeed, it is possible that the stylistic conservatism of the series was a deliberate ploy on the part of the broadcasters to emphasise the responsible manner in which the BBC was dealing with a politically sensitive subject. The programme takes an expository form and makes use of an unseen narrator, a man with an authoritative Scots voice who describes succinctly the outlines of the typical working week of a procurator fiscal. Immediately we find that the functions described in Chapter 3 as being typical of commentary fall into place. In particular, the voice-of-God acts as our guide, and everything it tells us is borne out by what we see and what interviewees tell us. From the start, the factual nature of what we are told is emphasised through a statistical summary of the number of arrests that are usually made during a weekend in the city. We are at once confident that we being led into a serious, sober-minded inquiry. That impres-

sion is confirmed by all the filmed sequences, which complement
and illustrate what the narrator says.

The programme's point of view is set up from the start in that the
only people who are interviewed are procurators fiscal. (In other
programmes in the series different participants in the system, such
as defence lawyers, express their points of view.) This is not to say
that the fiscals threaten the off-screen authority of the commentator. On the contrary, what they say is given the programme's tacit
endorsement as reliable information in that it always complements
and never conflicts with the narrator's words. Together, the two
parties carry the argument. And the core of the argument is that,
given the massive number of cases that pass through the procurators' office and the courts, a system of justice which is inevitably
rough and ready is the best that can be hoped for in most of the
cases concerned with the relatively minor crimes of drunkenness,
common assault and theft.

Two other important factors give the programme its structure.
First, to shape our sense of time, events are linked to a chronology as
the week's events go by. At the start of the week the emphasis is on
bail hearings for those who have been held in police cells over the
weekend. Five days later, our attention is focused on the trials of
those whose cases have finally come to court.

The second factor might be described as the programme's alternating rhythm. This adds to our sense of time, but it also – since we
are carried outside the courts into the streets, the police cells and the
procurators' offices – ensures that we know that the events covered
are taking place in Edinburgh. The rhythm of the programme oscil-
lates between rapid action and a more considered pace. Among the
swiftly moving sequences are the following episodes. On the city
streets by night the cutting and action is relatively fast as the police
wagons swoop on suspects and arrests are made. Though less
frenetic, the pace remains brisk as large numbers of people are led
into police cells and we cut to the procurators' office where the
volumes of paperwork that all these arrests have generated have to
be digested and processed. Cutting remains brisk – it is almost a
montage – as the bail cases are heard and most of the individuals
charged seek to get out of police custody as rapidly as possible.

Thus the editing illustrates the procurator's assertion that the pressure of numbers has the consequence that few cases – only the most serious – can be accorded a treatment that is more than cursory. Again, a similarly brisk pace is adopted in the coverage of the trials that take place on the Friday. Here the fiscal has described the system as being dependent for its functioning on eight out of ten people who are charged deciding to plead guilty. Were more to elect to stand trial, the system would jam up. We then follow the fiscal's case load of ten individuals, nine of whom plead guilty and are shown in a montage receiving sentence from the presiding sheriff.

These brisk episodes alternate with sequences which are paced much more steadily. There are broadly two kinds of less rapidly cut sequence. One consists of interviews during which procurators fiscal give an account of their work to an interviewer who is neither seen nor heard. As has already been indicated, much of what we see in the programme illustrates their words. The other comprises trials, which are covered at greater length – as in the case of a young man charged with drug dealing which runs for several days.

Where extended coverage of a court case occurs, we have leisure to perceive not only that the pace of cutting slows but also that a two- or three-camera set-up enables the crew to cover speeches from all parties in the court room without apparent interruption. The quality of sound is generally good throughout the programme, and certainly so in the court sequences. Here too, the clear and relatively high-key lighting reveals facial expressions clearly, in contrast to the footage secured on the streets, which has either been recorded through a night-vision lens or been electronically degraded to look that way. Lighting of the quality described in the courts matters because it enables the viewer to make out via facial expression the thoughts that underlie the words of the various parties. For example, the procurators and defence lawyers do not allow their faces to reveal anything in their poker game with witnesses and each other. But a judge allows a certain scepticism to play over his features while listening to a police officer insisting under cross-questioning on the accuracy of a blatantly improbable piece of evidence. By contrast, cutting to the young officer's face, we witness his discomfort (confessed by his wincing glance) at the realisation that he has made a fool of himself. And the expressions of the accused often reveal their personalities quite nakedly.

As we said earlier, the programme's structure and style are not innovatory. For the most part we get what we are led to expect. The procurator's account of the people whose cases he deals with as being mostly white, mostly male and mostly under twenty-three years of age reflects the title of the episode: a small proportion are mad, he says, a rather larger number bad, but the great majority are simply sad – frequently unemployed and without goals in life that matter to them. The majority of cases we see in the montage sequences amply confirm these observations. To this extent, *Sad, Bad and Mad* exhibits the kind of stereotyping to which we referred in Chapter 3. Not only the accused but also the police and the procurators are rendered as being typical of their kind – figures not altogether unfamiliar from countless documentaries about the law. It should be added that the programme also fits the classic properties of televised documentary discourse in that it could be seen to inform and educate. There is one further way in which it matches what we have described as the characteristic features of this mode: it shows the realities of the judicial system as if they were self-evident to anyone who happened to be in the right place to see them. In other words, it deals in mimetic realism; its themes are on the surface, not hidden away.

There are two other significant elements inherent in the programme. First, we cannot but be aware that we are looking in on real-life British court proceedings for the first time. This factor formed the basis of the advertising campaign designed to ensure that the programme grabbed the interest of viewers. Second, dramatic suspense is employed to discourage the audience from switching channels.

That suspense centres on the much fuller coverage given to the case against the suspected drugs dealer. We have no more idea than the procurator fiscal what verdict the jury will hand down, and although he shares his thoughts with us on how each stage in the case is going, we too have to wait for its decision. The process, as with most contests, is deeply interesting – one party will win and the other lose – and it draws us in. What is more, there is a twist in the tail. The young man is found not guilty – but then is unexpectedly taken back to his jail cell. We, like the jury, have been kept ignorant of the fact that he is currently serving a sentence for assault. The outcome is a genuine surprise.

For Richer, For Poorer: an observational documentary

Channel 4 transmitted *For Richer, For Poorer*, a fifty-five-minute programme, in its *Cutting Edge* prime-time documentary slot in 1995. An observational film, it is an excellent example of how careful control of time and place can do away with the need for commentary. This programme looks at the rituals of matrimony through the eyes of three English couples as they prepare for and go through with their weddings. The accounts of the respective pairs are presented through alternating, interwoven storylines in which we cut between comparable moments experienced by each group.[4] The couples appear to have been selected because they, and their immediate families and friends, live by quite distinctive sets of values. One couple are upper middle class, the second have newly attained affluence through a company they themselves have set up, and the third have no work and are living on the breadline. Not the least of the programme's fascinations is that we perceive each couple as being typical of large numbers of people in their social stratum, yet each family group lives hermetically sealed off from all other strata of English society.

Centring as it does on one of the most familiar of social rituals, the programme is typical of observational documentary in that it has a clearly defined topic which the audience can recognise instantly. It also has a built-in time line deriving from the events themselves. The programme begins with the couples musing on what they expect marriage will bring them. These thoughts give way to increasingly intense preparations for the wedding, and culminate in the great day itself, with its ceremonials, awful speeches and organised mayhem. Given that the programme has its own narrative time line (or, more accurately, three such entwined threads), it also provides the viewer with a strong sense of its contemporaneity through the way the participants speak about marriages, their social circumstances and, in particular, their attitudes to work or unemployment.

Notwithstanding the significance of time, it has to be said that in this programme the observation of place is dominant, as the film shows the three couples in the *milieux* they inhabit. It is one of the main elements that substitute for commentary. So, for example, we cut from the gilded luxury of the haunts of the upper-middle classes, where Elizabeth and Christopher are putting the finishing touches to their wedding-day preparations, direct to the grimy concrete tower-block where Julie and Peter live. It is just as much the places as what the couples say about themselves that comment on them. To hear Christopher mention that he is an investment banker confirms our sense that there is money behind him and Elizabeth, but we can see that they are having their wedding reception at the Ritz and that her parents live in a magnificent Queen Anne house – so the pictures tell us much of what we need to know. Meanwhile, Peter mentions that he cannot afford to buy stamps for the wedding invitations and that he has never held a steady job, but the camera alone gives us plenty of evidence that he and Julie are hard up.

Although there is neither voice-of-God commentary nor on-screen presenter (and for this reason the documentary is properly described as observational), the programme does provide a clear view of its subjects through other, ingenious devices. First of all, it uses irony. For example, the third couple, Jo and Rob, work together. Rob is a self-made business man, passionately interested in making money and having it define his individuality. He and Jo speak of their determination to have a wedding that is completely different from anyone else's, but as they do so, the camera pans down a row of identical mock-Georgian terrace houses to settle on their front door. They are not at all as unusual as they would like to be – which is no doubt why the programme's researchers chose them.

Even stronger irony – and much of the programme's thematic material – is revealed through the juxtaposition of the beliefs, values and attitudes of each couple (together with their families, since the parents also reveal their thoughts). These are delivered to an un-heard interviewer who sits out of frame. Most of these people (the financially poorest being the exception) are resoundingly sure of their values, however gently they express them. But the programme makers' device of cutting between them subtly undercuts their certainties.

Although the three couples do not meet, they are united by one belief: that marriage is worthwhile – although they want very different things from it. Elizabeth and Christopher say they are traditional and that marriage is a system that gives stability. Jo and Robert see it as a natural extension of their shared business venture, a kind of confirmation of their working lives. They each see themselves as likely to be working successfully in thirty years' time. Julie and Peter both appear to come from broken families and are determined that marriage will change their lives. They intend that their marriage should pull Peter away from the petty criminality of his adolescent years and give them both a sense of purpose which they feel they lack without it. It seems more like an act of faith than a plan – and its touching vulnerability contrasts sharply with the confident materialism of the other two couples. If this illusion fails Julie and Peter, they will have little left to rely on.

Pre-recorded popular music provides one other element of commentary. The film makers have chosen songs that add considerably to the sense of ritual; but at the same time they also add to the sense of irony as they date from the 1960s and earlier and therefore celebrate love and marriage from an outdated perspective. The songs introduce an incongruous note because they do not match what we know about the aspirations of our present-day couples.

Where *Sad, Bad and Mad* gives priority to information and education over and above entertainment, the reverse is the case with *For Richer, For Poorer.* Or, more accurately, it is the entertainment value that the viewer first enjoys, watching these people in their hermetically sealed worlds, almost all of whom have blind confidence that the values they hold dear are universal truths. But the simple act of juxtaposing the three couples gives the viewer the pleasurably vicarious power of seeing their quirks and whimsies exposed to the world. By the very same token, however, the programme is most informative; but it sugars the pill of its rather uncomfortable observations by making the experience of watching it so enjoyable.

This, then, is a programme which seeks to maximise its audience appeal while taking a fresh look at some peculiarly human foibles through an ironic lens that nonetheless respects the well-established canons of documentary value. It has the characteristic transparency of the observational mode and the sense of direct involvement as, for example, the camera crew freely move among the wedding guests and eavesdrop on their conversations. If, almost inevitably, it tends to highlight some of the obviously dramatic moments in these social rituals, its ironic stance enables it most effectively to avoid the kind of superficiality that (as we saw in Chapter 3) can limit observational film. (We will have more to say about irony at the end of Chapter 9.)

November Days: a reflexive documentary

The first thing to say about *November Days*, a long documentary that was transmitted in the BBC's *Inside Story* slot in 1990 and runs for two hours and forty minutes, is that it centres on a strong authorial presence. Like Nick Broomfield and Michael Moore, to whose work we referred in Chapter 3, Marcel Ophuls makes himself a player in the investigative drama he initiates. Like them he adopts a variety of masks when he approaches people: he too sometimes pretends to be inept, and he occasionally provokes humour at the expense of those he is questioning. An older man, however, his range of personae is broader and subtler than those of Broomfield and Moore. And it is affected in *November Days* by the fact that his personal history – as the son of a Jew who fled the Nazis – causes him to be involved in his subject in a way that Broomfield never is and Moore merely pretends to be. Ophuls shares the sorrow of some of those he interviews while he presses home the guilt of others.

November Days starts out as a chronicle of the events leading up to and following the destruction of the Berlin wall – events captured largely through news reports. But the chronicle with which we are concerned is actually played out through people's memories. And in pursuing those recollections it soon extends to cover a much longer period – back to the 1930s. Thus present-day footage is juxtaposed with memories of the way things once were. The film's structure is, loosely described, that of an investigation. However, it does not take a problem–solution format, not least because Ophuls, a moralist evaluating how people acted in the past, does not try to offer solutions. Nor is it shaped by the application of a logical progression. In this film x does not necessarily lead to y *en route* to z. Rather, the structure seems driven by associations. For example, something that somebody says may lead to an associated idea, and Ophuls will allow his film to be waylaid by the unexpected connection. That rhetorical style goes with an unreadiness to hammer home any conclusions to which the investigation might lead. Ophuls uses the reflexive style to reinforce the viewer's perception that not all the moral issues which he puts on the screen are easily judged.

The programme starts with what seems to anticipate a straightforward technique. Ophuls re-screens BBC news footage of the nights one year earlier, in November 1989, when the people of East Berlin crossed for the first time in huge numbers into West Berlin and so began the process that led rapidly to the destruction of the Wall and the eventual unification of Germany. Some months after those events, Ophuls traces some of the joyful individuals who featured in that coverage and asks them to expand on their thoughts now that time has passed. Some of these people are ordinary members of the public, and Ophuls explores with them their hopes and fears for the future as the old East German economy collapses and the ideals of Communism are swept aside by the overwhelming desire of so many to savour the riches of capitalism.

But other interviewees are senior members of the Party, and Ophuls uses all his personal and directorial skills to plumb their motives and their sense of responsibility for the events that overtook the nation. As an interviewer, he gets cosy with the subject; he asks a number of questions that are posed in a friendly, conspiratorial manner (as if to say, 'Given that we have to deal with such a difficult topic, let's do it in the easiest way possible') but which then open a deep trap (see Saynor, 1990: 46). He does this with Egon Krenz, the final leader of the regime, tying him into knots. Later he buddies up to a Neo-Nazi, Michael Kühnen, only dropping in the information that he himself is a Jew when they are well into the conversation. He gets close to Brecht's daughter, Barbara Brecht-Schall, who had been a political ally of Honecker. Ophuls reminds her of the former acquaintance of their parents, but then, when she claims not to have had anything to do with Honecker, ruthlessly cuts to footage of her in his company. To make matters more pointed, he underlays this episode with Bing Crosby's recording of 'The Song of Freedom' – a pop song which recurs through the film.

There is a certain irony in Brecht's daughter being discomforted in a film which respects the dramatic precepts of her father (described in Chapter 3). In fact, Ophuls's whole approach is Brechtian in that he deploys a variety of techniques to encourage a thinking response on the part of his audience. In one favourite device he constructs unexpected juxtapositions which interrupt the flow of his interviewees' arguments, undermining any feeling of trust that might have been building in the viewer. For example, he cuts away from an interview with a senior Party figure to a parrot whose cage stands in the same room and dubs words into the bird's mouth which mock its master. He underlays romantic Tin Pan Alley songs of the 1930s. He creates a tension between their benign fantasies of love and the chilling experience in Germany, both under the Nazis and, latterly in the East, under Honecker's authority. There, universal espionage (often with family members reporting on one another) destroyed free speech and was used by the state as a justification for ripping families apart.

There are many points where Ophuls inserts sequences from well-known feature films to comment on what his interviewees are saying. For example, Brutus is seen stabbing Julius Caesar in a scene from Joseph Mankiewicz's 1953 film of Shakespeare's play. Ophuls so places the footage that it comments by association on Honecker's expulsion from office by his former colleagues. This is typical of the manner in which, through the juxtaposition of interviews and film scripts, old newsreel footage and songs, he encourages us to doubt that we are being told how things really were.

With all its many features and extraordinary moments, the problem that *November Days* creates for the viewer is not unfamiliar in films made in the reflexive mode: it is to know what the film is actually trying to say, since so many different ideas are being introduced. Ian Buruma says that Ophuls probes into the myths, lies and horrors of the old German Democratic Republic (Buruma, 1996: 229). But there's more even than that: at various times, Ophuls discusses state terror under the East German regime, and it is compared with the terror of the Nazis. He talks about anti-semitism right across twentieth-century German history and interviews a present-day fascist. With industrial and Party workers he raises the issue of the collapse of the East German economy as it is swamped by the mighty machine of the West; and arising from that, he opens up comparisons between the morality of the communist and capitalist systems. Not only is there much and various material, but, as already hinted, with Ophuls discussions of these kinds do not result in clear victories of one moral position over another. So, not surprisingly given its diversity of ideas and the profusion of its elements, the film is a sort of maze, not altogether well shaped, but fascinating to roam through. It is a film which reminds one of the saying that it is more satisfying to travel than to arrive.

In the end the maze takes its core from Ophuls's investigation of himself. The moral conundrums he sets others are to some degree problems which he faces himself. Although he seldom expresses his own opinions, one occasion on which he does so falls at the very end of the film. Asked by one of his interviewees where he stands on the issues he has been discussing, he says the two immeasurable gains for East Germans are that they now have the same freedom of self-determination as everybody else, and that the Wall has gone. For him, all other anxieties pale into insignificance compared with this. And he ends his film with one of the workers who has just lost her employment nonetheless celebrating the twin freedoms she and her fellows have gained: to say what one wants and not to be exposed to state terror for doing so.

My Demons: The Legacy: a first-person documentary

Willa Woolston's documentary (transmitted by the BBC in 1992) extends the *Video Diaries* format beyond the confessional form (which it quite often takes) to the point where it has an explicit therapeutic function. Her film records a journey from London across North America. It takes her through Los Angeles (her daughter's home), on to Detroit (where her son lives with his wife and their infants) and culminates in Philadelphia, the city where she grew up and the rest of her family still live. Her purpose was to visit her sisters and her children with the specific aim of finding out more about herself by recovering memories of her childhood. The record of her travel across the States becomes the trail of an inner journey in which she goes back into the past to get to the psychological roots of the physical and mental torture she and her sisters suffered at the hands of her stepmother. That mistreatment has left her with a life ruled by savage apprehension and relentless traumas. During her all-too-frequent bouts in crisis she has found herself pushed to drink and suicide attempts; and all the intimate relationships in her life, not only with men but also with her own children, have been damaged.

The construction of the tape is not unusual for a *Video Diaries* programme, but it does draw attention to itself, given the nature of the subject material. Willa Woolston acts as her own narrator, and so the voice-over, far from being a dominating voice-of-God address in the manner of many expository documentaries, quietly utters the painful truths that have shaped her life for decades. At the core of the film are very long takes during which the camera rests, more or less static, on individual members of her family while she talks to them from behind the lens. Other moments of equal weight occur when she puts herself in front of the lens and resists cutting the shot until she has managed to utter all the horrors that are flooding her memory. These shots – which form entire sequences – record the moments when Willa probes her sisters' and her children's memories, and they quiz her about hers, all of them slowly moving together towards a fuller understanding of the woman who tortured them.

Together those of the older generation bring back the traumatised memories of childhood as uncomprehending victims of their tormentor. They recall being hanged by the thumbs from pipes in the basement and left there for the entire day. One sister was once tied to a chair and abandoned in the summer sun until her skin blistered. And they remember other terrible abuses and assaults. Worst of all, they remember the special horror of their father, whom they loved dearly, knowing that all this was going on and yet doing nothing for fear he might lose the vivacious young woman who had rescued him from widowhood.

Although Willa Woolston retained overall editorial control of her Diary, skilled technicians worked on the post-production. The editing has a professional finish (for example, cutting sometimes on actions to speed them up, delaying other moments for emotional impact by holding shots long after the action or conversation has ended). Other examples of good craftsmanship are seen in the sophistication of the film's internal form, which takes its outline from Willa Woolston's search through recollected family history. As we have said, most of these memories are covered in long takes in close up. They are therefore also harrowing for the viewer to witness. Into these prolonged takes the editor has inserted extensive home-movie footage taken by the father. In these shots the sisters and their stepmother are seen at the various periods to which their words refer – and they are always serenely happy. But this is not irony; rather, it racks up the pain and gives authority to the eldest sister's words when she says that, try though she might, she could never get the neighbours to intervene and help them in any way. Because the family looked as comfortable together as we see them to be, there was no compelling reason for outsiders to act.

The voice track alternates between words spoken direct to camera in the conversations just described and Willa's voice-over when she describes obstacles in her way, or the reasons for her moving from one place to another. When she moves between cities or houses, a montage of shots (invariably including airports, roads seen from moving cars and family greetings or farewells) marks the transition. These montages act as markers of time and place; but they also provide a change of tempo and mood to give the viewer some relief from the intensity of the intimate moments between members of the family.

The camera is always in Willa's hands (except when, very occasionally, one of her sisters turns it on her), and from time to time members of her family, either from mild embarrassment or when agonising memories thrust back into their conscious minds, request her to switch off. She seldom obliges – and the effect is to build up our respect for a group of singularly courageous people.

As is usual in this format, most shots were taken with nothing more than available light. Synch sound was recorded direct on to videotape, sometimes through a single microphone, and on other occasions with a pair of clip-on mikes. As it happens, the somewhat rough-and-ready quality of the pictures and the occasional imbalance in sound levels when Willa speaks to her family from behind the camera contribute to our sense of intimacy with these people. These accidental devices, which arise from the various technological, personal and economic constraints of the shoot, actually assist in the construction of a rhetoric – almost a language. This compares with two equally effective devices popular in previous decades. Then, hand-held camera and reframing via the zoom lens (both techniques plentifully used by Willa Woolston) developed a rhetorical signification. It derived from the fact that both practices were originally necessary in capturing documentary footage on the wing. However, they became means of giving the same feel of urgency to footage which had been quite carefully planned to look the way it did.

The tape has in this respect something of the surface texture of a home movie, although from the plain evidence of its careful preplanning it is anything but that. The blend of the apparent casualness of the shooting style with the high professionalism of many of the tape's aspects (including its editing and dubbing) builds the viewer's confidence that Willa knows what she is doing. In this way, the mix of professional and amateur elements locates *My Demons: The Legacy* in a strategically placed situation within television discourse. It offers itself to the viewer on the one hand as being deeply personal (as indicated by the amateurish elements), but is rendered acceptable (even trustworthy) in terms of familiar television practice by the professional control of its pace, structure and purpose.

One of the tape's strengths is the way in which its aesthetics complement Willa's journey of self-discovery. To understand this, we need to describe briefly what happens. As she looks further into herself, and her family reveals significant fragments of its history that she had not known, Willa becomes aware that the lives of each generation are connected by meaningful repeating patterns. First, she discovers that, although she never inflicted any physical injury on them, her children suffered quite grievously (feeling responsible, as children often do, for the parent's suffering) as witnesses to her hysterical outbursts and drunken rages. Able now for the first time to share her painful remorse with them (and to make her discoveries stick by recording them on to tape so that she can review and confirm them later), she eases some of the blocked channels for the love that they have found so difficult to share.

No less significantly, she begins to understand from what she has inadvertently done to her offspring that the abuser herself may be worthy of sympathy. This breakthrough is, to her astonishment, reinforced when her eldest sister and her daughter tell her that Ferris, her stepmother, had herself been the victim of a horrible family life. She was the only daughter of a father who absented himself on the birth of the infant and a mother who drifted into alcoholism as a consequence of his desertion. Ferris seems to have ended up both parenting her mother and taking the blame for her condition on to herself – just as Willa's children did two generations later.

All this information gives Willa the courage to contact the old woman in the hope of understanding her better. Although she succeeds in working up the courage necessary to make the initial telephone contact, and then rings several times during the last weeks of her stay in Philadelphia, Ferris will not allow her to get any closer and declines a visit. But Willa discovers that even talking to her on the phone builds her comprehension as she listens to her stepmother's persistent lies and self-deceits. Her growing understanding neutralises the sting of the demonic image which has terrorised her all her life. Willa returns to London and moves out of her old flat. Her film closes with an image taken through doors opening out from the houseboat she has made her home. As we look across the calm waters of the Thames, she tells us how her whole life has changed. For the first time in her adult life she is able to sleep without nightmares and wake without dread. She feels in control in a way she never did before.

The style of this tape enriches its themes in addition to adding, as we remarked above, to our sense of its authenticity. On the one side, its professional qualities complement the sense of ritual. We find ourselves following the route made familiar by psychoanalysis that leads into the realms of repressed memory. Eventually we perceive that recognition of the causes of deep pain can aid healing of the psyche. But on the other side, the amateur and obviously inexperienced aspects of the shoot convey in a deeply personal way the isolation of this brave woman as she maps and records what is to her (as to any individual who starts out alone on such a journey) the uncharted route to the terrified centre of what she must perceive to be her unique and wounded self.

The extent to which work such as Willa Woolston's has driven back the boundaries of documentary can hardly be overstated. When Dai Vaughan described how the documentarist makes use of the image of a horse (see Chapter 2), he remarked, 'You cannot make a documentary about a unicorn' (Vaughan, 1983: 28). This was a simple aphorism designed to underline the thought that the documentary must take the objective world we live in for its subject matter. At the time he wrote, it was broadly accurate, but today, although a *Video Diaries* programme cannot actually show fantasies unless it generates computer images, it can and does readily make them its subject.

Lido: a poetic documentary

Lido was directed by Lucy Blakstad, and transmitted by the BBC in 1996. It has the qualities of a deeply felt, personal view of her subject that one tends to associate with the poetic mode. This form of documentary making is, like the reflexive mode, often *auteur*-centred precisely because the poetic vision expresses itself in what the viewer takes to be a person-to-person register. Its way of looking at things (both photographically and thematically) is so unusual that we take it as the vision of an individual.

The subject matter of *Lido* is simple – the open-air public swimming pool that gives the film its title and the Londoners who frequent it during the hot summer of 1995. The entire film (with the exception of an introductory helicopter shot) was recorded within the perimeter of the swimming baths and surrounds. A strong sense of place is established from the start. All the footage was filmed outdoors and, apart from the nocturnal sequence with which it ends, in broad sunlight. Not the least of its delights for viewers living in a cool, sun-starved climate are the memories it leaves of the screen radiant with aquamarine blue and bathers lit by sunlight and its reflections.

Light is the first element that gives the film the strong poetic aura which underlies some of its themes. But if televisual poetry is to succeed in communicating the rich meanings that its sounds and images generate in the mind of the viewer, it has to be carefully structured. There are two main devices that give *Lido* its form. The first device is discreetly handled and consists of an implied movement through time as the baths, at first empty except for a few lone swimmers, gradually fill up when families, couples, people hoping to find partners, the old and the young join the afternoon rush. The film ends with its only night sequence, as a party of friends gather to share in a ceremony of commitment between a lesbian couple. The wedding vows exchanged, some of the guests dive into the pool to celebrate, and this symbolic consummation brings with it the idea that in the joyous moment of public union both the day and the summer season have come round to a close. It is typical of the poetic mode that it arouses emotion in the viewer – here one of pleasure at this culmination which so fittingly concludes the events the film has covered.

The second structuring device is more obvious, and through it we can reveal some of the means by which the film generates feelings in the viewer. It consists in an alternation between three kinds of footage: first, observation of the bathers, second, interviews with them – both from camera positions that are out of the water – and third, shots taken from submerged camera positions.

The bathers are observed as they undress, while they swim (some lazily, others for exercise, a few as if to break personal speed records) and as they lie round the margins of the pool taking the sun. In these scenes the camera is quiet, often static, and in many shots takes up a low angle, which catches the attention because it is unusual – as if it were adopting the point of view of someone sitting by the pool side. Ambient (that is, background) sound is handled distinctively in these sequences in that, although at times it gives a realistic perspective that complements what we are seeing, it is not always motivated by what the images show. For example, there are occasions when the baths are packed with people, but the level of summer sounds will suddenly be lowered or even cut to silence (which may be then softened by a quiet, luscious music).

Lucy Blakstad conducts the interviews herself from beside the camera. She is not seen, but some of her questions are heard on the sound track, and once in a while respondents address her by name as though they had got to know her during the period of shooting. This, and her presence near the margins of the frame, adds to the sense of an authored text. Around the pool she finds people of all walks of life – the powerful (senior civil servants) and the powerless (unemployed women and men); the well-to-do and the poor; gays and straights; and all races – and she talks to a representative selection. Her questioning tends to start with an inquiry about what attracts each individual to the lido, and then works round to encouraging people to talk about themselves and their wants and pleasures as well as what they know about the other people who come to the baths. She uncovers a diverse polyglot community, all wanting different things from their lives and their recreation but living together in an easy-going and contented mutual tolerance.

The sequences shot on the underwater camera introduce a compelling element of fantasy. Streams of bubbles and blue light embellish the swimmers as they fishtail past us in slow motion – a pregnant woman, a skinny old man, young men and women flaunt-ing their bodies, kids having a good time. A disembodied pair of spectacles floats down. Someone drifts to the bottom in the lotus posture. Individuals find the peaceful isolation they seek. Mean-while, silky music accompanies the weightless bodies and the camera too swims free, tilting and swaying in the shifting water. Some of the people we see in these sequences are known to us from earlier pool-side encounters. Thus the element of fantasy is seam-lessly joined to the sunlit life above. The fantastic light that falls on everything above and below the water line dissolves the boundaries between illusion and actuality. The fluidity and beauty of everything seen and heard beneath the surface make for a feeling of deep delight. It is infectious and colours our perception of all the people in everything they do. So the fluid underwater visions of the people become as integral a part of them as their earthiness. The film, by fusing the fantastic with the factual, offers the viewer a metaphor for wholeness – wholeness as the union of mind and body in the well human being, and wholeness also as the union of diverse people and cultures in the thriving community. These themes are drawn harmoniously together through the lesbian wedding that ends it.

Lido is not only poetic in its effect: it invites reflection on a number of themes – the nature of a community (so it has ethnographic overtones); the changing patterns in personal interaction in contemporary British society (for example, the lesbian wedding and single parenthood); and the need to escape from the public persona that each of us has to bear. However, the poetic element dominates. As we said when outlining the nature of the mode, the emotional affect of such a documentary seems to be designed to dominate the viewer's reaction to it. It is as if Lucy Blakstad wants her figures to people the viewer's imagination.

PART III

Fact, fiction and drama

Telling a story
FACT, FICTION AND DOCUMENTARY

Narrative and the creative treatment of actuality

Whatever the means by which documentaries engage with either the real world or an imagined one, they usually have some form of narrative structure. Although it is not inevitable that they employ narrative devices, it is common – and there is a reason for it. It is part of the shaping process whereby the documentarist transforms the fragments of reality into an account directed at an audience of viewers. Philip Rosen shows what happens when this process is missing, using the earliest actuality films to make his point (Rosen, 1993: 74–5). In their making, the camera was simply set down and pointed in such a way as to film whatever was in front of it (actuality) at the moment it was operated. So it recorded fragments selected from the space and time continuum of the real world, such as the onrush of workers emerging from the Lumière factory. The projector then presented what the camera had registered, and the significance of those shots lay in their photographic verisimilitude: they seemed to show fragments of reality to the audience. Such a means of proceeding, however, although able to convey some significance, did not provide the film maker with much opportunity to fill the text with meaning; in the instance cited we find out very little about the Lumière workforce other than that they are leaving the factory. Therefore, to give greater depth to these silent actuality films, exhibitors sometimes employed lecturers to tell the audience what meanings they should take from them. Sometimes they might have done no more than identify the places and actions in front of the camera; but on other occasions, it seems reasonable to guess, they must have acted as story-tellers, building a narrative around what was unfolding on screen. This may seem strange to us until we recall the present-day equivalent – the proud parent talking bored guests through home movies or videos of the family.

The documentary (as opposed to actuality) film is usually said to have first appeared with *Nanook of the North* (Robert Flaherty, 1922). Thus it occurs relatively soon after the mainstream feature film had become the norm for the industry. As John Grierson and his colleagues used to stress, the documentary took issue with what they regarded as the juvenile themes proliferating in Hollywood entertainments and their familiar escape from reality. But while it sought to innovate new, socially oriented themes, it nonetheless expressed them through some of the dominant mechanisms that had already been established for the production of meaning on the screen. So the documentary does in many cases depend upon the basic elements of narrative, which it uses as a means of dramatising its subject matter (see below). Documentarists have deployed narrative strategies in one form or another in each of the broad modes that we have described. It is one of the two basic methods of shaping meaning in documentary, moulding its constituent elements into story form. The other is the construction of an argument, a topic to which we turn later in this chapter.

Narrative, no less than argument, skews meaning: the very process of putting material into story form inflects it, since the film makers are making decisions to select certain aspects of what happened at the expense of others, and to present them in the specific way they now interpret them. Having captured fragments of reality, the film makers actively intervene by shaping those fragments into an artefact. Thus narrative is inevitably both selective and subjective. In addition, it has a fixative effect: the manner in which the narrative represents events as having occurred may well be accepted by the audience as being the way things were. If for no other reasons than these, it is a powerful and (if used irresponsibly) a potentially dangerous means of communication. In this regard it would be almost impossible to over-stress the potential ideological implications. By employing narrative, documentarists can sometimes lull audiences into a false sense of security about the authority of their account. A good story can lead viewers to believe that they are getting the only authoritative version, whereas it may in fact be just one of many possible perspectives on the topic. One step further, narrative deployed irresponsibly can be a potent instrument for convincing audiences that lying propaganda speaks the truth.

Narrative

What is the nature of narrative? It usually requires as a minimum a sequence of actions that have a goal or purpose, and these actions occur in a story world which occupies a specified time and place. This is true no matter whether that story world claims to be real, as in a news report, or entirely fantastic, as in science fiction. Narrative also requires that causal connections be drawn between the events that it brings together in the sequential chain. The first event is seen to bring about the second, and the second then bears on a third. Where 'characters' are involved they are likely to be shown both to have played a part in initiating the events and to have been changed by them. The documentary film, when it uses narrative devices, exploits these common principles of sequencing. It does so not only through the commentator's words but also by selecting and privileging certain times and places over others through both camera placement and cutting together the resultant footage (see Rosen, 1993: 74–5). This makes it possible, by bringing the parts into relation with one another, to construct and advance a story. These features are readily identified in the type of programme (to take a common format) that might carry the title '*A Day in the Life of* [let us say] *a Bank*'. It will have a beginning (perhaps at opening time), a middle (when the doors close) and an end (the early hours of the next morning), and there will be some kind of purpose to the story (to show the routine and the extraordinary activities of the day). A series of events will unfold as the twenty-four hours pass, which will implicate certain characters. The latter will usually be people (the staff and customers), but the place (the bank building) or the institution (the bank as a legal entity) may in documentary take on functions which make them resemble characters.

If the 'day in the life' format provides documentary with one of its basic narrative structures, another is the 'journey of discovery'. Much beloved of ethnographic and natural history documentarists, this format gives the audience the agreeable illusion that it is sharing with the programme's presenters the quest for knowledge new to Western humanity. But of course this structure is as much a narrative contrivance as the first. We mentioned in Chapter 1 yet another format, the problem–solution pattern (which we shall analyse further when dealing with argument below), and there are more. What becomes apparent is that documentary, no less than any other genre, makes use of formats and stereotypes because they are readily understood and enjoyed by viewers. Thus (to develop a point made earlier) it is not just the irresponsible documentarist who may falsify the truth. There is always a risk of skewing the representation of an event that happened in the social world in the very process of adapting it to the demands of narrative. To take an obvious example, the ethnographer or natural historian may not be taking the first steps into strange new territory, despite what their films appear to show. They may have been living there for months, and during that period their subjects may have adapted their lives to the intrusive presence of a camera crew (see Loizos, 1993: 106). In that case, what is shown on the screen skews what happened on the ground.

Narrative in classic fiction

In classic fiction the narrative structure will often give pride of place to main characters (usually people, but sometimes creatures or even things) who, at the start of the story, exist in a more or less stable state of being. Something disrupts this stability and causes problems for the protagonists. As a consequence, they spend the rest of the story working towards a new, different state of stability in which some difficulty or problem has been resolved. In this basic form of plot circumstances change the protagonists; as they undergo transformations they take actions which in turn set in progress further alterations in the story world. Characters and events interact, and both are changed as a result. Not the least of the pleasures enjoyed by the viewer is the experience of being teased and held in suspense while the intricacies of the story are being worked through and the fate of the characters hangs in the balance. The final outcome of all these transformations is frequently the establishment of the surviving characters in a new stable state, which is different from that in which they began. This is one of the principal goals of the narrative. Another, no less important, is to involve the viewers in this world of make-believe action and events in such a way that they experience a feeling of identity with one or more of the characters and are swept along on the tide.

Narrative and argument in documentary

The typical narrative profile of a documentary is rather different. Nichols accepts that narrative is indeed often found in documentaries but suggests that it is given less emphasis than in fiction. Rather, documentaries often exploit the problem–solution paradigmatic structure in which, as we said in Chapter 1, an issue or problem is first established. It is then examined so that its historical background and present dimensions can be clearly perceived. Finally, a solution to the problem (or, if that cannot be offered, possible ways to finding one) may be introduced.

This popular format suggests why documentaries frequently give prominence to evidence and argument. Sounds and images, rather than being elements of a plot occurring in an imaginary universe, stand as evidence and are treated as such. That tendency in turn gives priority to the structuring requirements of an argument, which call for an attempt to demonstrate a case on the basis of relevant evidence. In documentary that argument will usually concern itself with something external to the text (that is, relating to the historical world) rather than (as with a fiction) internal to it.

The consequences of these factors for the construction of the documentary text are far-reaching. In order to advance its argument a documentary has to employ a particular presentational strategy so that viewers are persuaded that evidence has been properly marshalled and fairly presented. This requires the deployment of logical, analytical and rhetorical skills. By comparison, fictional narrative will tend to concentrate on the motivation of characters, the plausibility of actions and events and the internal consistency of all the parts of the story (Nichols, 1991: 18–20, 125–6).

Although the framework of argument is likely to predominate, the evidence – that is, the information provided by camera and sound sources – may well be presented in story form, so questions of narrativity do still arise even when argument is in play. Certain devices that help to structure fictional narratives are also widely deployed in documentary. For example, in Michael Moore's *Roger and Me* the story revolves around Moore's attempts to arrange a meeting on camera with Roger Smith, the chief executive of General Motors. The audience is kept waiting to find out whether Moore will manage to get his interview. Delays, retardation and suspense are all in play. These devices have much the same role in documentary as they do in fiction – they engage the viewer's attention and seek to hold it.

The setting up of puzzles or enigmas can also have a role to play, although less dynamically in documentary than in the detective genre. However, viewers are offered much the same tacit contract – that if they keep watching, the solution to the puzzle established at the beginning will be revealed to them (Nichols, 1991: 123–5). In *Roger and Me* there is a kind of enigma which centres on the question of what a meeting between the two protagonists could achieve. Only at the end of the film do we register the anticlimactic truth, which has been facing us all along, that a meeting would have achieved nothing.

As is typical of documentary, then, in *Roger and Me* the construction of a story is far from being the end of the matter. Rather, an argument is developed from it,[1] which, in this case, concentrates on the indifference of a vast corporation to the way it destroys the lives of the people it has made redundant.

Although argument is one of the distinguishing characteristics of many documentaries, this is not to claim that documentaries express unchallengeable truths. As Nichols reminds us, more than one argument can be constructed around every fact (Nichols, 1991: 116–17). So even a simple matter of record (such as a statement of the names of the horses in a race and the order in which they passed the finishing post) is subject to interpretation just as soon as a commentator begins to explain why one did well and another faltered.

It is worth making the point that when the development of an argument is the main core of the programme, narrative can be dispensed with altogether. A good example of such a format is the so-called lecture film. This is a development of the old way of presenting (referred to at the start of the chapter), in which silent films were sometimes accompanied and explained by speakers. In the lecture film the voice of a narrator recorded on the sound track develops a theme and illustrates an argument. There is no story in such material as (to take an early example) *Housing Problems* (Edgar Anstey, 1935) or *Children at School* (Basil Wright, 1937) or their successors, and they resemble academic essays. As we shall see, significant types of television programme are given over to making statements and developing arguments.

Narrative in relation to fiction

If we think again about the 'day in the life' format mentioned above, we can readily perceive that it could just as well be found in television drama and feature films as in documentary. We need therefore to find out how narrative and fiction differ from each other before making the distinction between fiction and non-fiction.

As we have seen, narrative involves story-telling processes such as creating a scene of action around a cause-and-effect chain, setting it in a well-marked time scheme and mobilising characters in some shape or form. It is, Branigan suggests, a particular way of assembling and understanding information that is best contrasted not to fiction but to other ways of assembling information that do not use narrative. Examples of the latter include essays, lists and diagrams (Branigan, 1992: 1–2, 192).

While narrative concerns structure (the way in which information is assembled, presented and understood), fiction concerns its believability (the truth value that we place on what we are told).

Fiction

The key word 'fiction' is so common that it barely sustains contemplation – which makes it worth starting with what appears to be obvious: fiction is not fact. It ought, at first sight, to be quite easily separated from documentary, because the latter seems not to claim to be a product of the creative imagination. However, the concept of fiction has roots which are not so remote from the idea of fact. The word 'fact' derives from the Latin *factum,* a thing done or made. The term 'fiction' has had a number of meanings, but in one earlier usage it had the sense of an artefact – a thing made or invented with skill; so here its meaning remains close to that of fact. But it also referred to imitation (a copying of fact, so to speak). In addition, it meant to feign – which is particularly interesting since the individual who feigns creates with the imagination, and the resultant idea can be either truth or a lie, or, even more interestingly, neither.

In the context of story-telling, the meaning of the word 'fiction' does indeed fall between the two poles of truth and falsehood. For instance, even where we read a fiction title promising us 'a true story', we usually do not expect it to be exactly that, or we would be watching the news or a documentary or reading an honest auto-biography. It is helpful to think of fiction as occupying a middle ground in that it is often concerned with feigning the provisionally true. That is the burden of what John Searle says:

> Fiction is much more sophisticated than lying. To someone who did not understand the separate conventions of fiction, it would seem that fiction is merely lying. [But] what distinguishes fiction from lies is the existence of a separate set of conventions which enables the author to go through the motions of making statements which he knows not to be true even though he has no intention to deceive. (Searle, 1975: 326)

The conventions of fiction require from viewers a different kind of activity from that which is needed for narrative, according to Branigan. He finds our ability to understand a narrative (or for that matter a non-narrative) comparable to our ability to understand a sentence. That is distinct, however, from our *belief* as to its truth, plausibility, rightness or realism. We may understand a narrative that we do not believe. Conversely, a reader can learn from fiction without mistaking it for the real world. Fiction is neither an illusion nor a false belief; rather, it seems to require that the spectator or reader connect text and the world in a special way.

A fiction does not determine exactly which object or objects it represents, and this openness is what distinguishes fictional references from other sorts of reference. An element of choice is built into the text requiring the perceiver to search and exercise discrimination in assigning a reference to the fiction and in applying it to a more familiar world. (Branigan, 1992: 192–4)

This idea is brought to bear on our topic by Nichols when he argues that fiction offers the viewer access to a potentially unique, imaginary domain. Of course, it may bear resemblance to other fictional worlds to the extent that it belongs to a genre. And, equally obviously, it may bear resemblance to our world, particularly if, for example, it is made in a classic or transparent realist style (see Chapter 2). But it is always at the service of the creative imagination. By comparison, documentary claims to offer access not, as fiction does, to *a* world, but to *the* world. To be sure, in directing us towards the world, documentaries remain texts – and as such they (like fictions) are constructed and they convey ideological values – but that world is the social, historical world in which life and death are, at the extreme, inescapable actualities (Nichols, 1991: 109–10). In fact, we can test this from our own experience by recalling the impact of images of death. The representation of an actual death in documentary or news footage always affects us differently from the deaths portrayed in fictional screenplays.

Put more formally, we may say that in the fictional interpretation of a symbol it is necessary to recognise that the material presence of the symbol itself does not necessarily imply an immediate reference to an actual object. Fiction can evacuate the symbol of its social history as well as its basis in fact. This may sound complicated, but it is easy to understand if we consider an obvious example encountered every day in film and television. When we look at an image of a fictional character, we do not interest ourselves primarily in the actor who plays the role (that is, the historical person with a factual existence) but in the character represented. The person represented in such an image is simultaneously factually specific (for example, the actor Harrison Ford) and fictional (the character Indiana Jones). We could, of course, read his image as factual (which might mean a reading centred, for instance, on the actor's career and acting methods), in which case we would connect the shot to the actual person or object in the real world. There, we respond to the documentary imperative, the invitation to make connections from the filmic text to the actual person whose actions constituted the pro-filmic events.

In contrast, fictional images are not accompanied by any such imperative. With fictions we find that a different kind of invitation comes with the text and we are not asked to connect the shot of an actor to the actual person Harrison Ford. Rather, as Branigan says, we defer making the immediate reference from the text to an object or person in the real world. Instead, postponing making such checks, we consider the information yielded in the succession of shots within the film. In other words, to find out more about the character Indiana Jones, we refer in the first instance not to the real world but to the fictional text. It is what that character does on screen (and what others do to him) that gives us the most fruitful source of information with which to build an idea about him. So we need to wait until we have all the information that the film can give before attempting to reach a full understanding of him. As Andrew remarks, all moments in a fiction film are significant for the viewer who is constructing its meaning. He or she 'is asked to swim in a time stream, and ... cannot look away without the fiction threatening to disappear' (Andrew, 1984: 45). Thus the spectator's discovery of the meaning of a fiction is not achieved by immediate reference to an object but is deferred until the text has run on, has perhaps even been completed: 'Fictive meaning is typically judged not on the basis of a sentence or a proposition, but on the basis of a discourse, a network of sentences or propositions' (Branigan, 1992: 198–9). Because fiction is neither simply false nor obviously true but is initially indeterminate and non-specific, the challenge it sets us is to discover what it is about. Hence, one of its values lies in its ability to tempt us to explore our preconceptions and to suggest ways in which they might be altered to fit new situations (see Branigan, 1992: 196). This is a large claim, but it helps explain the considerable pleasures that fiction can give. Its value depends to a great extent on the needs and uses discovered for it by each viewer (see Chapter 9).

Distinguishing fiction from non-fiction

How do viewers know whether they are watching fiction or non-fiction? The answer seems to be that they recognise, whether knowingly or not, that a number of formal conventions are in play. Some of these derive from the cultural conventions through which knowledge is acquired in our societies. It has been argued, for instance, that documentary relies heavily on the conventions that allow us to reason about causality in the real world and which we experience in common with other people. The close fit between these social conventions and those which we find in non-fiction allows us to accept that references in documentary are to the specific world it designates (Branigan, 1992: 204). It is an idea developed by Nichols when he describes documentary as a 'discourse of sobriety' linked in this respect to other forms of discourse in which serious points are being made about society. He cites as examples written essays, scientific reports and weekly magazines devoted to politics, economics, education and the arts. Such discourses, like many documentaries, adopt a rhetorical stance, which persuades the reader that their connection with the real world is immediate and sober, that they deal in matters concerning access to, control and use of power (Nichols, 1991: 3–5).[2]

Turning from generalised social conventions to specific documentary forms, we can see that a number of their important structuring conventions are of an intertextual nature. That is, these conventions have been brought to the documentary screen from other kinds of text by film makers who recognised that they added to the authenticity of their work. For example, some documentarists have learned from journalists' chronicles of events how to use commentary to structure matters into a swiftly moving, chronological narrative that can be readily understood by the listening viewer. Others have derived, from such sources as written histories and the records of legal cases, the methods of weaving evidence and argument into their accounts so as to persuade us of their truthfulness. For their part, audiences make sense of documentaries by relating them to a corpus of other works with which they appear to share common features.

Television conventions in non-fiction programming

We are mainly concerned here with those conventions particular to non-fiction television programming which distinguish it from shows based on fiction. In Chapter 6 we shall have more to say about the increasing tendency towards hybridisation in televised drama-documentary.

First, a word has to be said about the presence of these conventions in the several modes of documentary. Since the modes are structured in different ways and therefore address viewers in various manners, we do not find all the televisual conventions present and functioning in every mode. We seem to be cued to read a programme as documentary when one or more of the conventions that are described below are in play, so we do not in practice look for the complete package before recognising what we are watching.

Argument
Documentaries, as we have said, are often in the business of making a case: 'Argument about the world ... forms the organizational backbone of documentary' (Nichols, 1991: 125). It often forms the logical basis for the text and makes it coherent. And it can take many different forms. An explicit argument may be openly presented by the narrator with the aid of examples that have clearly been chosen to illustrate the points being made. Alternatively, argument can be implicit, as when making the case includes presenting us with a number of carefully chosen examples on the strength of which we are invited to draw our own conclusions. Arguments can be presented in a variety of forms, including essays, diaries, notebooks, reports and descriptions, evocations, eulogies and exhortations. These forms are not specific to any one medium any more than tragedy, comedy and epic are. Not only can they occur in the documentary, but they can be found in any of its modes (Nichols, 1991: 125). We may recall, however, that television has long been in the business of making statements and developing arguments through many forms of programming, especially those given over to news and current affairs. Thus television documentary frequently feeds off viewers' expectations of the journalistic presentation of socio-political or economic events (which is not to deny that some-

times it leans on the expectations aroused by fictional modes of representation).

Documentaries operate, however, according to a different structuring logic from that of narrative fictions. In the latter, the viewer will expect, for a set duration, to suspend his or her disbelief and to be drawn in by a narrative that will frequently take daring twists and turns on the semi-concealed route to reaching a satisfying conclusion. As we have said, part of the pleasure of consuming narrative fiction is that of being teased and hoodwinked by the confusing turns that the story may take, while remaining sure in the knowledge that everything will ultimately be resolved. Documentaries, however, tend to be governed by a different set of principles. Narrative in documentary is generally aimed at enhancing the sense of developing argument, of presenting the documentary account in such a way that it will be rendered more memorable and persuasive for a viewing audience.

Argument, then, is a means of representing a case about the world. Nichols says it has two major parts – perspective and commentary. Perspective refers to the point of view established by the programme's depiction of the world. It is like style in fiction in that it implies rather than states the argument. It provides the (usually unseen) frame through which the viewer perceives the subject. A hypothetical example will make the point: two programmes cover the history of the domestic light bulb. The first adopts a formal approach in which distinguished historians and white-coated scientists are interviewed in their studies and laboratories. They deliver well considered pieces of information in educated voices, and an unseen presenter links their contributions together. The programme is illustrated with archive pictures of early light-bulb factories, with footage of lamps in every kind of setting and with an analysis of their efficiency. This is the traditional expository manner of a scientific series such as *Horizon.* As Roger Silverstone demonstrated in a detailed examination of one programme in the series, the rhetorical address to which its every element contributes reassures us that the research is detailed, the facts are accurate and the programme is offering us the most authoritative way possible of understanding the topic in question. In fact, the construction of such a programme is apt also to be calculated: first, to ensure that we believe the chosen topic is of central scientific importance; second, to inhibit us from recognising that some of the presentation may rest on disputed speculation; and third, to draw our attention away from ideological issues (such as the way the application of certain sciences serves the Western democracies at the expense of the rest of the world) (see Silverstone, 1987: 291–330). All told, programmes like *Horizon* make the scientific realm appear to be one in which scientists exercise an almost magical power and do science on our behalf.

The second programme features a working-class man in overalls demonstrating how light bulbs were made in different eras, and how effectively they worked. He has a rough and ready workbench in a shabby repair shop. There are no interviewees, and, with wry humour, he does his own presentation direct from the workbench. As we watch, he blows glass for a hand-made bulb and, while demonstrating the basic principles, makes a rudimentary filament and gets it to work. If something does not function, the presenter takes it in his stride and tries again – or cheerfully explains the failure. The casual style of this programme should not disguise from us the fact that it too has adopted a distinctive rhetorical address. It is a set-up in the sense that the guy in the repair shop (whether or not he acts in his own life in the way he appears to do on screen) is actually playing a variant on a role familiar to us. He is another version of the anchor man.

In each case, the topic is the same, but the perspective on it differs strikingly. The effect of the first programme tends to make science seem the remote domain of the super-boffin. The second approach brings science and technology into every viewer's home life and demystifies it. It relies on the appeal to simplicity and common sense: if this ordinary guy can both understand and enjoy science and technology, perhaps we can too. The two perspectives make the arguments about the science of light bulbs very different.

Meanwhile, commentary can occur in more than just its most frequently encountered form, which is, of course, direct spoken address by an on- or off-screen presenter. As we saw with *Sad, Bad and Mad* in Chapter 4, such a narration has the power to weld together images and ancillary speech so that they provide evidence for the argument which it both constructs and controls. However, commentary can also be offered via the juxtaposition of elements within the documentary. For example, in a documentary about social conditions shots of people living in grinding poverty might be intercut with sequences covering the sumptuous life styles of the well-to-do. This device could, for instance, provide unspoken commentary to illustrate the social effects of a government's fiscal policies. It is a method of using commentary which Humphrey Jennings developed in some of his war-time films, examples being *London Can Take It* (1941) and *A Diary for Timothy* (1944–45). We have already encountered its effective use in Ophuls's *November Days* (Chapter 4).

Commentary thus offers a particular statement about the world which complements a documentary's perspective. However, it is distinct from the latter in providing the viewer with a more overt and direct, as well as more conceptual, account of the argument (Nichols, 1991: 118).

Characters and documentary subjects

Fictions invariably have characters, who usually act as if unobserved. What they say and do and what happens to them make them the focal points of the typical fiction. Their actions change the course of the fictional story, and in return the events of that story impinge on and change them. However, characters in the documentary are seldom of this type, and we are placed in a different relationship to them. In general, the people who are allowed to speak in documentaries do so as witnesses or experts. Partly for this reason and partly because they are usually on screen in order to be observed, it is more common to refer to the people in documentaries as subjects than characters. It is rare for them to have the fully revealed personality of the fictional character, and the rhythms and shifts of their inner lives are not wholly governed by the events of the narrative in which they are set. Other things which we never see are going on in their off-screen lives, and they have long personal histories which we seldom even glimpse. The knowledge that a great deal of the subjects' lives is absent from the screen typifies documentary. By contrast, the feature film will often appear to give us insights into the public and private aspects of the lives of its main characters (i.e. we see them in a series of interactions with other characters, but we are also privy to their subjective responses and share in their emotional stirrings).

Among the traits which distinguish the principal documentary modes are the differing ways in which they represent their subjects. In the expository mode events are not focused internally by subjects in the manner just described as typical of fiction, but tend to be brought into focus, as if from outside, by the commentary. Subjects in the expository mode, unlike fictional characters, are therefore not the dynamic centre of narrative information. They are witnesses or participants rather than protagonists. Where they are observed speaking or acting, the meaning of their words and actions is given direction and context by the commentary. Or if they speak about their own lives, they may act as their own commentators, seeming to stand outside themselves and providing us with guidance on how to interpret their actions or words. This is something quite different from the way a fictional character speaks and acts within his or her role (Branigan, 1991: 204). The expository mode is not alone in offering us subjects with these characteristics: interactive documentaries often function in respect of their characters in much the same way, but, in complete contrast, the latter may also behave in this mode as though they were being observed directly.

Subjects in the direct mode, almost by definition, do act out their social roles (albeit inflected by the presence of the camera). As social actors (even though they only play out a fragment of their lives' activities), they are not treated as the witnesses of their own existences, as occurs in the expository mode and some interactive films. Nonetheless, although there may be no verbal commentary to come between them and the viewer, their words and actions are given focus by the programme's perspective. For example, many of Fred Wiseman's documentaries share a common look, which frames his subjects and provides the context in which we see them. Filmed in grainy black and white, they employ long takes which are shot with telephoto lenses in whatever light is available. The effect is to exaggerate the far from photogenic qualities of his subjects, so that the lives of those caught up in the institutions which he features (prisons, schools, the police, etc.) seem, by comparison with the images of conventionally beautiful people that occupy so much time on our television screens, to be ugly and impoverished.

In the reflexive and first-person modes the presenter usually ceases to be merely an on-screen commentator or interviewer and becomes also a 'character' in the programme (see Chapter 3). But since one object of the reflexive film is to make subjectivity strange, certain factors will provide an external focus on their characters. It may be the words that the presenter utters about his or her role, or the unconventional way in which they behave or in which the camera records their antics, or it may be the perspective constructed by the programme – but some factor or other will encourage us to look at the 'character' of the presenter as if it were registered in quotes. Once again we are invited to observe the subjects, but this time they – both presenters and their interviewees – are dealt with ironically, (see Chapter 9). Thus, for example, no matter what his ostensible target – motor manufacturer or banker – all Michael Moore's work in the television series *Video Nation* features him playing the role of a bumbling man who, despite his obstreperous manner, has simple moral right firmly on his side. His heavy-handed performance of this role leaves his audience the task of deciding whether it really represents Moore's personality and whether he is the mouthpiece of righteousness that he appears on first hearing to be.

The drama-documentary is, as might be expected, the one mode in which subjects may function in a manner similar to the characters in fiction. Even in this mode, however, there is likely to be some form of commentary on their roles; this may be required by the broadcasting authorities to make clear what is fact and what fiction. And even if there is not, the perspective on the subjects' actions that is provided by the audience's knowledge that it is seeing a hypothetical representation of an event drawn from the social world provides an external standpoint from which the characters are viewed.

There is, however, another way in which the subjects of a documentary may resemble the characters in a drama. Faced with a choice of people who might be filmed, many documentarists find it hard to resist the individual who shows signs of being able to perform for the camera (see also Chapter 8). Although it does not necessarily follow that the audience will identify with a 'performer' (because on the whole, in documentary programmes we don't identify with single characters so much as with what they represent), the favouring of such a subject is just another way in which actuality can be skewed by documentary intervention.

Blurring the boundaries – intertextuality
We have long since established the idea that the fiction film and documentary seem on the surface to represent opposed tendencies. The former, being a vehicle for entertainment, has the potential to distract audiences from the realities of life. Therefore, in general, it runs counter to the broad thrust of the documentary, which seeks to open the eyes of viewers to serious issues in the socio-historical world (Britton, 1992: 28).

In practice, however, things are seldom as simple as this. What actually often happens can best be described as an intertextual blurring of the boundaries. It arises because each type of film can borrow from the other. For instance, in order to heighten their impact and keep the viewers' attention in a screen world dominated by the many gratifications of drama, documentaries often employ some of the same rhetorical ploys as fictional narratives. In addition to narrative closure and continuity editing, these may include extravagant, eye-catching shots, expressive music and flamboyant cutting patterns. Conversely, the various features that characterise each of the documentary modes – such as their manner of address, camera style, choice and treatment of subject matter, dominant narration by a commentator – can be imitated by fiction films to enhance the impression of truthfulness. We deal with the drama-documentary in the next chapter, and will explore these issues further there. But it has been noticed that modernist films also tend to blur the distinctions between fiction and non-fiction (Rosenthal, 1988: 69). An example is Godard's *Tout va bien* (1972), with its long sequences in a meat-processing factory dominated by argument about the workers' conditions of employment. The construction of the film draws viewers' attention to what Godard chooses to show as the tendency of the feature film to falsify social actualities. In effect, by basing the work in fiction but masking it from time to time as a documentary, Godard has produced a thought-provoking amalgam: the cinematic essay.

The equivalent of this format in documentary is the reflexive mode. Here it is easy to fall victim to the blurring between the two worlds, as Nichols himself does. He argues that his own view that documentary gives us access to the world does not suit the case of the reflexive mode particularly well. Films such as *The Thin Blue Line* operate through multiple speculations. For Nichols, these produce what he calls the 'conditional tense' and refer us to a world that is an imaginary extrapolation from the real world (Nichols, 1991: 112). However, this seems to miss the point. The speculations of a film such as *The Thin Blue Line* (like the reflections on the film-making process that characterise all documentary productions in the reflexive mode) are distinct from fictions of the type we have been describing. They seek to demonstrate the extent to which views of the world have been shaped and constructed by those who made the film. Nichols's concept of the conditional tense is helpful but is not well applied. What the reflexive programme usually offers us is not a conditional view of an imaginary world but a conditional view of the world. The same is often the case with drama-documentary too. Both modes imply that the world does exist in the way they show it – provided (conditional upon whether) you look at the evidence gathered by their makers from the point of view they adopted.

Viewers' expectations
When all is said and done, however, we come back to the basic position that we established at the outset: that the distinction between documentary and fiction lies in the expectations of the viewers and in the kinds of activity they are prompted to perform. These differ in the two types of film: the most fundamental difference between the expectations prompted by narrative fiction and those prompted by documentary lies in the status of the text in relation to the historical world (Nichols, 1991: 25).

The documentary response is elicited in a viewer when the image is perceived as signifying what it appears to record. However, film and video tape not only record but also have a 'language' (Vaughan, 1993: 101). In semiotic terms this means that in documentary the sign (that is, the recorded sounds and images) is perceived as coinciding with its meaning. It has what can be called a metonymic function because the sounds and images partake of the same order of reality as that to which they refer (O'Sullivan *et al.,* 1994b: 181–2). By contrast, in fiction, meaning is constructed via a sign which has no necessary connection to empirical reality – although it may be rendered highly authentic by mirroring that reality. Fiction is perceived as yielding a metaphorical rendering of the real world (Crawford and Turton, 1993: 87, Nichols, 1991: 28).

Thus we have come round full circle to the question of documentary's meta-language to show once again how it signals to viewers the particular frame in which they should place their expectations of the programme in question. Having established that, we have to add that all the conventions that separate documentary from fiction (including those governing viewers' expectations) come under pressure in reality programming, which depends for some of its considerable impact on blurring the boundaries. We cover reality programming in the upcoming chapter after first analysing the nature and function of drama-documentary.

Making a drama out of a crisis

THE DRAMA-DOCUMENTARY
AND RELATED FORMS

In the preceding chapter, in which we explored the relationship between fact and fiction in documentary, we noted the use of a range of techniques employed by documentarists to lend greater coherence to their arguments and to heighten the dramatic impact of their work. We have also, elsewhere in this book, considered the extent to which documentaries can be regarded as enactments of real-life events. That is to say, viewers are given the impression that they are participating in a dramatic spectacle that has been prepared for their benefit rather than being positioned as witnesses to events which would have run their course in much the same way with or without the camera being present. Some commentators have even gone so far as to assert that one of the defining characteristics of documentary is its dramatising tendency. As Paul Rotha once observed, 'Documentary's essence lies in the dramatisation of actual material' (cited in Rosenthal, 1988: 21).

The aim of the present chapter is to look more closely at those forms of programming in which there has manifestly been a merging of documentary and dramatic components. Viewed from a certain perspective, this merging could be regarded as an extension of the constructivist tendency in all documentary. Documentaries are, after all, made, not found objects. We shall, however, concentrate on those instances where documentarists have consciously used dramatising ploys (in particular, techniques of re-enactment and reconstruction) whilst still claiming a factual basis for the work or sequence in question.

Drama in documentary

There are, of course, many ways in which dramatic and documentary elements are integrated. We shall therefore not just examine the type of work to which the labels 'drama-documentary', 'docudrama' or 'faction' have been routinely applied; we shall also – at the more micro level – assess the role and function of re-enactments and reconstructions in the wider context of factual programming. Within the last decade or so a number of hybrid formats have been developed, all of which include dramatic reconstructions as a standard component. In Britain, for instance, programmes such as *Crimewatch UK* (in which the public's aid is enlisted in the police's efforts to solve crimes) and *999* (focusing on re-enactments of real-life rescues by the emergency services) are good examples of a hybridised form of programming. From the broadcaster's point of view such programmes have the dual attraction of high audience appeal whilst still providing a measure of documentary-like enlightenment.

The dramatic imperative

In considering the variety of ways in which documentary and dramatic elements come to be conjoined one must first recognise the major importance of drama in late twentieth-century, media-saturated culture. In Raymond Williams's words:

> In most parts of the world, since the spread of television, there has been a scale and intensity of dramatic performance which is without any precedent in the history of human culture ... It is clearly one of the unique characteristics of advanced industrial societies that drama as an experience is now an intrinsic part of everyday life ... Whatever the social and cultural reasons may finally be, it is clear that watching dramatic simulations of a wide range of experiences is now an essential part of our modern cultural pattern. (Williams, 1974: 59)

If drama consumption is such an intrinsic part of modern cultural experience, it should come as no surprise to discover that today's producers of factual television programming – in all its many manifestations – should make such extensive use of dramatic simulation. The 'true story' has accordingly become a trusted weapon in the scheduler's armoury, and audiences have come to expect that nowadays most major headline-grabbing events – hijackings, disasters (natural or brought about by humans), military actions, etc. – will probably soon be transformed into what one writer has nicely described as 'instant histories' (see Nimmo and Combs, 1983: 75). Indeed, so powerful is the dramatising impulse that we are beginning to see it appearing in sectors of programming hitherto not closely associated with dramatic presentation. News and current affairs reporting, for instance, – particularly as practised in the United States – is now so entertainment-oriented and employs such a wide range of dramatising techniques that we are fast approaching the point where it could be legitimately classified as an off-shoot of factually-based drama!

If one thinks of the voracious appetite for 'true-life stories' or 'real-life drama' on television as being a late twentieth-century phenomenon, one does well to remember that the impulse to provide factually-based dramatic retellings has a very long historical tradition. Television and other mass-media forms may have significantly increased the number of opportunities for representing past events through various types of restaging. The fact remains, however, that dramatised retellings, as a cultural or artistic enterprise, go back a long way. It would, for instance, be possible, by only slightly expanding the term 'drama-documentary', to make it apply to a large proportion of humanity's creative output. Early Greek theatre, Shakespeare's historical plays, together with the majority of Hollywood biopics, all deploy a range of dramatising techniques in the production of plays or stories based on (more or less) documented facts.

Issues in the drama-documentary debate
The integration of disparate (dramatic and documentary) elements into a single composite format has often led to heated debate as to the legitimacy of such a practice. Major controversies have flared up around the making or screening of particular documentaries (for details, see Kilborn, 1994a). Likewise, politicians have never been

slow to voice their doubts about a broadcast form which they claim
has always been prone to 'monkey[ing] around with actuality' (Holt,
1978). We shall be examining the criticism to which drama-
documentaries have been exposed later in the chapter. For the time
being we shall simply remark that most of the argument has centred
on: concerns about the status of the historical or factual data which
provide the basis for the dramatised retelling; worries about the
manner in which the documentary and dramatic elements are conjoined; and misgivings about how much poetic licence film makers
have allowed themselves in putting together their accounts. In this
respect it is by no means insignificant that the whole drama-
documentary controversy has much in common with the centuries-
old debate about how history itself is recorded: How much of what
we call 'history' results from the subjective interpretation of historians? And to what degree does the act of telling inevitably tinge and
skew the accounts that are rendered? (Carr, 1961, McArthur, 1980,
Allen and Gomery, 1985.) The writing of history is frequently
accompanied by conjecture concerning the accuracy of sources or
documentation and by questions about the underlying ideological
purpose of the project. Similarly, with drama-documentary the focus
of critical attention has often been on the attempt to distinguish
between those parts which appear to have their origins in factual or
verifiable information and those where some imaginative or narrative embroidering seems to have occurred.

Why mix drama and documentary?

Given some of the problems which have surrounded the hybrid
formats under discussion, it is fair to enquire why such formats
should have been so regularly employed. The first and most obvious
point is that a dramatic reconstruction – of whatever kind – allows
an account to be rendered in cases where, for whatever reason, no
recording of the event has been made.[1] In the earliest days of
cinema film producers would regularly resort to reconstructions of
events, principally because cameras at that time were simply too
cumbersome and unwieldy to be conveyed to the relevant venues.
Georges Méliès, for instance, one of the pioneers of the cinema,
produced in 1899 a series of short films based on newspaper reports

and photographs of the famous Dreyfus Affair (see Christie, 1994: 98). Similarly, in the 1930s the American production team responsible for the series *The March of Time* combined dramatic simulations of events with newsreel and documentary presentations to produce what one critic has described as a 'new form of compelling journalism' (Jacobs, 1979: 107).[2]

Seen from a slightly different perspective, not only did dramatic or filmic reconstructions allow for new forms of collaboration between film makers and journalists, but film makers with a political message to proclaim also began to turn to dramatisation as part of a consciousness-raising or propagandist exercise. It is, however, a moot point whether one can in all cases apply the term reconstruction. Sergei Eisenstein's perhaps most famous film *Battleship Potemkin* (1925) is only very loosely based on historical events. It is basically an invention of incidents that did not happen, larded with a few historical details, much aggrandised in significance and deploying the full range of cinematic techniques – especially what Eisenstein refers to as 'dialectic montage' (Lovell and Hillier, 1972: 25–7; Roud, 1980: 314–28). The films of John Grierson also make extensive use of restaging or dramatising ploys, often aimed at drawing the attention of the audience to the underlying social message. In other words, the employment of reconstruction techniques did not just result from the physical difficulties of getting the camera to the original scene; it was also born of a recognition that, in the process of restaging, the film maker could intervene or inflect the work in such a way as to draw attention to the wider significance of the event or events portrayed (see also Winston, 1995: 88–9).

Both Eisenstein and Grierson regarded dramatisation as an essential feature of documentary or factual filming as they conceived it (Winston, 1995: 54, 99). By the same token, audiences accepted it as one of the means by which their interest was engaged. Problems have occurred, however, in those cases where dramatisation – or, more properly, methods of dramatic reconstruction – have been employed but where there has been no open acknowledgement of the fact. In the case of Robert Flaherty's *Nanook of the North* (1922), for instance, which is one of the great pioneering works of the documentary tradition, it soon became apparent that, in putting together this simple tale of Inuit people, Flaherty had made extensive use of re-enactment. As we have commented (see Chapter 3), by getting Nanook and his relatives or friends to act out long-abandoned hunting practices, Flaherty produced a romantically skewed account of what life had been like, rather than what it was like now (Rosenthal, 1988: 216, Winston, 1995: 102).

The range of uses for drama-documentary
As already indicated above, one of the main reasons for using dramatic reconstruction in documentary has been to provide audiences with access to material or events which would otherwise have remained locked away in archives, personal memories or official documents, leaving many questions unanswered about how or why particular events occurred (Scannell, 1979: 101–2). It is, however, important to recognise that, over the years, the reasons for employing reconstruction techniques have changed. In the early days of documentary, re-enactment was used principally to overcome the physical barriers posed by cumbersome equipment or the difficulties of accessing certain types of documentary evidence. Nowadays these 'logistical' problems have been largely overcome by the development of ever-more sophisticated lightweight cameras. Having the technical ability to film in previously inaccessible places is one thing, but being granted permission to do so is another: one of the situations in which some form of reconstruction has been most regularly employed is where documentarists have been denied access to the people and places they wished to film. They have therefore seen no alternative but to recreate events on the basis of the best available information.

Consider, for instance, the not uncommon situation where institutions, or even governments, have been reluctant to let the cameras in – either because they have something to hide or because they fear they would not have sufficient control over the filmed account of their activities. In these cases programme makers have frequently resorted to dramatic reconstruction to overcome the problem of access. For instance, during the Cold War period a series of drama-documentaries was made because documentary crews from the West did not have access to countries 'behind the Iron Curtain'.[3]

Whilst one does not wish to be overly prescriptive in suggesting that film makers, almost as a matter of course, turn to reconstruction in tackling certain subjects, one can nevertheless indicate some broad categories in which the reconstruction mode will be preferred. It goes without saying that all events which, for whatever reason, did not come within the camera's purview when they occurred will have to be re-created (if, that is, the producer thinks it important to give a visual–verbal enactment rather than rely on a narrator to activate our imagination into the task of re-creation). The history of film and television is littered with examples of such reconstructions.

In measuring their function and effectiveness one always does well to consider the film maker's underlying objectives in employing these techniques. Peter Watkins's acclaimed drama-documentary *Culloden* (BBC, 1964), for instance, is conceived as a critical, sobering reassessment of the circumstances surrounding this bloody battle (1746), in which thousands of Scottish clansmen perished at the hands of the English army. Against the background of the preparations for military engagement and its aftermath, actors representing protagonists from both sides of the battle-lines speak direct to camera and give their view of events. It is as if they are being interviewed by a contemporary news team filing a report for an extended news item. (These scenes gain a special poignancy in that some of the actors are descendants of people who fought in the real battle.) *Culloden* is the very antithesis of costume drama. What we are presented with is a series of historically authenticated eyewitness accounts in which the emphasis is on analysis and reflection rather than on action for its own sake. To be sure, there are some re-enactment scenes of the battle itself, but Watkins's primary motivation in making *Culloden* was to strip away some of the romantic myths that had surrounded Bonnie Prince Charlie and his Jacobite army and to shed new light on ways in which this conflict may have shaped subsequent historical developments.

In the case of *Culloden* the access to historical events is provided by dramatic reconstruction solidly founded on a body of historical evidence in order to provide insight into a set of past events. The implicit aim is to get the audience to reconsider its own view of this myth-enshrouded phase of Scotland's history. In his next work, *The War Game* (made for the BBC in 1965 but not transmitted), Watkins again employs drama-documentary techniques, but to rather different ends.[4] *The War Game* documents the horrific consequences if a nuclear device exploded over an English city. Just like *Culloden*, it was meticulously researched, and every scene is based on the latest scientific information (much of which is introduced in the film through charts, graphs and statistical displays). The emphasis is on providing a cool appraisal of the likely outcome rather than on extracting the full dramatic potential of this nightmare scenario. Nevertheless, the very fact that it combines dramatic and documentary approaches was one of the reasons used by those in institutional authority (in this case the higher echelons of the BBC) for deciding to withhold the programme from transmission. Thus, as in so many subsequent controversies surrounding the drama-documentary form, it was the form itself which was considered problematical rather than the fact that certain sensitive issues were being addressed (see also below).

What the example of *The War Game* also illustrates is a particular use of the drama-documentary in those cases where much may already be known about a situation or event, but where a certain amount of hypothesising may be necessary to complete the argument or make the case. In one sense the Cold War documentaries mentioned above belong to this category. In each case the production team was involved in a process of reconstructing a plausible account of events using 'leaked' information from a variety of sources (smuggled diaries or statements from those who had fled to the West) to which they had gained access. By the same token, dramatisation techniques have also been regularly employed in instances where there may be abundant documentary evidence relating to a person or event, but where certain pieces of vital information are missing and where the relevant gaps have to be imaginatively filled. In these instances dramatisation takes the form of informed speculation as to 'How it might have been' or even 'Who the guilty person(s) might have been'. (Such drama-documentaries as these obviously have additional appeal to broadcasters in that they have much in common with those highly popular 'whodunit' or mystery stories!) A good example of this type of drama-documentary is provided by *The Trial of Lord Lucan* (ITV, 1994). Lord Lucan, it will be remembered, was a peer of the realm who vanished in mysterious circumstances in 1974 following the murder of the family's nanny. The ITV dramatisation brings Lucan back in order to examine the events surrounding his disappearance, about which there had been much speculation during the intervening time. It also allows a jury to form a judgement on the basis of all the known evidence.[5]

The Trial of Lord Lucan was able to capitalise on the fact that Lucan's disappearance had become one of the Great Mysteries of the Century. In other types of drama-documentary the basic facts of the case are never in contention and the dramatic element has a different role to fulfil. Take, for example, *Thatcher – the Final Days* (ITV, 1991), the drama-documentary which traces the final chapter in the political demise of Britain's former prime minister. Whereas the course of the events which had been played out in the public domain were familiar enough, there was, not surprisingly, a much less detailed picture of the series of behind-the-scenes crisis meetings and the general emotional turmoil as a political era was drawing to a close. The programme attempted therefore, as would a totally fictionalised account of a politician's rise and fall, to give viewers a more three-dimensional picture of a public figure and to satisfy the audience's appetite to know more about the private world behind the public mask.[6]

Reaching the parts that other documentaries cannot reach

By introducing a dramatic dimension into their account documentarists are also able to reflect or comment on areas of experience not always illuminated by the traditional documentary. In particular, a dramatisation may help to highlight the role played by emotional and psychological drives in determining human action. It can give us insight into a protagonist's mind and thus help us to understand why a particular step was taken or a decision made.

The claim, then, which is made for drama-documentaries is that they facilitate a different level of understanding and a qualitatively different level of viewer involvement in the drama as it unfurls

(Kilborn, 1994a: 66). They encourage viewers at one level to relate to these events as they would to any other drama while remaining aware that in the majority of cases what is being enacted has its roots in a series of 'real life' events. In so doing, drama-documentaries allow, at best, for a considerable measure of empathic identification on the part of the audience, whilst at the same time encouraging it to reconsider *how* a particular chain of events was set in train.[7] As David Edgar, himself a seasoned dramatist, has commented:

> The dramatic power of drama-documentary lies in its capacity to show us not that certain events occurred (the headlines can do that) or even, perhaps, why they occurred (for such information we can go to the weekly magazines or the history books), but *how* they occurred: how recognizable human beings rule, fight, judge, meet, negotiate, suppress and overthrow. (Edgar, 1982: 23)

Viewed in this light, many drama-documentaries can have a clear dual focus: they can be powerfully dramatic, but can also stir their audiences in other ways. Consider, for example, the case of *Hillsborough* (ITV, 1996), scripted by Jimmy McGovern and retracing events that led to disaster in the Sheffield stadium where ninety-five soccer fans died in April 1989. The film is on the one hand a taut, harrowing drama centred on two or three of the families most directly affected by this tragedy. It uses all the tried and tested dramatic conventions to intensify our emotional involvement in the pain and anguish experienced by these families. At the same time, the knowledge that everything that happens or is said in the film rests on the most meticulous research enabled *Hillsborough* to assume the force of a documentary *exposé:* in this case, attributing a considerable measure of responsibility to the police for grossly inadequate crowd control. The screening of the film thus led to a vigorous debate as to whether hitherto unknown information, which had come to light in the course of making the film, was sufficient grounds for reopening the original inquiry into the disaster. (For more on documentary's effects, see Chapter 9.)

'Drama-documentary'? 'Documentary-drama'? 'Faction'?

So far in this chapter we have referred to those artefacts in which there is a mixing of documentary and dramatic impulses as if they constituted a single category. The truth is, of course, that there is a multiplicity of ways in which the 'dramatic' is inserted into, aligned with or merged with the documentary. To illustrate this point let us for a moment consider just a few of the different ways in which an individual's life can be portrayed using techniques which would be recognised as broadly 'documentary'.

One of the most popular methods of portraying a life is to use traditional documentary means. Friends and relatives will give their memories. Letters to and from the person will be cited. Photographs from family albums or excerpts from home movies will be shown. All these fragments will be moulded into a coherent, aesthetically satis-fying narrative account in which the main contours of the subject's life emerge. As often as not, the life story will be recounted by a narrator figure who may have been chosen on account of their close relationship with the person in question. In *Edward on Edward* (ITV, 1996), for instance, the Queen's son Prince Edward presents a personal account of the life of his great-uncle, Edward VIII, who abdicated to marry an American divorcee.

An equally popular form of television biography involves the mixing of standard documentary techniques with a number of dramatised reconstructions. More often than not, an anchoring narrator figure will again be employed, and likewise the reminis-cences of friends and acquaintances will once more form the backbone of such a programme. Interpolated into this discourse of retrospection, however, there will be a series of dramatised sequences during which key episodes in the life of the person are enacted.

The logical extension of this type of mixed formatting is the fully-fledged, factually based drama in which all the documentary elements have been subject to a thoroughgoing creative transforma-tion. The broad outline of the life in question remains, but every-thing is rendered in such a way as to push it in the direction of a piece of dramatic entertainment. Hollywood biopics and the 'faction' formats favoured by the American networks are the best examples of this type of dramatisation. These faction formats have been the butt of much hostility in that critics have often complained that too many liberties have been taken with the known facts in order to maximise the dramatic potential of the piece. They have also been subject to the criticism that when they tackle serious or complex subjects they often over-simplify or sanitise matters to what is seen as an intolerable degree. Here one might cite the example of *The Day After* (ABC, 1983). Describing (like *The War Game*) the aftermath of a nuclear attack, it employs the standard conventions of television drama to assist audience identification with the characters. In the eyes of some critics, however, the employment of such means was not justified, because they felt it would reduce the deeply serious issues being addressed to the level of just another soap opera.

In reflecting on the various ways in which drama and documentary elements coalesce one must not assume that there is a necessary connection between the extent to which dramatic techniques are employed and the work's impact on the audience. Many factions or biopic presentations, for instance, – for all their attempts to inject pace, drama and even suspense – can easily appear flat or insipid, especially if they slavishly follow the long-established set of 'true-life drama' conventions. Accounts which, on the other hand, attempt more subtle kinds of dramatic reconstruction can often be far more evocative in their impact.

Take, for example, one of the most acclaimed documentaries of recent years, Jon Blair's Oscar-winning account of the life and legacy of Anne Frank, the girl whose diary of her two years of hiding from the Nazis in Amsterdam during the Second World War had already provided the inspiration for many stage and film adaptations. In *Anne Frank Remembered* (BBC, 1995) Blair employs a method of documentary reconstruction in which he makes extensive use of original archive material (diary extracts, photographs, letters, official files, etc.) and the memories and testimony of those who were near to Anne, especially her father. The film's particular achievement is to have selected and edited the documentary material in such a way that the memories and significance of Anne's life are most poignantly re-invoked. The off-screen narration (using the voice of Kenneth Branagh) sets the various eye-witness accounts in context, but Blair also employs other techniques to secure a measure of viewer involvement. Chief amongst these is the use of subjective camera to convey the sense of claustrophobia and entrapment in the Amsterdam house in which the Frank family once hid. Nowhere in the film, however, is there any attempt to overplay the dramatic. Indeed, one of the strengths of *Anne Frank Remembered* is that, unlike other treatments of the Holocaust theme (such as the American television series *Holocaust* (CBS, 1978)), it deliberately eschews conventional dramatic techniques. Nevertheless, by quietly reconstructing the conditions under which Anne lived during her two years of hiding, and augmenting this with the testimony of survivors, the film allows viewers to re-create in their mind's eye something of the terror of this ordeal.

Two sides of a coin: drama-documentary and documentary-drama
The above discussion highlights some of the problems which all critics encounter in categorising works that fuse documentary and dramatic impulses. So multifarious are the ways in which these elements can be combined that in practice it has proved very difficult to draw meaningful distinctions between different hybrid categories. Hoffer and Nelson, in their study of American docudrama, claim to be able to distinguish between no fewer than nine forms 'ranging from the "pure" form based on investigatory and trial records recreating events in the lives of actual persons ... to programmes utilizing historical personages or themes which include some fictionalization' (Feldman, 1986: 346). Likewise, Goodwin *et al.* operate with the notion of a sliding scale spanning a 'hard line category involving a fusion of the practices and conventions of drama and commentary at all levels and the soft line category ... essentially documentaries with a minimal use of dramatic reconstruction' (Goodwin *et al.*, 1983: 4).

Just how productive such taxonomies are in critical terms is very much open to debate, especially since there is almost constant experimentation with new hybridised forms. Nevertheless, one can still draw a useful distinction between two broad categories: on the one hand the drama-documentary and on the other the documentary-drama. As the terms suggest, it comes down to different shades of emphasis. With the former, a body of information or evidence is gathered about a particular event, which is then worked up into an account that may well employ the standard conventions of dramatic discourse (Caughie in Goodwin *et al.*, 1983, 69; Petley, 1996: 18). In documentary-drama, on the other hand, the documentary element has less to do with the presumed authenticity of the subject matter and more to do with the styles or techniques employed by the production team. As Paul Kerr has commented:

> Documentary drama takes its 'documentariness' from its form or style, which is often associated with the visual rhetoric of *cinéma vérité* ... [The] camera therefore often gives the impression of being 'surprised' by the action. Other examples of the documentary drama 'style' include improvisational acting, gritty, grainy, unglamorous lighting, and a rough, raw sound quality. (Kerr in Goodwin and Whannel, 1990: 83)

Still a sensitive area?
As already intimated, the practice of combining documentary and drama in a single hybridised format has over the years been heavily criticised. The nub of much of the criticism has been that, in the hands of more unscrupulous producers, drama-documentaries can be used to distort rather than to illuminate reality, particularly in their treatment of political or historical subjects. For instance, in an article that roundly castigates what he refers to as 'faction television' Paul Johnson declares:

> The object, quite brazenly, is to influence opinion on contentious matters. The viewer does not know whether he is getting theatre or documentary. In fact, he is getting a bit of both, inextricably mixed. (Johnson, 1981: 363)

Whilst it cannot be denied that particular care has to be exercised by producers when working in this form, there is little evidence to suggest that they adulterate the truth in the way Johnson suggests. What is clear, however, is that most of the criticism that has been levelled at drama-documentaries has been directed more at their subject matter than at their format. In other words, the more politically sensitive the subject matter, the more likely it is that the programme will be considered dubious. It is for this reason that drama-documentaries have often featured prominently in the ongoing struggle between those who set a high premium on the 'public's right to know' and those who believe that broadcasters should display some self-censoring moderation when sensitive issues are being treated. (See also remarks in Chapter 7.)

Most critics are agreed that the fears about audiences being hoodwinked are much exaggerated. Moreover, in the majority of cases the hostility seems to have been occasioned more by the commentator's dislike of the views expressed than the allegedly ambiguous or misleading format of the programme itself. (It is in this respect quite significant that the 'behind the Iron Curtain' drama-documentaries alluded to earlier met with no adverse comment whatsoever when they were screened.) What those hostile to drama-documentaries have also failed to recognise – or perhaps, more accurately, have not been prepared to accept – is that one of the reasons for producers turning to the drama-documentary form is their desire to break the established mould of representation, whether dramatic or documentary. The declared aim is to challenge the audience to new ways of seeing (Corner, 1995: 92–3).

In this respect we would also argue that, far from confusing viewers, drama-documentaries have the potential to encourage a reflective, critical response. Television audiences have never been so easily duped as many politicians would often have us believe (see also Chapter 9). And as far as contemporary audiences are concerned, the often sophisticated knowledge that viewers have about how programmes are made, coupled with a considerable insight into the processing of information and material by media institutions, has meant that the claims of programme makers are subject to what we can only regard as a healthy degree of audience scepticism. (It is possible to argue that greater audience knowledge, together with the proliferation of hybrid formats, is why there is nowadays much less controversy over the legitimacy of mixing drama and documentary than there once was.) (See also Petley, 1996: 19.)

The situation today

In making the case for drama-documentaries one must, however, be careful not to accord them a status which overestimates their importance in contemporary television programming. True, they allow the broadcaster or programme maker to play the 'reality card' while at the same time providing considerable scope for creative or imaginative elaboration (Corner, 1995: 93). True, they can be employed, especially in their more popular 'true story' forms, to generate large audiences at peak viewing times. On the other hand, whatever the format in which the dramatic and documentary components are combined, the resultant programmes are always going to have to compete for a place in the schedule like any other type of programming. In short, they are expected to deliver the size of audience commensurate with their production or acquisition costs. This has placed particular pressure on the drama-documentaries of the classic mould (those which follow in the tradition of *Cathy Come Home* (BBC, 1966)), which have always been a relatively high-cost form of programming. As Ian McBride, Head of Factual Drama at Granada Television, observes:

> The transmission opportunities for drama-documentaries are so few. They are big, difficult, expensive things to make. They're not things in which the producer makes a quick profit. They cost as much as full-blooded drama, and more because you have all the journalistic work in advance ... Styles have also changed. Earlier, styles were closer to documentary. Now they're closer to film. For a two-hour drama-documentary, a scheduler will be paying six or seven times as much as he or she would for a one-hour traditional documentary. (Interview with authors)

An extension of current affairs journalism?

Producers of factually based drama not only seek to attract audiences by virtue of the programme's dramatic appeal, they also frequently trade on the audience's knowledge of the subject acquired through other forms of factual programming (most notably news and current affairs but sometimes other documentaries). Indeed, one of the most popular forms of drama-documentary in recent years has been the 'instant history', a format in which all the known facts of a widely reported and preferably dramatic event are gathered together and packaged in a standard dramatised format (Kilborn, 1994a: 64–5).

Much of the work produced by the Drama-Documentary Unit at Granada Television falls into this category, and its production *Why Lockerbie?* (ITV, 1990) provides a good case study of how this sort of drama-documentary is made. The stark and brutal 'facts' of the Lockerbie tragedy, which occurred in December 1988, had already been very widely reported in all the news media, so what Leslie Woodhead and the *Why Lockerbie?* production team planned was to gather together all the existing information, couple it with the latest findings of police investigators and come up with what they described as a 'dramatised investigation' of events leading up to the destruction over Lockerbie of Pan Am Flight 103. The team's primary motivation in making the programme was the desire to provide what they hoped would be a credible and compelling account of how and why the tragedy of Lockerbie came to pass. In Woodhead's words:

> We want[ed] to show why it happened and we have some new answers to the question which is still the focus of the biggest murder investigation in history. Our researches, which trace the 20 months leading up to Lockerbie, have uncovered disturbing evidence of warnings ignored and safety sacrificed to expediency – adding up to a picture of a tragedy which could and should have been prevented. (Woodhead, 1990: 12)

Equally interesting for our present concern, however, are the reasons why the drama-documentary form was chosen. Like most other Granada drama-documentaries, the origins of *Why Lockerbie?* lie in television journalism. Producers working for Granada's *World in Action* team had already produced a thirty-minute current-affairs investigation of the Lockerbie tragedy, but it was clear that certain areas or aspects of the investigation could only be satisfactorily explored through the form of dramatised reconstruction. As Woodhead observes, 'It was apparent that the subject presented formidable problems of access to key sources in areas of aviation security, terrorism and police surveillance' (Woodhead, 1990: 12).

For a time, the *Why Lockerbie?* production team considered whether 'a hybrid mix of documentary interviews and dramatic reconstruction might be the most effective technique for exploring the background to Lockerbie' (Woodhead, 1990: 12), but they opted in the end for the 'fully-fledged', ninety-minute drama-documentary format, principally because key witnesses working in airport security were unwilling to be interviewed on camera. The other equally compelling reason for choosing this format was the realisation that the story of the events leading up to the Lockerbie tragedy was ideally suited to dramatic treatment.

Why Lockerbie? therefore has a multiple appeal to audiences. First, it parades its documentary credentials, claiming that all the material included in the dramatised account is based on meticulous research. Second, it keys into viewers' extra-textual knowledge of a set of historical events as reported in the news media and into the profound sense of disturbance unleashed by the Lockerbie tragedy. And third, it appeals because of its dramatic impact, with echoes of the detective story but also of the disaster movie. Its nature illustrates what some would regard as one of the more problematical features of these hybrid texts. If they move too decisively in the direction of becoming glossy, fast-moving dramatic entertainments, they may forfeit the respect that viewers might otherwise be prepared to accord them as well-researched statements about historical or contemporary reality. If, on the other hand, they move too far in the direction of becoming purely documentary discourse, there are dangers that certain audience expectations of the pleasures to be delivered by factually-based drama will not be fulfilled (see Petley, 1996: 18).

The regulation and policing of dramatised reconstructions

Given the intensity of the debate over the legitimacy of mixing documentary and dramatic modes (Paget, 1990: 97–9), broadcasting institutions have displayed a nervousness about the drama-documentary form. It has always been recognised that those working in purely fictional modes have had a degree of licence in the production of their stories – in particular, that they have sometimes used the cover of fiction to express certain political ideas which would not be countenanced in news and current-affairs categories. With factual drama, on the other hand, there has, if anything, been suspicion in some quarters that the introduction of documentary elements into a partly or predominantly dramatic vehicle might expose the broadcaster to charges of possible bias or audience manipulation.

As a consequence, broadcasting institutions and regulatory bodies have produced sets of guidelines to which programme makers are required to adhere when operating in this mode. They also have to exercise caution in not running foul of libel and defamation laws, especially when dealing with living persons and contemporary events. The principal instruments of regulation, however, take the form of the published (and regularly updated) guidelines and codes which all producers are obliged to take account of when working for a particular institution. The BBC *Producers' Guidelines* make the following stipulations:

> When drama realistically portrays living people or contemporary sit-
> uations in a controversial fashion, it has an obligation to be accurate
> – to do justice to the main facts. If the drama strives for a fair, impar-
> tial and rounded view of events, no problem arises. If it is an accurate
> but, nonetheless, partisan and partial portrayal of a controversial
> issue, the commissioning executive should proceed only if convinced
> that the insight and excellence of the work justify the platform
> offered; and that it will be judged honest, thoughtful and stimulating.
> (BBC *Producers' Guidelines*, 1993: 25)

The advice to producers in the *ITC Programme Code* is couched in very similar terms. The key stipulation is that 'the dramatised docu-mentary which lays claim to be a factual reconstruction ... is bound by the same standards of fairness and impartiality as those that apply to factual programmes in general' (*ITC Programme Code*, 1995: 17). Whilst both sets of guidelines, not surprisingly, alert pro-gramme makers to the dangers of overstepping the mark, there is also a clear recognition that an all-too cautious approach can be the recipe for blandness. Producers are therefore effectively required to perform a delicate balancing act. On the one hand, they may intro-duce fictional elements as necessary to effect dramatic economy or achieve narrative coherence; on the other, this must be done in such a way that none of the known facts is distorted or viewers potentially misled.

One of the specific recommendations to producers of 'factual drama' is that appropriate use should be made of labelling or sign-posting devices so that viewers are made fully aware of the status of the material being screened. Viewers should never be in any doubt that what they are seeing is a dramatised reconstruction, or that parts of what is so re-enacted are based on conjecture or surmise. Labelling is one of several strategies employed by programme makers to forestall any criticism of dangerous merging of fact and fiction. An additional strategy is to ensure, through a variety of means, that the claims of the programme in question are viewed in relative terms. The audience is thus encouraged to see it as but one interpretation of a set of events and not as a definitive statement. Quite frequently, this is achieved by arranging for a particular drama-documentary to be screened as part of a series or season of programmes dealing with a particular subject or event (for more on this, see Chapter 9). In this way audiences are more inclined, so it is argued, to see the programme in a wider context and less likely to jump to any false conclusions (see also Feldman, 1986: 351).

Macro- and micro-reconstructions

When broadcasters first drafted guidelines concerning the blending of factual and fictional modes they were thinking primarily of programme-length reconstructions. Nowadays, however, shorter dramatised reconstructions are just as likely to be found embedded in other factual and entertainment strands of programming. And just as broadcasters are required to pay careful attention to the specified guidelines for full-length 'macro'-reconstructions, so too with the interpolated micro-re-enactments the same principles have to be adhered to.

In this section we examine the role played by dramatised reconstructions in the context of two popular strands of factual programming and consider the extent to which these new hybrid formats are supplanting the more traditional forms of documentary.

Crimewatch UK

Crimewatch UK, which became Britain's top-rated factual series in the mid-1980s, is one such hybrid format which uses a variety of techniques and strategies to maintain the interest of its multi-million strong audience. The programme employs a tried and tested formula involving a certain amount of scene-setting by the show's resident presenters, appeals for information by a number of uniformed police officers and the screening of three or four dramatised reconstructions of particular unsolved crimes.[8] (In the 1990s this has been supplemented by often rather blurred video recordings of felons caught in the act by surveillance cameras and by a short sequence, known as Aladdin's Cave, in which a collection of stolen property is displayed in the hope that it may be identified and reclaimed by a member of the *Crimewatch* audience – a special incentive for viewing!)

The heart of the *Crimewatch* programmes remains, however, the reconstructions of the crimes, which detail the circumstances in which they took place. The purpose of these dramatised reconstructions is twofold. First, by addressing the viewers as responsible public citizens, they attempt to enlist their support in the 'collective' battle against crime (the citizen informant as opposed to Grierson's earlier notion of informed citizenry!). To an equal degree, however, they constitute short, action-packed bursts of dramatic entertainment – valuable (from the broadcaster's point of view) in helping maintain the attention of an audience in today's increasingly competitive environment.

Although legitimised by the doubtless worthy intention of encouraging the public to assist the police, these reconstructions have, from the outset, been subject to various forms of criticism. Some of it relates to what we refer to elsewhere in this book as the issue of 'typicality' (see Chapter 8). The following questions are asked:

- Does what is depicted or re-enacted in the dramatised reconstructions constitute a representative cross-section of crimes committed, or do other criteria (the production of compelling mini-dramas) play a more significant role in determining what viewers get to see?

- Does the bundling together of so many reconstructions which depict 'crimes against the person' give the impression – mistaken and in no way borne out by official statistics – that the whole country is awash with violent crimes of this type (Schlesinger and Tumber, 1993: 26)?
- Can there be any certainty as to what frames of reference viewers might be using in decoding the short dramatised sequences?
- To what extent are audiences being manoeuvred into positions where their response is determined as much by the emotional persuasiveness of a dramatic presentation as by the informational value of a documentary reconstruction? (See also Chapter 9.)

There are no easy answers to these questions and, as we shall discover in the following chapter, determining how audiences or viewers respond to media texts is a much more complicated issue than many would have us believe. The producers of *Crimewatch,* however, are acutely aware that they are involved in a difficult balancing act: having to combine the best traditions of responsible investigative journalism in the field of crime reporting with the desire to engage the viewer's attention by deploying a series of techniques ranging from direct personal address to the action-packed, fast-moving re-enactments (see Ross and Cook, 1987: 155–8).

   In an effort to forestall criticism that they are merely appealing to the more voyeuristic instincts of the television audience, the producers of *Crimewatch* always take care to avoid sensationalising or over-dramatising the reconstructions which feature so prominently in the programme's menu. They are required to do so. Regulatory authorities and broadcasting institutions are deeply conscious of the criticisms which the re-enactment of crime can arouse. For instance, in August 1994 ITV decided to discontinue Michael Winner's *True Crimes* series, partly because the programme's crime re-enactments were thought to be too luridly sensational and partly because it was feared that they might possibly heighten public fears about crime. The producers of *Crimewatch* on the other hand have always been at pains to emphasise the documentary character of the reconstructions. As Schlesinger and Tumber have commented:

Where documentary reconstruction is involved, the ability to convince an audience needs to be rooted in the detailed authentication of the events portrayed ... In the realist documentary framework it is precisely the establishing of correct detail that counts. (Schlesinger and Tumber, 1993: 24)

The producers of *Crimewatch* have always, understandably enough, insisted on the public service credentials of the programme. As we have already suggested, however, *Crimewatch*, and programmes like it, are consciously trading on the audience's familiarity and fascination with the many other forms of crime fiction which are such a regular feature of mainstream programming.

Reality programming

With *Crimewatch* it is the mixing of various components which has proved to be such a winning formula in terms of audience ratings. In this respect *Crimewatch* has more than a little in common with another category of programming which, since the late 1980s, has enjoyed considerable popularity. We refer to the type of programme to which the generic label 'reality programming' or 'reality television' is often applied (Kilborn, 1994b). Although these terms are notoriously imprecise, what is implied are programming formats in which documentary and dramatic elements are blended together in what has proved to be a very popular mix.

Just as *Crimewatch* relies for its impact and popularity on a hybrid structure with a mix of components, so the various types of reality programming bring together different but complementary elements in what their producers trust is a particularly audience-friendly package. Short, action-packed sequences that concentrate on the work of the police or the emergency services are reality television's stock in trade. A typical programme will consist of up to five segments, each of which is relatively self-contained in that it will focus on a particular incident or event (a drugs raid or a rescue). Some of these 'reality bites' will have been recorded as the actual events unfurled and will have been filmed by members of the police, fire or ambulance services specially detailed to produce blow-by-blow accounts. Some will have been filmed by a one- or two-person

'documentary' team shadowing those emergency or rescue operations. Still others will take the form of material submitted to broadcasters by camcorder-owning amateurs who have filmed bizarre or
harrowing incidents.

Where no such material is available, producers will resort to some
type of dramatic reconstruction. Here every effort will be made to
extract the full dramatic effect from the episodes of bravery or
derring-do which are being re-enacted. Most reconstructions will
make plentiful use of techniques familiar from the world of dramatic
fiction. A particular aim is to create an atmosphere of suspense.
The fact that as viewers we are frequently aligned with those who
are carrying out the rescue or tracking down the alleged wrong-
doers might also be claimed to contribute to the appeal of such
programmes, by adding a sense of voyeuristic, identificatory
pleasure.[9]

Because reality television is unashamedly populist in its aspirations, it also – as one might have expected – has close connections
with other types of programming, especially television soaps. Each
encourages strong forms of audience involvement in the lives of
characters or in *milieux* with which we are mostly familiar. Each will
regularly feature the 'puncturing' of ordinary routine by some
dramatic event. There is also a structural affinity. Soaps have inter-
weaving story lines; reality programmes rely on an accumulation of
separate stories, but they all have a common thread (e.g. police
hunting criminals) running through them. Both forms of programme are therefore well suited to those 'distracted' forms of viewing about which we shall have more to say in the following chapter.

What, then, is the relationship of reality programming to other
forms of documentary? It does, after all, bear many of the hallmarks
of documentary realism. These 'reality bites' also appear to have
much in common with sequences in fly-on-the-wall documentaries,
in that both bear witness to events in the world 'out there' about
which the viewer might like to discover more. The often difficult
conditions in which the images and sounds have been recorded reinforce the sense of authenticity. Picture wobble, temporary loss of
focus, problems with framing and sound distortion are all an index
of spontaneity and enhanced reality status. The impression of

heightened realism can, however, be deceptive. Though evoking a strong sense of events occurring in the 'here and now', these reality bites effectively bracket out those wider areas of social concern to which classic documentary attached so much importance (Nichols, 1994: 54).

Packaging the real

Just as *Crimewatch* relies for its popularity on a characteristic mix of components, so do the various forms of reality programming depend on the way in which the multiple ingredients (reality bite, reconstruction, surveillance material, presenter talk) are brought together in a fast-moving, audience-friendly package.

Most programmes of this kind will also have their own resident anchor-person who introduces the clips. He or she comments on the events depicted or enacted and generally acts as the programme's master of ceremonies. Occasionally there will be an attempt to reflect more seriously on the implications of individual 'reality bites'. For the most part, however, the anchor simply performs the function of a narrator, setting the scene for the next action-packed sequence.

A good illustration of a reality programme which relies on careful packaging is the British series *999* (BBC). Closely modelled on *Rescue 911* (the successful American show), *999* concentrates on the work of the emergency and rescue services. Like its close relative *Crimewatch*, it employs a similar hybrid format with 'live' footage, dramatic reconstructions, life-saving tips and various forms of commentary incorporated into a carefully orchestrated programme package. Once again, however, it is the reconstructions which lie at the heart of the programme.

Because the watchword is 'accessibility', the dramatic reconstructions featured in *999* will closely follow modes employed in dramatic fiction (Kilborn, 1994b: 432–3). Just as a television soap will produce a dramatically enhanced – and thus necessarily skewed – picture of everyday life, so a series such as *999* will focus on those episodes and incidents which can be represented in the most dramatically appealing fashion. In one programme, for instance (BBC 1: 21 June 1996), the dramatic reconstructions included a policeman impaled on railings, a diver fighting for life in a decompression chamber and a paraglider who had fallen 200 feet down a cliff on the Isle of Wight. The drama does not merely derive from the creative treatment of the events, it inheres in the subjects themselves!

Although 999's dramatic reconstructions are a primary source of its appeal to viewers, the producers have always been at pains to underline the programme's claims to be 'responsible' factual discourse. To start with, the programme is introduced, and the reconstructions contextualised, by the well-known journalist, Michael Buerk. Buerk's presence, it might be argued, adds further credibility to the accounts, since he has acquired a reputation as a reliable and trusted BBC reporter and newsreader. In addition, viewers will at some point be introduced to the 'real-life' individuals who have featured in the rescues or near-disasters. Not only does this provide a measure of reassurance to viewers who might otherwise have been concerned for the well-being of these individuals, it also quells any lingering doubts among the audience that what the reconstructions project is firmly based in reality (see Bondebjerg, 1996: 39). In short, with a programme such as 999 some of the problems encountered with those macro-reconstructions, where the boundaries between fictional and factual may sometimes become blurred, do not arise.

Tabloid television?

One problem with the new hybrid and reality formats is that – for all their attempts to establish their public service credentials – they are seen as exemplifying the inexorable move towards tabloid television, in which the commercial imperative to maximise audience ratings makes it difficult to produce anything other than relatively superficial accounts. The emphasis always has to be on dramatic – as opposed to documentary – reconstruction, and the major objective is to produce gripping entertainment.[10] Thus, although a programme such as 999 may well open the public's eyes to the *modus operandi* of the emergency services, it will seldom set these activities in any wider social or political context. Indeed, the sort of probing analysis that one might expect from a traditional documentary account seems effectively to be ruled out (Kilborn, 1994b: 433).

On the other hand, some critics take the view that these new reality strands should be seen in a far more positive light. They claim that these reality formats have enabled producers to break free from the stranglehold of the older expository modes (with their authoritarian overtones) and to develop new ways of perceiving the relationship between the public and the private sphere. As Bondebjerg has commented:

> In a way ... it could be argued that what we are witnessing through hybridization and new reality and access genres is the democratization of an old public service discourse ... and the creation of a new mixed public sphere, where common knowledge and everyday experience play a much larger role. (Bondebjerg, 1996: 29)

Concluding remarks

There is no question that in the coming years we will see further experiments in the mixing of factual and dramatic modes and the introduction of new forms of hybridised programming. Debates about the legitimacy and effectiveness of such forms will doubtless continue, but in the new digital and deregulated age it seems likely that the emphasis in the debate will shift. The concern will be less with the alleged confusion which can arise in viewers' minds when 'fact' and 'fiction' are merged in these hybrid forms. Rather, it will centre on the consequences of the populist imperative: the need to create factually-based dramatic entertainments where the aim is not so much to raise consciousness as simply to discourage the viewer from switching to another channel.

PART IV

Documentary production and reception

'Just do it our way!'

INSTITUTIONAL CONTROL AND PRODUCTION ECONOMICS

Our aim in this chapter is to consider a number of issues relating to the production of television documentaries, especially the relationship between the producers of documentary material and the institutions or companies that employ them or give them commissions. Documentary has always been subject to a whole series of institutional and economic constraints, and it is our intention to consider what impact they have on the type and range of work that gets broadcast. We shall also be exploring the vexed question of what threats are posed to documentary by the radical transformations that have taken place in late twentieth-century broadcasting structures. Will documentary be changed out of all recognition by increasing deregulation and commercialisation? Can it still continue to play the role it allegedly once had in the golden age of public service broadcasting? Or do the new commercial imperatives make it much more likely that documentary will be condemned to a more marginal role, its survival being dependent on its acquiring the entertainment potential of other televisual forms?

Political and institutional control

Documentaries, like any other cultural artefacts, are the products of particular sets of historical, economic and cultural circumstances. It is for this reason that distinct national traditions of documentary have developed that reflect the different priorities of broadcasters and, by extension, of governments. Though it is beyond the scope of this book to chronicle the various historical developments and national traditions, let us at least consider some of the ways in which documentarists operating in particular systems have come to produce the work they have.

Throughout the history of documentary there have been various groups and bodies that have exerted considerable influence on the forms which documentary has assumed and the functions which it has been called on to fulfil. Film makers in what used to be called the Western democracies (there are Eastern ones too now!) have regularly had to seek different types of sponsorship to provide them with the funding or time necessary to finance their projects. And since the rules of sponsorship dictate that there shall always be a pay-off for the sponsoring agent, documentarists have found themselves – to a greater or lesser extent – involved in acts of compromise.[1] By the same token, in times of war, crisis or national emergency, when governments or regimes have sought to impress upon their people the need for action or compliance, documentarists have regularly been drafted in to make propaganda films at the government's behest (Lovell and Hillier, 1972: 31–2, 151).

Areas of sensitivity

Given the political and/or economic constraints to which they have always been subject, documentarists have frequently found themselves in the position of having to assess how far they could go in contesting accepted views of history or other established 'received' ideas. It should therefore come as no surprise to learn that the most serious and bitter controversies involving documentaries have occurred when governments or official institutions have challenged the rights of progressively minded documentarists to produce work which revealed things or voiced sentiments that the former would have preferred not to enter the public domain.

One of the most (in)famous examples of institutional censorship was the banning by the BBC of Peter Watkins's powerful documentary *The War Game* (1965), a drama-documentary account of the likely effects of a nuclear attack on a British city.[2] Made at the height of the Cold War, *The War Game* was banned, officially on the grounds that '... the effect of the film [was] judged to be too horrifying for the medium of broadcasting' (BBC Press release). Of course, much more lay behind this decision than simply the desire to protect the public from being exposed to horrifying images. As has subsequently been shown, there was a degree of involvement by the government in the decision not to screen the film. There was clearly a recognition in high places that such a film could have a negative impact on the public's attitude to the nuclear deterrent (Aubrey, 1982: 48–54).

The case of *The War Game* – which was, incidentally, first screened on television twenty years later in 1985 – is a classic instance of how vulnerable some documentarists can be to censoring intervention.[3] It also emphasises a general point about why institutions – whether in the shape of television organisations themselves or outside bodies that have a controlling influence over them – feel a need to put the brake on certain types of documentary activity. In contrast to fiction films, where censoring authorities are principally concerned with scenes of sexual or violent activity which can allegedly disturb or deprave the easily impressionable, the censorship of documentaries has mainly centred on the withholding of views or information which, if released, would be judged to be detrimental to perceived institutional interests.

The issue of censorship is extremely complex, and one cannot do justice to the topic here. As has already been suggested, however, censorship can take many forms, some of them emanating from the broadcasting institutions themselves and some from external agencies. There is, for instance, an important distinction to be drawn between those forms of pre-emptive control which are legally enforced (in the UK by means of government D-notices and the like) and the various forms of internal censorship which a broadcasting institution imposes out of a recognition that it might incur the wrath of some higher authority (political or economic) if it transmitted certain types of material.

The question of how documentarists have negotiated windows of opportunity for themselves in often difficult circumstances and the reprisals they have had to endure when governments have clamped down is worthy of a study in its own right.[4] It takes us into the whole area of censorship and also into the debate about what impact a documentary can be presumed to have (see Chapter 9). The point we would like to reinforce for the moment, however, is that succeeding generations of documentarists – in whatever political system they have found themselves – have often had to operate in conditions that placed severe constraints on their ability to communicate with audiences in ways they deemed appropriate. This does not mean to say that every documentary project is accompanied by an agonised debate on what is politically expedient or what might raise the hackles of a commercial sponsor. It does imply, however, that in their attempts to get work produced or commissioned documentarists have had to show considerable sensitivity as to what would be considered acceptable within the bounds of the system in which they were operating. Expressed in more explicit terms, film and programme makers have often been prepared to indulge in various forms of self-censorship to ensure that their work finds an audience. It also explains why a number of independently-minded film makers have chosen to turn their backs on mainstream film and television production and have opted instead to produce politically and/or stylistically challenging work which is circulated, often in 16-mm or video format, to special-interest groups.

There are bound to be differing views on how we should judge the various accommodations that 'mainstream' documentarists make in seeking to get their work screened. Some critics will take the line that the merest hint of self-censorship constitutes an act of political expediency, whereas others will see it as exemplifying the unavoidable compromises that are forced upon most film and programme makers who wish to work in so public a medium as television. Suffice to say that, at whatever period of documentary one casts one's eye, one can almost always come up with examples of film makers making what we would see as accommodations to the perceived needs of sponsoring agents (in whatever sense one understands that term).

At its most extreme, this accommodation will involve the film maker in a blatant propaganda exercise. The well-known German film maker Leni Riefensthal (born 1902), for instance, made a considerable name for herself with *Triumph of the Will* (1935), her monumental depiction of one of Hitler's party rallies in Nürnberg. Much of what we see in this film was in fact especially orchestrated, with government assistance, in order to maximise its impact when captured by Riefensthal's cameras. Even though she has vigorously disputed the degree of direct involvement by the Nazi party in the film-making enterprise, Riefensthal can hardly have been under any illusions about the kind of account which would find favour in the prevailing political conditions (Jacobs, 1979: 136–40). Even John Grierson does not escape criticism or the charge of being unduly respectful to sponsors' needs. As we have already seen, for all his proud claims that documentary (his documentaries) could have a major democratising function in raising public awareness about social issues, the critique of society which he offered was far more muted than he would have us believe.

Sometimes the 'adjustments' that a documentarist makes in response to external pressure are of a different order. They will involve him or her in the devising of strategies or ploys to overcome the influence of some controlling agent. During the period of the Cold War, for instance, a whole generation of documentary film makers working in the former Communist states of Eastern and Central Europe had to negotiate a particularly difficult course. They were all too aware that the major function of the officially sanctioned documentarist was to project robustly positive images of the State and its achievements. At the same time, no small number of them wanted to indicate to their audience that all might not be as it actually appeared. Thus, whilst seeming to toe the party line, they developed techniques for sending out coded messages to an audience which had for its part learned the art of reading between the lines.

Relations between documentarists and broadcasters

The vast majority (over ninety per cent) of documentaries are nowadays produced directly by, or at the behest of, television organisations or channels. It follows therefore that with respect to the formats used, the styles and approaches employed and even the subjects tackled, it will be the respective institution (a term here used to refer to the television company, organisation or network) which will have a determining impact. The institution in turn is shaped by, and continues to be exposed to, a series of different forces (economic, political and cultural), some internally generated, others externally enforced. And when the institutional priorities of the organisation change as a result of political intervention or in response to a new economic situation, then sooner or later these changes will have an impact on the programming strategies of that institution. (For more on this, see below under 'The situation in the UK'.)

If it is true that documentary film makers are beholden to institutions to this extent, there are different ways in which one can characterise this relationship. The first and most obvious is to single out the economic power that institutions exert over what documentarists produce. As we know, television is a rapidly changing industry and the programming demands and institutional practices of today are very different from those of the late 1970s. For one thing, as a result of the progressive deregulation and commercialisation of broadcasting, documentary production teams, many of them operating on a freelance, independent basis, are now pitched into a far more competitive relationship with one another as they vie for commissions from television broadcasters. In this respect there has been a clear move away from the explicit or direct forms of control which institutions exerted on in-house production teams towards a less explicit but no less tangible form of control whereby commissioning editors of broadcasting institutions have acquired major powers in deciding which independent producer receives preferment in the increasingly cut-throat business of getting projects funded or commissioned.

The documentary tradition
For all the controls that institutions exert, and in spite of the tensions that arise out of having to compete with one another for funding and commissions, contemporary documentarists are bound together in one important respect: most will be aware that they are part of a larger or longer tradition which goes beyond the present-day exigencies of individual institutions. There is a sense of belonging to what Bill Nichols has aptly characterised as 'a community of practitioners' (1991: 15). The commitment to produce representations of the socio-historical world within the limits imposed by

broadcasting institutions gives documentarists a sense of common purpose, which may possibly have been strengthened in recent years by the awareness that the current broadcasting climate is not always conducive to the documentary cause. There is a further common-ality in that they are all, to a greater or lesser extent, conscious that they have inherited from former generations rules and conventions which inform their present working practices. There is, in short, an awareness that documentary itself represents an institution to which the documentarist has certain obligations that stand quite apart from their obligations towards the subjects they treat and to the organisations they work for.[5]

The attempt on the part of institutions to exercise control over both form and content of documentary programming has inevitably led to strains and stresses in the relationship between documen-tarists and broadcasters. In particular, there is a growing feeling amongst documentary film makers that the contemporary ecology of broadcasting has made it increasingly difficult to uphold some of the principal aims of documentary as they have traditionally been conceived. This is, however, matched by an equal awareness amongst independent producers that getting their work screened on television may confer on that work a kind of institutional authority it would not otherwise acquire. Thus, while the majority of docu-mentaries are nowadays made by independent producers, they are still marketed and promoted as institutional products (e.g. 'the latest Channel 4 documentary') and not as the work of a particular director or documentary team.

Changing priorities
The main sources of conflict in relations between documentarists and broadcasters lie, as suggested, in the new priorities which now prevail in this progressively deregulated broadcasting era. Nowadays there is an increasing expectation that most factual programming will have to have passed an 'accessibility threshold' to allow it to attract what is deemed to be a reasonable size of audience. The fear on the part of the documentarist is that, in the process, ever more popular formats (especially the various forms of reality program-ming) will gradually gain the ascendancy, thus leading to wide-

spread trivialisation and a dearth of opportunities for the serious, challenging or 'creative' documentary.

For some documentary film makers, then, television is seen as something of a *bête noire*, which, whilst seeming to increase the number of factual/documentary slots, has proved an unreliable servant of the documentary cause. This criticism, however, needs to be seen in its historical context. The first point to make is that before the advent of television, documentaries fulfilled a very different function: in the pre-television era film documentaries and newsreels were the only vehicles for providing moving-picture accounts of events of the day. With the coming of television the situation changed quite radically, as this reporting function was taken over by the new medium, which quickly established itself as the major provider of news and current affairs coverage.

Once cinema had lost the sole responsibility for documentary, the genre quickly began to develop along significantly different lines (see Chapter 1). This inevitably led to tensions between those who felt that any departure from the values of cinematic documentary was a kind of betrayal and those who considered that the whole future of documentary depended on adjusting to the demands of the new medium. These tensions, although they are perhaps not felt as keenly nowadays as they once were, still tend to surface quite regularly, especially in cinematic cultures such as in France, where the traditions and values of *auteurist* cinema remain firmly entrenched. In general, however, there is now a recognition amongst documentarists that television has become the key force in determining the present and future course of documentary and that such economic realities have to be confronted. This does not mean to say that these realities are always openly embraced. There is, for instance, a continuing resentment that the standard television formats do not allow for the more expansive treatment of certain subjects that was previously possible in the feature-length documentary targeted at the cinema audience.

Whilst no-one can deny the impact of television, opinions do differ on the extent to which it has actually transformed the documentary landscape. Some take the view that, in spite of television's notorious 'branding and stranding' policies, there will still be windows of opportunity for the one-off creative documentary (Bourelly, 1993: 49). Others are far less sanguine and believe that television's commercial imperatives will make it increasingly difficult to find a slot for any programme which does not fit in with standard expectations concerning length and the demands it makes on viewer attention. It is this desire on the part of broadcasters to pigeon-hole individual programmes into pre-existing slots in the schedule which many documentary film makers still find very difficult to accept. To them, it is as if they are being required to meet the demands of a fully industrialised process characterised by the need to conform to one of several available moulds. The optimum requirement is for a standardised product which can be easily accommodated into the channel's schedule. (See also Chapter 9.)

New developments in documentary: secondary markets and new delivery systems

If we maintain that television has had such a huge impact on the development of documentary since the 1950s, we should ask what are the ways in which documentarists have responded or adjusted to the changing needs of television itself. Broadly speaking, there is general consensus that in the heyday of public service broadcasting documentary received a form of artistic patronage from television on which it can no longer rely in the current market-led broad-casting climate (Chanan, 1995: 41). As they have adapted to what is generally seen to be a much harsher climate, documentarists – like all other producers of cultural artefacts – have been forced to subject some of the traditional modes to searching examination. The conse-quence of this has been that, slowly but surely, new styles and modes have come to the fore – partly born of the economic necessity to reach a larger audience, but partly attributable to the need of any genre to regenerate itself as some of the established approaches begin to reveal their limitations. One might also regard this inno-vatory drive as part of that wider artistic endeavour to forge a means of expression which does justice to the subject being tackled. As Brecht cannily observed:

> Our concept of realism must be wide and political, sovereign over all conventions ... Methods become exhausted, stimuli no longer work.

New problems appear and demand new methods. Reality changes; in order to represent it modes of representation must also change. (Brecht, 1980: 82)

To illustrate the transformational capacity of documentary one could cite the example of what some refer to as a European documentary 'New Wave'. The chief characteristic of this New Wave is not so much that it represents a wholly new approach to film making as that it picks up on and reworks older, no longer fashionable forms. In the words of one observer:

> The idea of a 'New Wave' refers to a renaissance of the '*documentaire de création*' – authored films which replace the observational approach (Direct Cinema, *Cinéma Vérité*, Fly-on-the-Wall) with work that is telling an overtly personal and constructed story. It is typified by strong narrative. Many of the techniques are those of drama, yet the films remain firmly rooted in reality. (Marshall, 1995: 12)

It is, however, not just ideas on the form and content of documentaries that are changing: as we shall discover in the final chapter, new strategies are being devised for the scheduling of documentaries. We are also seeing the gradual emergence in Europe of so-called niche providers: television channels wholly dedicated to the screening of documentaries (see below). Whilst all these developments bear witness to the fact that television is still regarded as a key player in the funding, production and exhibition of documentaries, one must also draw attention to other means of marketing the documentary product. There are two aspects to the development of secondary, non-broadcast markets. The first involves exploiting additional means of delivery in order to extend the life of the otherwise all-too transient television documentary. These can be tried and tested systems, such as 16-mm or video cassette. They can on the other hand involve using the new technologies of video CD, CD-1 and similar systems. The second relies on documentary producers or broadcasters teaming up with publishing houses in order to produce multi-media packages capable of being exploited in this new and rapidly expanding sector.[6]

The economics of documentary production

Viewed historically, the documentary has been closely identified with the aspirations of socially concerned film makers to provide some form of cultural enlightenment. It has also – in its more negative manifestations – been associated with attempts to persuade and cajole through various forms of propaganda. Looking upon documentaries as a vehicle for the expression of social concern has, however, sometimes had the effect of underplaying their importance within the broad economy of contemporary broadcasting.

As should already have become clear in the course of this chapter, documentaries in the television age are now seen as commodified items in exactly the same way as all other forms of programming. They are bought, sold and exchanged in the international media markets, and the conditions under which they are produced are subject to the most rigorous scrutiny in terms of production turn-around times, budgetary requirements and potential consumer and/or advertiser appeal. By the same token, documentaries are also subject to a diverse range of pressures and constraints resulting from the increasing competitiveness within the television sector. All this has caused broadcasters to gravitate generally towards tried and tested formulae in their programming and to opt for 'safe' subjects and conventional treatments where there is the least element of risk. An additional consequence of this competitiveness has been a marked increase in the incidence of 'cloning' (Wood, 1996: 18–19). This militates against the creation of distinctive documentary strands on the major channels, since – as we shall see – programming ideas or styles that prove popular with audiences on one channel are very rapidly copied by other broadcasters.

Another consequence of the transformations currently taking place in broadcasting is that media organisations are being increasingly internationalised (Stenderup, 1995). This may bring economic benefits, but it also makes it more likely that broadcasters will prefer certain types of 'lowest common denominator' programming that have broad, international appeal. This situation is clearly one that favours large producers in large countries who derive particular benefits from economies of scale. Conversely, the small producer –

the two- or three-person independent company, of which there are literally hundreds scattered throughout Europe – has an increasingly uphill struggle to remain viable. This again gives rise to fears that there will be insufficient diversity in documentary provision and a marked tendency to favour the safe, standardised product. In the words of one critic:

> Documentary splits into separate camps: at one extreme are the big production houses. These groups are compelled to seek economies of scale and are pulled towards series production, where overheads can be spread across more screen hours, but where the film-maker's individuality is inevitably submerged. At the opposite end of the spectrum is the small producer who thinks in terms of individual artistic production. (Chanan, 1993: 40)

Buying and selling documentaries

As television executives become ever more cost-conscious in decisions relating to production funding and programme acquisition, so documentary is exposed to another type of cost-benefit analysis. It is, for instance, generally accepted that the cost of generating one's own programming is almost always going to be more than that of acquiring imported material. Executives and programme directors are therefore for ever weighing up the cost advantages of buying in 'foreign' material against the possible negative consequences of such programming being of lesser appeal to a home audience.[7] Another problem facing cost-conscious controllers when buying and scheduling documentaries is that, broadly speaking, they find themselves spending significantly larger sums per viewer than with other forms of programming. In the words of one commissioning editor:

> It wouldn't be difficult to find a Controller of Factual Programmes at a British broadcaster who was having to spend a dollar for every ten of his or her documentary viewers. Across the corridor, his/her colleague in light entertainment could expect a thousand viewers for the same dollar. (Haws, 1995: 16)

Although documentarists can, in defence, claim that the costs of documentary production are significantly lower than those of quality drama, the economic arguments remain stacked against the more traditional documentary. This is one of the reasons why we have witnessed since the late 1980s an increasing hybridisation in television documentary as producers attempt to build into it the more successful features of other genres. This also explains the growth of those low-cost, self-made productions which exploit the potential of video/camcorder technology. In addition, as we shall discover in the next chapter, there have been significant changes in working practices, many involving an element of multi-skilling, which have enabled documentarists to reduce the size of their crews and to produce certain types of documentary for a fraction of their former costs.

One must, however, guard against giving the impression that documentary making, for the reasons listed above, has completely transformed itself into a slick, technology-driven industry with the emphasis on rapid throughput and rapid response to the latest consumer demand. In spite of its having become part of a highly industrialised production process, documentary making has remained a relatively labour-intensive form of media production. It is a highly skilled craft demanding high levels of patience, commitment and dedication. Even with the benefits brought by new technology (especially in the field of editing), the time taken to put together a well-researched documentary has not decreased significantly.

The changing face of European documentary

Given some of the points made in the preceding section concerning the much harsher broadcasting climate in which documentary has been required to operate in recent times, there might be some justification for believing that documentary is indeed (as some would claim) an endangered species. The fear is that, as the commercial imperative becomes ever more insistent, so broadcasters will take the least line of resistance and seek refuge in ever-tackier forms of factual broadcasting, with the emphasis on infotainment, to the virtual exclusion of more challenging, innovative forms of documentary (Kilborn, 1994b). How serious are these threats? Or have documentarists succeeded in adapting to the new economic realities of broadcasting without having to compromise themselves too severely? In the following section we shall be looking at the changing face of European documentary in the attempt to pinpoint developing trends and to show how documentarists, including those working for public service organisations, have responded to the challenge to produce more accessible forms of programming.

As television executives make ever more insistent demands that factual programming should compete with other forms of programming for a place in the schedule, it may come as something of a surprise to learn that there are some who are convinced that documentary has a relatively bright future (Kilborn, 1996: 142–3). Viewed in purely statistical terms, the position of European documentary looks quite healthy. In one 1994 survey, for instance, it was calculated that in the previous year more than 20,000 hours of documentary programming had been produced and transmitted. The fact, however, that some 10,000 companies were competing for this business immediately puts this figure in a slightly different perspective, as does the discovery that both production and screening of documentaries are very unevenly spread across the European states. Significantly more documentaries, for instance, are screened in Britain, Germany and the Netherlands than in Italy and Spain, where they have largely disappeared from prime-time schedules. As we have already noted, documentary still tends to fare best in those countries with a strong tradition of public service broadcasting.

Niche providers

Whilst it cannot be denied that commercial imperatives in broadcasting have put pressure on documentarists, it should be pointed out that developments in the cable and satellite sector have provided a series of new opportunities. In particular, we have – during the 1990s – seen the emergence of a number of channels specialising in documentary. These so-called niche providers have spotted a market opportunity arising out of the problems that the more commercially oriented terrestrial broadcasters have had, both in positioning documentary within mixed programming schedules and in justifying the costs involved in funding a type of programming that normally appeals only to a relatively small domestic audience. Though still to make a major impact in Europe in terms of overall audience share,

the arrival in Europe of the Discovery Channel (which started broadcasting via satellite in 1989), the History Channel (start-up date,
1995) and two smaller networks, Planète and Documania (broadcasting in French and Spanish respectively) has increased audience
access to documentary and, in the case of Discovery, has given a
fillip to documentary production. With their largely populist programming designed to capture and hold the attention of today's
channel-hopping viewers, these new channels have not been uni-
versally welcomed, primarily because they are regarded as providing
mostly a bland form of programming which will not stir up controversy. In their attempt to reach the widest possible audience, however, these networks do cover quite a wide range of subjects that do
not always feature in the schedules of other channels. At present,
these niche providers do not present a major challenge to the terrestrial broadcasters, but with the rapid expansion of cable and satellite
provision and with further developments in the field of multi-media,
this situation is set to change. By the turn of the century, for
instance, it is estimated that sixty per cent of the UK's television
audience will be reached by cable and satellite, thus encouraging the
appearance of more niche providers wishing to specialise in factual
programming.

Satellite channels clearly have a different set of priorities compared with nationally and regionally based terrestrial broadcasters.
The former will always be concerned to maximise the outreach of
their programming, whereas with the latter there is at least some
expectation that they will produce work which in some measure
addresses issues that are more specific to the interests or concerns of
their national or regional area. Because all broadcasters are aware
that they are now operating in an increasingly global media environment, there is growing pressure to produce programming which
transcends national boundaries. The challenge which more and
more documentarists confront, therefore, is to produce documentaries that are identifiably rooted in a particular time and place and
at the same time have the capacity to speak to a much wider
audience (for instance, by not presupposing too much culturally
specific knowledge on the part of the viewer). This is one of several
broadcaster-imposed constraints under which documentary film

makers have to operate nowadays, another being that they are almost always required to tailor their films to the specifications of an individual broadcaster and thus, in effect, to make made-to-measure films.

Reversioning

One of the difficulties – some would say challenges! – which documentarists have to confront in producing work for trans-national providers, such as Discovery, is that programmes will often have to be refashioned according to the perceived demands of different national audiences. Consequently, makers of documentaries may be called on to produce multiple versions of a particular work, a process known in the trade as 'reversioning'. For understandable reasons, many documentarists are reluctant to become involved in such a market-driven exercise, which they see as compromising the artistic integrity of their work. All the signs are, however, that they will be required by economic necessity to dance to the broadcaster's tune.[8] As one commissioning editor has commented:

> Unfortunately, the real world demands standard durations and local stylistic conventions ... The question therefore is whether the film-maker and broadcast partners can agree on what the essence of the documentary shall be and the extent of reversioning required. (Haws, 1995: 17)

As one might imagine, such meeting of minds does not always occur, the worst-case scenario being when decisions about the reshaping of a work are made without the documentarist's consent.

Co-production

One of the other 'facts of life' that makers of documentaries have increasingly had to accept is that few projects get off the ground without the striking of a co-production or co-financing deal. This trend towards co-production is regarded by most commentators as an endemic feature of broadcasting in today's world. As John Marshall has observed:

> In an increasingly global media environment, where broadcasters are under financial and competitive pressures, international co-

production is as inevitable as it is desirable. Few broadcasters can contemplate fully funding high quality documentaries – not because the genre is particularly expensive, but because there are so many competing budgetary demands ... For the producer, co-production offers the possibility of more production and of making films in the way he feels right. The bigger the market, the more variety is demanded, and the more chance of finding a broadcaster who will share a particular approach or aesthetic. (Marshall, 1994: 50)

What cannot be disputed about the trend towards various forms of co-production is that they have their origins more in economics than in any desire to assemble the most talented group of film makers from diverse backgrounds to work on an artistically ambitious project. It is, however, not just the larger production houses that are being drawn into co-production; there is growing evidence to suggest that an increasing number of smaller producers is having recourse to co-production out of economic necessity.

As with any form of co-production, so with co-produced documentaries there is much argument over the gains and losses in an artistic sense. The purist view is that any co-production is going to involve the partners in various forms of compromise which will necessarily result in a bland, homogenised product. The fear is, therefore, that documentarists will increasingly be forced into producing work according to 'lowest common denominator' criteria and that this will jeopardise deserving projects that do not meet the criteria of the internationally oriented media market-place.

There are some film makers, however, who take the contrary view: they maintain that co-productions can bring greater autonomy. As the French film maker Jacques Bidou suggests:

When funding is diversified, the film maker has to avoid the trap of bastardising the film by trying to please everyone. I think in completely the opposite way. When you have a strong idea that's worth defending, you should find the people who are interested. That is what co-producing is about; not making a standardised product that appeals to the lowest common denominator. Remember that the documentary programme directors, who are fighting for their share of channel budgets, are really interested in original and high quality films. (Cited in Bourelly, 1993: 51)

A further point to make about genuine co-productions (that is, productions in which several partners are, from the outset, involved in the creative shaping of the project) is that they enable certain issues to be addressed from a set of different perspectives. It might be contended, for instance, that the BBC co-produced series *Living Islam* (1993) avoided falling into the trap of stereotypical representations of culture because it was partly looking at the subject from an Islamic perspective.

Co-financing

Such examples as *Living Islam* tend, however, to be few and far between. Much more typical are instances where individual producers or television stations strike co-financing deals. As the term suggests, co-financing involves documentarists in an often very time-consuming quest to assemble funding for a project from a variety of sources: pre-sales monies (linked in with broadcasting or distribution rights), television financing and, possibly, subsidies from various cultural agencies (see also Chanan, 1993). Amongst documentarists there is a recognition that 'co-production' in these cases amounts to little more than a spurious device for raising money.

Though film makers are often sceptical about the reasons for their entering into such 'partnership' arrangements, most of them accept that, without such devices, many of their projects would simply not get off the ground. Whilst the majority of such deals are straightforward commercial transactions, there have been various initiatives since the late 1980s – at both the national and the wider European level – to help documentarists to put together funding packages for their projects. In various parts of continental Europe, for instance, film makers have been able to draw on state and/or federal subsidy funds (e.g. in Germany and in Scandinavia). Likewise, for several years until its curtailment in 1996, there was a scheme which attempted to stimulate the 'creative' documentary through a series of supportive or enabling measures under the auspices of the European Union's MEDIA programme. The same scheme also brought together broadcasting representatives and documentarists at special events where the latter could pitch ideas for projects at the commissioning editors from diverse European television channels. In 1995

– after the withdrawal of more targeted support for documentary under the new MEDIA 2 arrangements – there was a move to set up a European Documentary Network, a self-help mechanism to assist the smaller independent production units in their search for co-production funding (Stenderup, 1995: 31–54). A similar scheme that has been running for some years is the Atlantic Co-Production Alliance, which – as the name suggests – attempts to establish productive links between broadcasters in Europe and North America.

Support mechanisms such as these clearly have a role to play in helping film makers to strike partnership agreements or to alert them to additional funding possibilities. The problem with such schemes is that they may not be sufficiently focused on the economic needs of documentarists in an increasingly competitive environment. With the European Union's MEDIA initiative, for instance, there was often uncertainty amongst film makers about whether the primary objectives were cultural or economic. In the words of one observer:

> It's not clear whether our priority is to preserve our own cultural identity, or compete on a business level with the US industry. But it is clear to me that with the amount of money MEDIA has available to invest, there's no chance of taking up the economic challenge. (Thomas Stenderup in Bourelly, 1993: 50)

Other commentators are of a similar opinion, suggesting that European Union schemes such as the DOCUMENTARY initiative are always going to be torn between on the one hand the aspiration to promote documentary projects which reveal the local and regional diversity within the EU countries and on the other hand the need to be seen to be supporting the European audio-visual industry, which is striving to assert itself against international – especially US – competition.

Given the many problems in setting up partnership deals, some documentarists are wont to take a simpler, more radical view of the whole issue of co-production. Film makers such as Paul Watson, for instance, are of the opinion that advances in technology – in particular the small cameras, which deliver high-quality images, and the new generation of digital editing equipment – will radically alter documentary production as we have known it hitherto. Watson believes that production costs will fall to the point at which many types of innovative documentary work will become possible without the tiresome search for co-production funding. In his own words:

> We will be able to make programmes that have national conviction and which are more attractive for this reason ... Blockbuster series depending on international co-financing deals will still be made, but these will be increasingly absorbed by CD-ROM technology. (Contribution at the 1996 Sheffield Documentary Film Festival)

The situation in the UK

In the UK, as elsewhere in Europe, the new commercial imperatives have had a tangible impact on documentary film making in both the privately and publicly funded sectors. All broadcasters have been forced to rethink their production and scheduling strategies, which has led to much uncertainty among both in-house and independent documentary producers. As one of us has commented elsewhere:

> The BBC – forced into a more competitive relationship with its commercial rivals and subject to growing financial pressures – is transmitting a higher proportion of popular or accessible documentaries. The ITV companies meanwhile have gone even further down this road, which has led to fears being expressed in some quarters that serious documentaries could disappear completely. And even Channel 4, which since its inception has been particularly committed to the documentary, may no longer be the Eldorado it once appeared to be, now that more market-place influences are beginning to exert their malign influence. (Kilborn, 1996: 144)

ITV

In the case of the commercial ITV channel the marginalisation of serious documentaries has, in the eyes of some critics, already reached crisis proportions. Whereas in previous decades there were a number of dedicated slots for serious or challenging documentaries (*First Tuesday, Viewpoint* and *Disappearing World*), in the current decade this has been reduced to one (*Network First*), which occupies a relatively unfavourable late-evening position in the schedule. This change can partly be laid at the door of the 1990

Broadcasting Act, which gave a measure of protection to current affairs but no longer specifically required of new ITV franchise holders that they should include documentaries in their programming schedules. The major criterion for scheduling a documentary nowadays on ITV is its ability to deliver an appropriately sized audience. In the words of ITV's one-time Controller of Factual Programmes, Stuart Prebble:

> Most factual programme producers understand that ITV has been put into an environment which is more commercial and difficult than ever before... The choice facing us is simple: we either remain competitive, which means reaching desirable numbers and types of viewers, or we go out of business. (Prebble, 1993: 6)

The consequences for factual / documentary programming on ITV have been plain for all to see. ITV executives and programme planners now have to be convinced of the (high) ratings potential of any documentary programme destined for prime time before they will even think of acquiring it or agreeing to support its production. The result has been the ghettoisation of more challenging documentaries in that single late-evening slot and the occasional appearance of softer forms of documentary in peak time. The latter are generally programmes which place heavy emphasis on human interest and are conceived more as diverting entertainments than serious explorations. A further repercussion of this less favourable climate has been that 'serious' documentarists now find it much more difficult to obtain funding for those projects with long gestation times, which necessitate extensive preliminary research and where the final outcome of the whole filming exercise may be uncertain. It also goes without saying that the new regime in ITV has led to much greater competition between documentarists themselves, much of whose time is now spent in developing appropriate skills and techniques for making the sort of pitch which will attract the attention of a commissioning editor.

Channel 4

Whereas documentaries have never figured high on ITV's list of scheduling priorities, the same could not be said of Channel 4. The screening of documentaries has always been an important part of the channel's identity, though some critics have lately been moved to express anxiety that this situation may change now that the channel is required to sell its own air time for advertising purposes. It would be no exaggeration to say, however, that Channel 4 has been a major source of funding – some would say of inspiration – for many documentarists. The channel does of course have a very different remit from BBC 1 and ITV, its major objective being to complement the service provided by the mainstream channels. Nevertheless, Channel 4 has succeeded in creating a number of very distinct documentary strands, including one or two which have become acknowledged brand leaders – at least as far as British television is concerned. *Cutting Edge,* for instance, has become both a popular and critical success, whilst the series *Undercover* has given a new twist to the investigative documentary by getting disguised reporters to expose crimes and misdemeanours with the help of hidden miniaturised cameras and microphones.

BBC

As far as the BBC is concerned, the corporation – like all other public service institutions in Europe – is having to make major changes in order to adjust to the new broadcasting ecology. First, a radical restructuring has taken place of the departments responsible for the commissioning and production of documentaries. Second, Producer Choice, whereby producers acquire much greater say over budgetary allocation – including deciding whether to use in-house personnel or outside facilities – has introduced a much more competitive element into the production process. And finally, the increasing pressure to generate respectable ratings for programming on the mainstream channel (BBC 1) has led to more emphasis than hitherto being placed on the notion of accessibility.

All this has had implications for BBC documentaries, as relevant departments have had to compete with other types of programming (drama, light entertainment) which can generally be relied on to generate a larger audience. At the same time there is some justification for claiming that the corporation is more reluctant than it once was to commission the type of documentary which would tackle a controversial subject in a hard-hitting manner.[9] Certainly, if one surveys the range of BBC programmes that lay claim to being documentaries, one can gather evidence to suggest that popular appeal is a high priority. Hybrid forms that combine a fly-on-the-wall approach with that of serial drama presentation have been designed to attract and hold the attention of viewers, as in the case of *The Living Soap* (BBC, 1993–94) or, more recently, *Soho Stories* (BBC, 1996). Similarly, there has been a tendency to introduce some of those softer forms of documentary-like programmes (e.g. *Animal Hospital* or *Children's Hospital*) into the early evening schedule.

If factual/documentary programming with greater popular appeal has been one characteristic feature of BBC output in the mid- to late 1990s, there have also been one or two attempts to break new ground. As Paul Hamann (head of BBC documentary) has remarked: 'We are always looking to re-invent ourselves and the formats we work in' (BBC, 1994: 4). As mentioned in Chapter 3, the BBC's pioneering of the 'video diaries' format, where individuals are given camcorders and asked to put together a filmed account of an episode in their lives with the minimum of institutional or professional interference, has added an important new dimension to documentary expression. Compared with Channel 4, however, BBC's documentary output across a range of modes and formats has not been especially innovative. Indeed, there has been something of a tendency to clone or copy the formulae which others have established. The most recent example of this was the launch of the series *Modern Times*, which, on closer investigation, shows a remarkable similarity – with respect to the style adopted and the subjects tackled – to the highly successful Channel 4 series *Cutting Edge* (see Wood, 1996: 18–19).

The BBC can be seen to be responding in other ways to some of the pressures of having to operate in an increasingly global broadcasting environment. With its international reputation for producing quality programming it has, for instance, been particularly keen to enter into co-production deals, mostly with American or European partners. One such project was *People's Century* (1996), which was made in conjunction with the American broadcaster WBGH. The series consists of twenty-six episodes chronicling major twentieth-century events as experienced by ordinary people from a wide range of cultures and backgrounds. Though it was generally given a favourable reception, *People's Century* points up some of the problems that are almost invariably encountered with such large-scale projects. Whilst providing an impressive account of major historical developments, the documentary could sometimes be seen to be trying too hard to adopt an equitable approach in order not to prejudice its chances of being well received in all the countries where it was to be marketed.

Concluding remarks

In reviewing recent developments in documentary we have tried to be even-handed in our judgement of how the genre is faring in the final years of the century. There are, as we have already intimated, reasons for being guardedly optimistic. Whilst no-one can underestimate the pressures that having to produce so much tailor-made work places on documentarists, these constraints are far from being a total stranglehold. Television, together with those other media outlets to which we have referred, still affords film makers with talent, energy and perseverance considerable scope for making their mark. (Some would argue that there are now many more opportunities than there were in what is alleged to have been documentary's heyday.) Added to this, documentarists themselves have, as ever, been adept at spotting new opportunities for placing their work. A case in point is the re-emergence of the feature-length, made-for-cinema documentary (e.g. *Hoop Dreams* (1994) and *Crumb* (1995)), a development which has allowed at least some film makers to tackle subjects in ways that would not have been entertained if the works had been commissioned by television.

One other point needing to be underlined is that television has been responsible for encouraging a rich diversity of documentary forms. It would be wrong to give the impression that developments in the 1990s had merely pushed documentary in the direction of bland uniformity. Nothing could be further from the truth. Notwithstanding those examples of cloning to which we have referred, there are still regular attempts at stylistic experiment and innovation.[10]

It is of course the case that these developments have resulted in certain changed priorities. Challenging documentaries, such as those made by John Pilger and David Munro, which confront their audiences with some of the more uncomfortable or shocking realities of the modern world, are still made. Nowadays, however, this type of politically or socially 'campaigning' work accounts for a much smaller proportion of total documentary output than it once did. Moreover, if documentaries that voice social concern are made, it is likely that they will be dressed up in more accessible formats. By the same token, historical subjects which in the 1970s might have been treated in a pontificating, celebratory manner are now tackled in far more imaginative, audience-friendly styles. A good example of this was *The Last Machine* (BBC, 1995), a documentary series that provided a stimulating and highly instructive account of how cinema originated.

Many more examples could be cited which show the diversity of current documentary output (see, for instance, our analyses in Chapter 4). By way of summary, however, let us conclude with the following assessment by two practising film makers of documentary's position at this stage in its history:

> As the documentary enters its second century, it finds itself less constrained by the ideological and aesthetic dogmas which have by turns driven and hindered its development. At their best, today's documentarists pick and choose from the forms of the past ... and produce films which are more varied, imaginative, and challenging than anything we've seen before. At their worst they churn out thousands of hours of virtually indistinguishable 'reality television'. (Macdonald and Cousins, 1996: 311)

How do they do it?

ASPECTS OF DOCUMENTARY PRODUCTION

Whereas the focus in the preceding chapter was on how documentaries are shaped by a series of institutional determinants, it is now time to consider the production process from a slightly different perspective. In the present chapter we consider various aspects of documentary production itself, from the early planning phase through to the final post-production stage. Though the emphasis throughout will be on 'nuts and bolts' concerns, the intention is not to provide a detailed manual for aspiring documentarists[1] but rather to highlight a series of issues which practitioners and critics alike consider of some importance in the study of the documentary process. The chapter will therefore focus on issues which have often been regarded as problematical or controversial: the sometimes fraught relationship between film makers and their subjects or the difficult ethical decisions with which documentarists are frequently confronted during the editing of recorded material.[2]

In discussing these issues we would like to stress that certain types of documentary are going to require production strategies and techniques that are very different from those used in other types. There is a world of difference between the production of a large-scale series such as *People's Century* (BBC, 1996) – where much of the emphasis is on compiling an account from existing archive footage – and the making of a highly personalised, self-generated video diary. One must also bear in mind that documentary production techniques themselves are changing. The development of cheap digital video cameras and editing equipment is already having a marked impact on the manner in which some documentaries are conceived and made.

The rapid changes in the structures of broadcasting have also brought greater pressure to deliver work against ever-tighter deadlines and often with reduced budgets. It is now generally accepted, for instance, that as much time (if not more) will be spent in attempting to secure commissions as in actual production. The requirement to complete projects within much shorter periods than hitherto is felt by many producers to be particularly invidious, since it has been long considered that a vital prerequisite for a successful documentary is the opportunity to pursue detailed research. Documentarists have always claimed that one of their functions has been to produce more considered, reflective accounts than would be possible in news and current affairs, but there are signs nowadays that some broadcasters look on documentary merely as an extension of journalistic reportage.

The documentary process

A collective enterprise?

As with all forms of cultural production, documentarists have evolved a particular set of working practices appropriate to the subject matter, the budget allocated, the equipment available and the deadline imposed. In addition, they often have the constraint of needing to produce work that accords with the specifications of a commissioning editor. In spite of being required to operate within such tight constraints, most documentarists will wish to underline their individual, authorial contribution. It is indeed this creative input which in no small measure results in a wide range of distinctive styles and approaches. But whereas the notion of authorship is usually associated with the ability of one or more members of a creative team to stamp their distinctive imprint on the work in question, documentary – like all other forms of media production – clearly remains a collective enterprise. Success depends on the close collaboration and understanding between all involved in the production process (see O'Sullivan *et al.*, 1994a: 196).

Crews involved in documentary production may well be much smaller than they once were (partly for economic reasons and partly thanks to improved technology), but there still tends to be a division of labour, whereby particular roles are allocated to individuals with specialist knowledge. We are, however, beginning to see some erosion of this model of production with the introduction of new multi-skilling practices, whereby members of a team take on a number of different production roles. Although documentarists welcome the 'streamlining' benefits these changes bring, they are still aware of the advantages which an allocation of roles can bring. Having a specialist editor work on the editing of the film, for instance, brings a fresh pair of eyes to the material which others have filmed. Those who shot the scenes or recorded the sound may sometimes be too close to the material to allow them to be sufficiently dispassionate.

Views of documentarists

Film makers themselves have decided views on what is important in putting together a documentary. The following passages show what two or three contemporary documentarists have singled out as significant aspects of their working practices. The British film maker Michael Grigsby, talking about the making of *Hidden Voices* (1994), a documentary exploration of life in contemporary Britain, has this to say about the importance of operating together as a team:

> We are all freelance and try to work with the same group as much as possible. That means there is a basic group who understand one another ... There's a lot of unspoken communication going on in research, shooting and editing. (Grigsby and McClintock, 1995: 6)

For Grigsby the particular advantage of working in such a team is that it allows for a concentration of effort at key moments in the production process. Thus in *Hidden Voices* the interviews which form the backbone of the film were shot in an intense fifteen-day period. Such economy could only be achieved, however, after extensive initial research, during which time the team formed a clear and focused idea of what it was seeking to express through the film. In Grigsby's words:

> It's extremely important for us to be clear about what we're trying
> to say, why we're trying to say it, and then work out a way to say it ...
> Half of what a documentary is can be more about your attitude to
> the subject than the subject itself. (Grigsby and McClintock, 1995: 6)

Lest readers should interpret this as signifying that documentarists
always go in with preconceived notions about the people they are
interviewing or the subjects they are addressing, let us quickly add
that most film makers – including Grigsby – see documentary production in terms of a slow evolutionary process that is critically
dependent on an understanding relationship between film maker
and subject. As Grigsby himself observes:

> Documentary film-making for me is a process of evolution. We will sit
> and talk about an idea, but after two or three months on the road the
> idea will still be there but a great deal will have changed. And a lot of
> our preconceptions will have been turned on their heads ... Things
> have to grow. That's why the long development period is necessary.
> (Grigsby and McClintock, 1995: 6)

Roger Graef (still best remembered for his ground-breaking fly-on-
the-wall series *Police* (BBC, 1982)) views the documentary process in
a different light. He sees it essentially as an evidence-gathering
activity in which the major aim is to come to an understanding of
the subject through the process of filming. In Graef's words:

> The term I offer for what I do is contemporary archaeology. We offer
> fragments of what went on which we try to pull in to a whole, like an
> archaeologist making a Roman vase. The problem is many viewers
> only get to see the fragments of the fragments. (Rayner, 1993: 45)

For Graef the documentary process is one of painstaking, almost
scientific, observation in which the documentarist is (or claims to be)
a relatively unobtrusive presence. The aim is to uncover in the
course of filming a sufficient number of telling details to be able to
fashion them into a persuasive, revealing account.

Whereas for Graef and Grigsby the emphasis is on the type of
observation in which members of the production team will attempt
to remain discreetly distanced, other film makers take a markedly

different approach. For film makers such as Paul Watson and Molly Dineen there is a recognition that the relationship established between documentarists and their subjects should itself be reflected in the documentary account. Watson's forceful presence during the filming of his much-cited work *The Family* (BBC, 1974) and his later *Sylvania Waters* (BBC, 1993) clearly had some impact on what his characters said and how they interacted. Similarly with Dineen: her working method centres on striking the sort of rapport with her subjects which persuades them to unburden themselves to her.[3] To do this she relies very much on operating single-handedly, with the occasional assistance of a sound recordist. As she explains:

> I do it this way because, ultimately, the most important thing is the individuals – the way they come across, what they say. They are not going to be themselves if they are hindered by machinery ... Mine is not an old-fashioned way of doing it. The traditional documentary has been treated more like fiction: shoot your shots and cut them in to recreate a situation. I am dictated to entirely by what a person does in a room. That will determine everything – my frame size, when I turn on, when I turn off. It's a constant gamble and it's why I shoot so much. (Dunn, 1993: 18)

Research

Most documentaries – with the exception of certain types of 'video diary' project – necessitate detailed, wide-ranging research. Indeed, having the time to conduct this research is crucial to the success of the whole enterprise. It can be the factor which separates the ground-breaking documentary from the merely run-of-the-mill. As far as the viewers are concerned, there is also an assumption that much more research effort will have been invested in documentaries than in other categories of factual programming.

Research can take many different forms and covers a range of activities. Finding a subject or a story may in itself be considered a form of research. Documentarists will need to know whether there is a sufficient body of evidence or number of accessible witnesses to make a project viable before they pitch an idea to a broadcaster. This can require that they spend time in libraries and archives, talk to witnesses and informants, conduct preliminary interviews and consult acknowledged experts in the field. There was a time when research assistants would take on this role, but in the current climate of ever-tighter budgets it is becoming customary for the film makers themselves to conduct this inquiry. The history of documentary is also full of examples where film makers have researched their subjects by going to live for some time amongst those whose lives are under investigation.[4] Robert Flaherty, one of the great pioneers of documentary, spent years living and working with the Inuit people in the wastes of the Canadian north before producing his *Nanook of the North* (Jacobs, 1979: 7–9). The great Dutch documentarist Joris Ivens and his collaborator Marceline Loridan likewise immersed themselves in Chinese society around the time of the Cultural Revolution before producing their epoch-making film *How Yukong Moved the Mountains* (1974). Such attempts on the part of documentarists to familiarise themselves with the world which their subjects inhabit are calculated to ensure that the subsequent account becomes a significant statement rather than just another lightweight journalistic inquiry. It also goes without saying that where film makers have won the confidence and respect of their subjects the latter will feel far more inclined to open up when being interviewed on camera.

Once a work has been commissioned, research takes on a slightly different aspect in that it becomes much more targeted. It also tends to blend in with various other pre-production activities, consisting of the preparation for the shoot and other logistical arrangements. It is during this phase of the production process that documentarists often gather ideas about the best way of shaping and structuring their accounts and what mode of presentation to adopt. For instance, two informants with very different views on a particular topic can sometimes be played off one against the other. A set of old prints found in an archive might be used as a way of introducing the various 'chapters' of a historical chronicle. The discovery of pieces of home-movie footage might provide a means of establishing some telling contrasts between the then and the now.

It is important to remember, however, that all these ideas for structuring a documentary are made on the basis of the extensive research already conducted and of experience gathered from working on other projects. As one experienced practitioner has noted:

> The depth of thought you invest [during pre-production] and the
> extent to which you foresee problems and obstacles go very far
> indeed to ensure a successful shoot ... Directing a documentary ... is
> less a process of spontaneous inquiry than one guided by conclusions
> reached during research. In other words the shoot may largely be
> collecting 'evidence' for underlying patterns and relationships iden-
> tified earlier. (Rabiger, 1987: 27)

Just as with any cultural product, much of the research that has
gone into the making of a documentary remains hidden from view
in the final transmitted version. We simply take it on trust that the
film account we are watching has been soundly researched. In certain types of documentary, however, this process of searching for
and acquiring information, of tracking down reluctant witnesses or
seeking out hidden truths, becomes part of the filmic structure. The
whole documentary account becomes a simulacrum of research
activity. In other words, the documentary is structured and narrated
in such a way as to create the illusion that we are following the
movements of the intrepid botanist, archaeologist or explorer as he
or she uncovers revealing pieces of historical evidence or clues as to
the existence of some lost tribe. Some of those recent 'undercover'
documentaries where documentarists go out on an investigative
mission with camera and microphone hidden about their person
work according to the same principle. Here the excitement of the
hunt for information and the hazards that the documentary
reporters encounter during the quest become part of a narrative
package.

Gaining access

The success of many documentary projects rests to a large degree on
the production team's ability to gain access to the people who have a
story to tell or the places where revealing evidence can be found. It is
one of the undoubted strengths of documentary film that it can
evoke a powerful sense of 'being there'. Moreover, a continuing
attraction of documentary for many viewers is the vicarious enjoy-
ment they experience at witnessing events to which they themselves
would probably be denied access (Loizos, 1993: 67).

For all these reasons, documentarists have over the years placed high priority on the negotiation of good arrangements concerning access. The key word here is 'negotiation', since there will very often be a conflict of interest between the persons and institutions which come under the film makers' scrutiny and the latter's desire to uncover hitherto unknown facts or information which may not always reflect positively on the individual or institution in question.[5] Responsible documentarists will therefore always need to have the full consent of their subjects before filming commences, and the latter have to be fully apprised of what the recording of their words and actions entails. Roger Graef, for instance, has been allowed unprecedented access by promising the people in his film that they have a 'guarantee that they get to see the film to correct factual errors, to remove any confidential information and to raise issues of balance' (Rayner, 1993: 5). In other types of documentary production the granting of access can be connected with wider political considerations. With Phil Agland's revealing view of modern China, *Beyond the Clouds* (Channel 4, 1994), permission to film was only obtained after a long campaign in which Agland and his co-producer patiently negotiated the terms on which filming would be permitted (Waldman, 1994: 48).

The nub of the problem is that, once subjects or institutions have given their consent for filming to take place, control – in terms of power relationships – clearly passes into the hands of the documentarist. There have been very few instances where film makers have been duped by publicity-seeking individuals (even though an increasing number of contemporary documentaries delight in focusing on various types of exhibitionist or eccentric behaviour). On the other hand, there have been numerous cases where subjects have felt exploited, victimised or abused by the documentary's representation of them.

One widely reported case of breakdown in relationship between a documentarist and those whose lives he was recording involved Paul Watson and his series *Sylvania Waters* (BBC, 1993) (see also chapter 3). The Australian husband and wife protagonists were bitterly resentful of the totally distorted image which they claimed the series gave of them and their family. Thus, whilst Watson felt that the access he had been given allowed him to produce a study which was 'properly anthropological' (Selway, 1993), for their part, Noeline and Laurie considered that the picture which was projected to the world was a highly selective and stereotypical account, which emphasised what they regarded as 'cruel and vicious editing' (Selway, 1993) in the quest for maximum dramatic effect.

The ethical problems surrounding what the film maker makes of the material once it has been gathered will always remain a bone of contention (see below). So far as gaining access is concerned, however, some would argue that the introduction of lightweight, 'go-anywhere' recording devices has meant that filming can now take place in both public and private places without the documentarist appearing to disrupt or otherwise affect the 'normal' flow of events. One must be careful not to take this argument too far, however, since access to many places – in particular, executive boardrooms, political offices and the like – is still categorically denied.[6]

Improved access has also resulted from the generally more enlightened view that institutions now have about the work of documentarists. Whilst many are still wary of the negative publicity certain types of documentary exposure can attract, others are now recognising that to allow the cameras in can bring its own rewards. A searching behind-the-scenes documentary can result in viewers revising long-held or prejudiced views. It can also – it may sometimes be claimed – go some way to correcting the distorted impression created by more sensationalist news reporting.

There will always remain situations where, for very understandable reasons, access will be denied. The documentarist will then often have to resort to various forms of subterfuge (donning disguise and secret filming) to obtain the revealing or incriminating footage, such as where those suspected of being involved in criminal activity actually condemn themselves out of their own mouths. Secret filming does, however, raise some difficult ethical issues, and broadcasting institutions have tight guidelines governing its use. It can accordingly only be justified when the subject under consideration is of important public interest and where the footage could not have been obtained by any other means. There is, however, a fine line between going undercover to obtain evidence of nefarious or questionable practices and using the 'public interest' argument to gain access to situations where the resultant material merely panders to the audience's voyeuristic inclinations (see remarks on reality television in Chapter 6).

Recording events

As with any other form of filming, documentary film makers will have given the most careful thought as to how to position themselves, their cameras and their sound-recording equipment to obtain what they consider to be the best results. (For more on this, see Rabiger, 1987: 72–9.) In some instances the events may need to be specially orchestrated to make them more amenable to capture by the camera. In other cases subjects will be directed in such a way that their 'contributions' fit in with the film makers' preconceived notions of what is required. On these occasions documentarists can be seen to be very actively interposing themselves.

It is important to remember, however, that even when documentary film makers are claiming a neutral observer status, as with fly-on-the-wall modes of filming, they must still be regarded as intervening. However carefully they negotiate the terms on which they are allowed to film people and events, their presence is bound in some measure to have shaped or influenced the course of these events. (See also Nichols, 1991: 25–8 and Rosenthal, 1988: 70–4.)

Interviewing

It goes almost without saying that interviewing lies at the heart of much documentary work. It is worth remembering, however, that for every screened interview or talking-head sequence that is featured in the completed work, there will have been many more informal interviews, all of which form part of the trust-building and information-gathering process which is such an essential part of each documentary project. Therefore, every on-screen interview or eye-witness account constitutes the tip of a very large iceberg whose precise dimensions will always remain unknown. It is, for instance, not generally known that potential interviewees are often subjected to an auditioning process in the course of which they are assessed for their telegenic qualities (clarity of speech, etc.) as well as for their ability to make telling statements or provide important evidence.

On screen the interview is a basic and versatile implement in the documentarist's rhetorical equipment. The probing questions of an interviewer can elicit from subjects responses which may provide evidence for a case being made by the documentarist or possibly contradict a view being put forward by other witnesses. Similarly, by conducting an interview on camera, the film maker can reveal something of the process by which information was elicited and the audience can judge – by studying the subjects' facial expression or other gestures – what credibility to attribute to what is being said (see remarks in Chapter 3 on the 'interactive mode'). In many cases, however, in the final edited version of the documentary the figure of the interviewer is merely an implied presence. We are led to believe that the subjects are responding to questions put to them by persons occupying that invisible space behind the camera, but we often remain ignorant about the identity of the questioner or the manner in which the questions were framed and phrased (see also below).

Interviewing itself can take many different forms, and the documentarist will often be confronted with a series of choices concerning how best to conduct the interview. All of them will have an influence on the interviewee's readiness to respond and, ultimately, on the documentary audience's own response.

- In what setting will the subject feel most relaxed?
- To what extent should the interviewer alert subjects beforehand to the type of questions to be asked?
- Should the interviewer be seen in frame with the subject?
- What level of formality should the film maker adopt in conducting the interview?
- Would the subject be more at ease within the bounds imposed by a structured interview or would it be more productive to opt for a more open-ended form of questioning, where an initial inquiry might prompt an extended flow of thoughts and recollections?
- How far can the documentarist go in teasing out responses from subjects, where the pain of remembering may be almost too much to bear?

Whilst it may be important to reflect on how the various types of interview may have been obtained, there is no disputing the powerful impact that such material can have. In many cases the ability to extract the revealing, challenging or even harrowing response from subjects is predicated on the trusting relationship which documentarists have been able to build up with their subjects. As Michael Rabiger has commented, 'Documentaries are only as good as the relationships which allow them to be made' (Rabiger, 1987: 31). It is often only on the basis of this trust that interviewees will feel able to express thoughts or memories which they might otherwise have found impossible to articulate. Claude Lanzmann, for instance, in his magnificent, moving documentary *Shoah* (1985), having persuaded survivors of the Holocaust to return to the locations of Nazi death-camps, extracts from them the most poignantly painful recollections of those times.

The fact that documentarists rely so heavily on gaining access to officials, representatives or witnesses ready to talk about their involvement in certain events raises a number of important general issues. The first of these concerns the ethical dimension of film making. The main questions to be answered here are: How far can a documentarist go in setting up interviews with potentially reluctant witnesses? How much does one need to tell an interviewee about the larger project, of which his or her contribution is but a part? And finally, and perhaps most crucially, what factors govern the use of interview material at the editing stage? (See in particular our analysis of Ophuls's *November Days* in Chapter 4.)

If interviewing in all its many guises is regarded as part of the process by which information or opinions are sought and given, then it is not surprising that it often assumes key structural significance in documentaries. One of the most popular ways of structuring an account is to build it around a series of contributions by 'talking-heads', where a number of witnesses or experts will have been interviewed and their comments (whether delivered direct to camera or in the form of voice-over) interpolated into an account that will typically switch between talking-heads and location or archive footage relating to what is being discussed. A further illustration of the structural importance of the interview is where the quest for the key witness or potential information-giver itself takes on major narrative significance. Many ethnographic documentaries are arguably based on this principle, in that they take the form of a journey into the relative unknown in search of those who may throw light on that which will often, in the eyes of the target audience, be regarded as exotic. In such cases the final, illuminating interview with the representative of the fast-disappearing tribe acquires the same status as the discovery of the lost gold of the Incas in a fictional adventure yarn. In recent years some of the work of the British documentarist Nick Broomfield has likewise assumed the form of a search for the elusive interviewee (see also Chapter 3). In *The Leader, his Driver, and the Driver's Wife* (1991) it is the white Afrikaner's right-wing leader TerreBlanche who is the target of Broomfield's quest. In *Tracking down Maggie* (1994) it is the former British Prime Minister and Conservative leader Margaret Thatcher. In both cases the focus of attention centres on Broomfield's constantly thwarted attempts to set up an interview. (For this reason these films might be regarded as narcissistic self-studies on the part of the documentarist rather than investigations of a particular political figure!)

In many cases, however, the function of the screened interview is to underline the credibility of the account being rendered. Having witnesses respond to questions put to them can be a key factor in helping viewers to assess the strength of an argument or to question the received wisdom on a topic. The particular structural advantage of the interview is that it can be used as a starting-point for, or a bridge to, other forms of verbal and visual testimony. Thus a documentary may begin with subjects being interviewed in an appropriate setting, but, as they develop their ideas or unfurl their memories, plentiful opportunities are afforded for pulling in other material to illustrate, complement or even contradict what they are saying. In other words, the 'memory work' of interviewees is often used by the documentarist as a cueing device for the screening of, say, relevant archive material. A good example of this is provided by the early episodes in the large-scale BBC/WGBH co-production *People's Century* (BBC, 1996). These episodes feature a number of carefully chosen eighty- and ninety-year-olds responding to an interviewer's questions on how they experienced key events at the dawn of this century. Right on cue come the visual, documentary records of these same events in the form of photographs, flickering archive footage and early newsreel material – all of which embody the official (as opposed to personal) memory of those times.

Whilst some of the points raised above appear to relate to the logistics of interviewing, they also have a bearing on wider issues of documentary discourse. In the example of *People's Century*, and in many other documentaries, the interviewer's questions are mostly edited out of the final transmitted version and the respondent's utterances presented as if they were a pseudo-monologue. One does well to remember, however, that the interviewer has always a decisive influence on setting the original agenda. Or, to put it in slightly different terms, he or she remains a structuring absence. In this respect the placing of a televisual frame around the subject's head provides an objective correlative for another type of framing that is occurring. Whether they are conscious of it or not, interviewees appear in documentaries not on their own terms but on those of documentarists; their contribution thus becomes part of someone else's agenda and is therefore subject to a host of controlling influences which may give a whole new meaning to the subject's utterances.

Editing

Of all the activities involved in the putting together of a documentary it is generally acknowledged that the editing process will have a crucial impact on the meanings that audiences will derive from the account in question.[7] As one critic has observed:

> It is in the editing room that many directors find their greatest challenge and fulfilment. It is in the editing room that documentary, unlike story-board based fiction film, is more often than not conceived, structured and born. (van Lier, 1994: 3)

As with the editing of any other media artefact, so too is the editing of documentary founded on two basic principles: first, the selection of a number of items from what is often a large store of available material, and second, the integration of these items into an account which will make sense on its own terms (the whole always being greater than the sum of the component parts).

Although the bulk of the editing work will be carried out during the post-production phase (i.e. in the editing room), some form of editing occurs at each stage of documentary production. The initial process, in the course of which the documentarist entertains various possibilities for treating the subject, can be regarded as a form of editing – as can the decisions on what to include in the frame while filming and when to run the cameras. Our present interest, however, is concentrated on the post-production phase, not only for its intrinsic importance but also because it is an aspect which is not frequently subjected to critical scrutiny.

As we have already seen in Chapter 4, the way in which editing is handled will vary according to the type of documentary. In a drama-documentary, for example, many of the editing decisions will effectively have been taken at the scripting stage, whilst in a fly-on-the-wall account the editing process only really begins when the material accumulated during weeks or even months of shooting is viewed and assessed. In the majority of cases, however, editing involves the paring down of an excessive amount of material to the length required by a particular format of programme. At the same time, careful thought will be given to how best to structure the material to fit in with standard narrative requirements or other presentational demands.

In the case of television documentaries the editing process will often have to take account of the fact that most material will be broadcast as part of a larger series. With documentaries which are going to be transmitted in a specified slot, such as Channel 4's *Cutting Edge* series (where each programme is different in subject matter from the rest), the material will have to be edited in accordance with an accepted house style and with a set of conventions that have been established for that particular documentary slot. Other types of documentary make different demands on the editors. For example, in *People's Century,* an account of the twentieth century serialised in twenty-six episodes, each episode had to be free-standing to some extent but also had to contain features which would invite viewers to return to the story as it unfolded. Another task for the editors who prepare documentaries for screening on commercial channels is to structure the account in such a way that it will accommodate the various advertising breaks. In countries such as New Zealand, where commercials take up fourteen minutes of every hour, documentaries have to be very carefully shaped so as to ensure that viewers return after each of the commercial interruptions.

Whatever specific form documentary editing takes, it is almost always a very time-consuming process. In many cases it takes longer than to produce the original footage. For example, the producers of the landmark US documentary *An American Family* (1973) shot more than 300 hours of film over a seven-month period, but the editing of the material took a full twelve months (Rosenthal, 1988: 203). Whilst digital editing systems (such as Avid and Lightworks) have brought some time-saving benefits in recent years, the creative, challenging aspects of editing remain as time-consuming as they ever were. As one producer/director has observed:

> The two great advantages of digital technology ... are speed and creative flexibility. Using non-linear editing, a film can be cut in perhaps half the time it used to take on celluloid. But smart producers are not in fact cutting back their editing budgets by 50%. They are using the time savings to explore more alternatives in the cutting room and to create a higher quality product. (Whitby, 1994: 45)

Although, as already indicated, documentary editing has a good deal in common with the methods employed in the construction of other artefacts, there are some significant differences. Consider, for instance, the editing of a documentary compared with that of a fiction film. With the latter many decisions relating to the structure of the work will have been made during the script-writing and storyboarding phase. The major concerns of fiction film editors, therefore, will centre on such issues as how to heighten the drama or how to create a more effective transition between scenes. Documentary editors will also be concerned with such matters (especially in accounts which have a strong narrative impulse), but at the same time they will often be more involved in the basic structuring task of finding a suitable presentational mould for the material gathered.

As we saw in Chapters 3 and 4, editing procedures are also closely linked with the particular function that each of the main documentary modes is required to fulfil. One can, however, make a distinction between two broad approaches to editing, each depending on the type of documentary and the effects being sought. In the first the guiding principle is to create for the viewer the sense of 'being there', and in the second the attempt is more to shape the material in such a way as to highlight an idea or develop an argument. The first approach will tend to prevail in certain types of observational documentary (e.g. a fly-on-the-wall account) where the documentarist wishes to reinforce the 'realism effect'. With the second, which is sometimes referred to as 'expressive' or 'constructivist' editing, the intention is more to align or combine images and sound sequences in such a way that the meanings emerge more through the contrasts, echoes and reverberations *between* shots. The sense of a single, convincing argument is reinforced by the words (voice-over, commentary, dialogue), which are also carefully edited together to accompany the flow of images.

Editing therefore involves more than simply the desire to produce an argument; it can also play a crucial role in the desire of some documentarists to build from isolated fragments wholly new units of meaning. In the words of Dziga Vertov, one of documentary's pioneers:

> The Kino-eye is a means of rendering the invisible visible, of making obvious that which is hidden, of manifesting that which is masked ... It is not enough to show isolated fragments of truth on the screen, separate images of truth. These images have to be organized thematically in such a way that truth results from the whole. (Cited in Niney, 1994: 18)

There are several other aspects of editing which are worthy of further exploration but which – for reasons of space – we can merely signal here. The first of these concerns the status of the footage that is not included in the final edited version of a documentary. Does such discarded footage lose any significance once the documentary has been transmitted, or does it retain value as part of a larger archive of potentially accessible material? The debate on this issue has gained momentum as it has gradually become possible to store such material in forms (CD-ROM, etc.) in which it can be accessed much more easily than hitherto.

A second question relates to the subject of style. To what extent has the editing of a documentary programme been determined by the desire to fashion it in accordance with certain aesthetic principles? Of particular interest here are considerations of balance, pacing and rhythm – indeed the whole manner in which all the separate components are integrated in order to achieve a particular artistic effect (see Chapter 4).

A further area of debate relating to editing concerns the whole status of the material in its finally edited form. One of the defining claims of documentary has always been that the raw material is 'captured from reality'. Whatever forms of manipulation were practised at the editing stage, one could at least rest assured that the information contained within the individual frame had not been interfered with. In this age of electronic imaging, however, even these consoling certainties have disappeared. What can now be achieved in post-production is much more far-reaching than ever before. The possibilities for image manipulation are now literally limitless. In the words of one critic:

> In an era of limitless electronic tricks, seeing two characters in the same frame is not always sufficient to guarantee their physical existence in the same space. (Niney, 1994: 23)

Finally – and possibly most crucially – the process of editing draws our attention to the responsibilities that documentary producers have to the institutions who commission their work, to the audience at whom the work is directed and to the individual 'subjects' who feature so prominently in most documentary accounts. These responsibilities have a strong ethical dimension and it is to ethics we turn in the following section.

Ethics

Discussion of ethical issues has always featured prominently in debates about documentary. Producers of documentary, like all journalists and programme makers, are bound by certain professional obligations to conform to certain norms and standards. Fundamentally, documentarists and journalists share a common code of practice in that both are obliged to maintain certain reporting standards. Both have a duty to produce fair-minded critiques and not to skew their accounts in such a way as to make the evidence fit their particular interpretation of, or perspective on, a situation or event. They are also governed by similar ground rules pertaining to the ways in which information or footage is obtained and the uses to which it is put. In particular, they may be confronted with that 'classic' journalistic dilemma – namely: How far can they go – and what means can they employ – to gain the footage they wish to incorporate in their attempts to bring something to the attention of a wider public? Likewise: What considerations should guide them when they have to decide whether to carry on filming or to intervene to provide help to a threatened subject?

Most of the broadcasting institutions which commission and screen documentaries have codes of practice that are intended to guide programme makers on these matters, but in the progressively more deregulated system it is not always easy to achieve absolute compliance. There is also the difficult question of deciding where the responsibilities of film makers lie. Are they primarily to the broadcasting institutions, to the documentary subjects, to the audience, or to that more nebulous group – the collectivity of fellow documentarists (Nichols, 1991: 186, Rosenthal, 1988: 129–30)? There is no easy answer to this question. And, just as in other walks of life, there are differing views amongst practitioners on where their priorities lie. At the one extreme are those with a 'smash and grab' mentality, who move in on subjects and situations in distinctly predatory fashion. At the other are those who will always be mindful of the impact which any documentary intervention can have on the lives of their subjects and who will want to make them aware, even before filming begins, of the possible adverse consequences of such exposure. Moreover, most documentarists are, for their part, aware that the trusting relationship they develop with their subjects imposes a moral obligation on them not to betray that trust.

Probably one of the most important ethical issues for documentarists is whether (and if so, how) they should signal their own involvement. It is an issue which has to be addressed in all documentary modes. Furthermore, certain ethical considerations will tend to surface more frequently than others in particular modes of documentary. In the expository mode, for example, the mere fact that a voice-of-God commentator has taken it on him- or herself to speak with authority on behalf of many others may in itself be seen as ethically problematical. Likewise, in the observational mode film makers may well have to reflect on the consequences of their intervention in the subject's life, while at the same time concealing their own involvement. In the interactive mode, however, there would appear at first sight to be fewer problems: here at least we are led to believe that the documentarist is interacting on a more equal basis with the subjects and is allowing them the opportunity to expound their own views and ideas. What we as viewers do not know, however, is the exact manner in which this filmed exchange was set up. Was it part of a larger discourse? Was the documentarist being deliberately provocative in order to elicit a particular response? And, perhaps the most important question of all, to what extent have the responses been edited so as to make it more likely that the interchange will be seen in a particular light?

Some would claim that many of the ethical problems alluded to above are less pressing now than they once were, given that we live in an information-saturated age with a high level of media awareness. They argue that the public knows that it is relatively easy for reporters and programme makers to produce skewed or unbalanced accounts and that it is therefore more likely that subjects will seek to secure, if necessary, written agreement on the conditions under which recordings can be made and even the uses to which the resultant material can be put. However, even when subjects and film makers have entered into such agreements, it does not take much to sour once-friendly relations, especially when the final edited version of the documentary falls too far out of line with the subjects' expectations (see the discussion on *Sylvania Waters* above).

Most documentarists, recognising the need for honest dealing with their subjects, will seek the *informed consent* of those they intend to film.[8] The manner in which consent is obtained and the range of activities covered by the consent will differ according to the individual project and film maker. Some film makers make a contract with their subjects that gives the latter the right to view material prior to final transmission in order to check for distortions or factual errors. Others, like Paul Watson, will agree the general terms with their subjects as to where and how filming will take place, but will not seek their 'co-operation' in any of the later production stages. Still others take the view that subjects should be consulted and involved throughout the production process to guard against any complaints about distortion and manipulation (Grigsby and McClintock, 1995: 9–10).

Problems of an ethical nature are often encountered with fly-on-the-wall accounts where subjects have not always anticipated the outcome of this type of media exposure correctly. For instance, the students who volunteered to participate in the BBC documentary serial *The Living Soap* (BBC, 1993) were warned that, as a consequence, their private lives would become in effect public property. Although they were initially content to trade the glamour and certain material benefits (rent-free accommodation) for the constant intrusion into their private lives, the students soon found that they were being placed under intolerable pressure, particularly when it became clear that they were expected to produce performances of a sufficiently entertaining kind to maintain audience ratings.

It must also be remembered that producers of documentaries have a special responsibility to those subjects in whose lives they intervene, given the publicity that inevitably ensues from such exposure. When a documentary exposes the dubious dealings of an institution, broadcasters may decide that they are performing a public service by transmitting the programme. With private individuals on the other hand, they may have to show greater sensitivity. In 1993, for example, the first programme in a documentary series *Real Life* (Scottish Television) had severe repercussions for one of the featured families. The remarks of some family members about 'theft being a way of life' in that community led, soon after the documentary was screened, to the family being drummed out of the village in which they lived. Here one might claim that the broadcaster had a responsibility to alert the individuals concerned to the likely consequences of the public airing of their views.

Allowing subjects to preview material before transmission cannot, however, guarantee to alert them to the programme's possible impact. A memorable illustration of this was provided by Channel 4's *'Cutting Edge'* documentary *The Club*, broadcast early in 1994. This 'warts and all' behind-the-scenes account of Northwood Golf Club had been well received by senior committee members of the club at a specially arranged preview. When it was screened, however, the programme proved to be anything but the profile-raising exercise they had hoped for. Focused on the interaction of members both on and off the course, it provided a devastating exposure of the chauvinism, hypocrisy and prejudice which lay not far below the surface of seeming harmony and *bonhomie*. Public reaction to the programme's screening led to the mass resignation of the entire committee.

The issue of typicality

In the case of *The Club* the production team was not confronted with serious ethical problems in that the evidence gathered from dozens of witnesses all pointed in one direction: that social prejudice and class bias were endemic amongst many of those who had a controlling influence over the club's affairs. The (self-)condemnation arose from the words of the members themselves and was not an instant rush to judgement on the part of a small group of incomers. Film makers are placed in a more difficult situation, however, when they have to decide what credence can be given to statements made by, say, just two or three members of a large organisation. How representative are these views? Do they usefully contribute to a broader understanding of a situation or event? And, by extension, to what extent can filmed sequences that detail a particular episode in an ongoing situation be regarded as typical of events which occur on a regular basis?

The issue of 'typicality' is one that has been regularly discussed by both practitioners and critics of documentary (Corner, 1996: 136, Nichols, 1991: 40). It goes to the heart of documentarists' attempts to produce meaningful accounts of, or statements about, the socio-historical world, and it highlights the tension which exists between this objective and the means they deploy to achieve it. In short, the question arises: With what confidence can one generalise from the series of particular examples selected by the documentarist?

Some of the most bitter debates in recent years have centred on 'typicality'. Take, for instance, the controversy that flared up after the screening of *The Dying Rooms* (Channel 4, 1995), a documentary describing the parlous conditions in a number of Chinese orphanages. Much of the controversy centred on whether the maltreatment of orphans in China was as widespread as the programme appeared to make out or whether – as the Chinese government angrily asserted – a deliberately distorted impression was given through a highly selective sample of hard-pressed institutions. The charge against the British team that produced the documentary was that it sought out a limited number of worst-case scenarios, from which the viewer might infer that this was the general state of all Chinese orphanages.

Encouraging viewers to draw general conclusions from a limited number of examples is one aspect of typicality. The issue can, however, be viewed from a different perspective by considering the criteria according to which the allegedly representative examples were chosen in the first place. To be more specific: particular problems occur in documentaries when incidents or events which might very well be regarded by viewers as representative prove on close inspection to have been included because they satisfy the requirements of dramatic story-telling or because they fall in line with certain stereotypical images. For example, the programme *Summerhill at 70* (Channel 4, 1992), a study of a progressive independent school, allegedly distorted its subject by seeking out a series of dramatic and atypical events rather than concentrating on the more mundane – and more typical – lives of students and staff. Those working at the school felt that the picture offered by the documentary bore scant resemblance to what they experienced on a day-to-day basis. The particular criticism, however, was that the film makers began their work with various preconceived and stereotyped notions of what the school stood for. Not surprisingly, in the fifteen weeks that the crew spent at Summerhill, they were able to record a series of incidents and exchanges which neatly fitted into this prefabricated framework. In the words of one of the allegedly misrepresented teachers:

The picture which emerged was a rather violent, unstructured gang-land with scant regard for property or persons ... [It] bears little relation to the Summerhill I have worked in for 17 years. (Johnson, 1992: 8)

The charge against the makers of *Summerhill at 70* therefore is that, focusing as they did on a series of dramatic situations where trouble had flared or conflicts had to be resolved, they were acting according to a ratings-oriented agenda rather than digging a little deeper below the surface to try to reveal more about the nature of the educational experience the school delivered.

Whether it be in the form of fly-on-the-wall accounts of the trials and tribulations of family life (*The Family; Sylvania Waters*) or of behind-the-scenes *exposés* of institutional life, issues of typicality and representation continue to be central to the documentary debate. They give rise, among other things, to discussions about what codes of practice should be adopted in the course of filming and what rights of reply subjects should have after transmission. Once again, the argument as to what constitutes 'fair representation' will depend on who is delivering the judgement (filmed subject, documentarist or some external arbiter). It is interesting to note in this connection that a significant number of moves has been made to encourage subjects to become much more involved in the production of their own accounts. In the field of ethnographic documentary, for instance, subjects who were once treated as exotic objects of the incoming documentarist's gaze have themselves taken to producing their own chronicles of tribal or community life (Loizos, 1993: 169–89). There has, in short, been a marked increase in more participatory forms of film making.

Whilst new developments in camera and sound-recording technology have undoubtedly provided an important impetus for various forms of self-chronicling, an equally significant motivation has been the democratically inspired desire to allow individuals and groups a greater sense of ownership of the films that are made about them. Viewed in this light, the act of filming takes on a decidedly political aspect in that it will often help the participating individuals to discover or redefine their feelings of what it is to be members of that community or collectivity. Likewise, the documentaries produced over a number of years in the context of the BBC's 'Open Door' access programming also provide a good illustration of this desire to help groups towards a better self-understanding through the process of self-reporting (see also remarks on *Video Diaries* in Chapter 3). They are a further instance of the wish to redress the balance in a relationship which has always traditionally favoured the documentary producer.

Concluding remarks

In studying various aspects of documentary production we have emphasised how much of what documentarists do is determined by the requirements of particular programme formats. As we discovered earlier in the book, many of these formats have evolved out of the programme maker's need to find the types of formula which will meet with high audience appreciation. In some respects it might be argued that certain calculations about the audience are built into each phase of documentary production. Estimating how much knowledge one can expect the audience to have about a subject and discussing how to structure the material to achieve maximum impact will never have been far from the production team's thoughts. In the following chapter we shall be looking in more detail at the strategies that broadcasters have devised for reaching out to this audience, as well as considering ways of describing the impact that documentaries make on those who watch them.

Is there anyone out there?

AUDIENCES FOR DOCUMENTARY

Our main aim in this chapter is to consider the relationship between documentary output and members of the television audience. In the first half of the chapter ('Broadcaster–audience relations') we will focus on the various promotional and scheduling strategies which broadcasters have devised to secure the attention of an audience. In the second half ('Audience/viewer response') we will reflect on the ways in which viewers make sense of documentaries: what enlightenment or pleasure they derive from watching them and what impact, if any, individual documentaries might have on influencing their views on a range of contemporary or historical issues.

Broadcaster–audience relations

Targeting an audience

In today's increasingly deregulated and commercialised broadcasting environment decisions on what kinds of programming to include in a channel's overall menu of offerings are largely determined by what are regarded as the scheduling requirements of that channel. Documentarists, like all other programme makers, will be constantly reminded that they are producing work that constitutes one element in a programming package which is being used to target a particular audience. It is sometimes claimed that the judicious scheduling of a programme has a greater bearing on its likely impact on an audience than any intrinsic merit of the programme itself.

As we have commented in the preceding chapter, the targeting of an audience arguably informs the whole production process. Right from the outset programme makers are having to ensure that their work, once commissioned, will conform to the specifications of the slot in question (including such matters as style of presentation and mode of address).[1] Documentarists often express misgivings about the compromises they have to make in conforming to individual house styles and length specifications. They also voice concern at sometimes having to make their work more populist, thereby laying themselves open to the charge of trivialisation (Rosenthal, 1988: 35–6). Given the funding arrangements of contemporary broadcasting, however, film and programme makers have little choice but to bow to the broadcasters' requirements.

During the period when television was dominated by a relatively small number of terrestrial public-service channels operating in clearly defined national spaces, documentaries were regarded as a valuable programme resource. From both the broadcasters' and the audiences' point of view documentaries were seen to perform a valuable function in giving due weight or seriousness to a mixed diet of programming which contained more than its fair share of relatively lightweight escapist entertainment. The inclusion of documentaries was predicated on the assumption that the audience would respond positively to material which encouraged a thoughtful or reflective response, and that this would act, in some measure, as an antidote to the large swathes of programming that made little or no demands on the audience's intelligence.

Scheduling documentaries today

As long as television remained dominated by certain public-service ideals, documentaries seemed assured of a continuing place within the broadcasting schedules. They were regarded as an important educational and informational resource. Not only could they be defended on the Griersonian grounds that they contributed towards a well-informed citizenry, but, from the broadcasters' perspective, they also commanded respect as examples of 'quality' broadcasting. There was also a readiness on the part of public-service broadcasters to commit resources to documentaries with 'challenging' subject matter which did not always generate large audiences.

In the new, increasingly deregulated age of broadcasting, however, documentaries no longer have the measure of 'protection' they once had, and they are required to compete on equal terms with all the other forms of programming. As a consequence, the whole basis on which the documentarist communicates with his or her audience has changed. Film makers have now become obsessively concerned with accommodating their work within one of the available documentary strands (see Rosenthal, 1988: 38–9). This is well illustrated by clearly discernible moves within the BBC to broaden the base and diversify the range of its factual/documentary programming (see remarks in Chapter 7). To be sure, the worthy, more traditional forms of documentary still get an airing, but we are also witnessing the introduction of forms of programming (e.g. reality shows) which combine the crowd-pulling attractions of action-filled dramatic entertainment with residual commitment to public service (see Chapter 6). Such programmes may well command the attention of large, enthusiastic audiences, but they have also been implicated in what some critics have seen as the steady devaluing of the 'documentary' currency. Occupying, as they often do, some of the most sought-after slots in the prime-time schedule, their presence makes it that much more difficult – so the claim goes – to make the case for more traditional but less popular forms of documentary.[2]

Traditionally, television schedulers have always employed a variety of means to attract and hold the attention of audiences, but in today's multi-channel broadcasting environment all scheduling decisions will be governed by the knowledge that the viewer has a much greater number of programmes to choose from (in spite of the frequently heard complaints that what is offered is essentially more of the same rather than a more diversified range of options). The earlier idea of a 'set meal', where viewers would settle down to partake of the evening's viewing provided by their favourite channel, has been replaced by the notion of 'cafeteria provision', where consumers largely put together their own meal, selecting from a wide choice of channel offerings. In other words, scheduling, always an imperfect art, has nowadays become a much more hazardous business. Even the most carefully constructed schedule is likely to be torpedoed by (first) the carefree, channel-hopping behaviour of many viewers and (second) the increasing use of video recorders for time-shifting purposes, thus effectively rendering redundant the work of the scheduler. (For more on this, see Ang, 1996: 58.)

There was a time when the position of serious documentaries within the schedules of mainstream channels looked unassailable. In some ways they had, as we have suggested, become almost synonymous with the serious aspirations of public-service broadcasters. All this has changed, however, in today's commercialised environment. Nowadays they are regarded more as useful weapons within the scheduler's armoury and, as such, are used for a variety of strategic and tactical purposes. Their inclusion in the schedules is no longer determined by public-service requirements, but rather by the criterion of their likely performance. The irony is that, contrary to the expectations or fears of some critics, various categories of factual/documentary material have proved to be a valuable resource, especially in these cost-conscious times when some of those 'softer' types of documentary reportage have shown that they can perform well against serious competition on rival channels (especially programming that is much more expensive to acquire or produce).

In spite of all these attempts to find a new role for factual/ documentary offerings, broadcasters still adhere to certain long-established practices when it comes to scheduling this type of programming. Certain assumptions are made about the times within the weekly and evening schedule when viewers will be more inclined to tune in to documentaries. As far as British terrestrial broadcasters are concerned, the Monday to Thursday evening slots are regarded as the best times to schedule them. Similarly, within the confines of the evening schedule different types of factual/documentary programming will be introduced at different times to achieve particular scheduling ends. Thus on the mainstream channels, blockbuster documentary series (*World at War; People's Century*, etc.), in which large amounts of money have been invested, will almost always occupy prime-time slots (after the mid-evening news). Material which centres on popular life-style subjects, together with the glossier type of natural history programmes and the more action-packed documentaries, also find their natural home at this point in the schedule.

Broadcasters have also – over the years – developed other strategies designed to extract maximum advantage from the fact that
documentaries are usually part of a diverse range of programming.
On certain occasions, for instance, documentary explorations of a
particular subject will precede or be followed by one or more fictional
accounts.[3] Another favoured strategy is to take an issue that has,
over a period of time, received extensive coverage in news and
current affairs broadcasts and to make it the subject of a longer,
more probing documentary investigation. Here programme makers
are capitalising on the continuing interest of viewers in such topics
and can even presuppose a certain familiarity with the story or event
in question.[4]

By the same token, documentaries will also be scheduled to co-
incide with the anniversary of a well-known historical event.
Anniversaries of famous battles regularly trigger documentary reassessments, and the fiftieth anniversary (in August 1996) of the
dropping of the atomic bomb on Hiroshima was commemorated by
a number of factual/documentary programmes which examined
both the background to and the aftermath of this horrific event. In
less sombre vein, other series have their origins in the desire to
celebrate some major technological achievement or invention.
For instance, the BBC series *The Last Machine* (1995), a four-part
exploration of early cinema, was timed to exploit the celebratory
atmosphere occasioned by cinema's centenary. Still other documentaries gain a place in the schedule by being linked with a major event
about to happen. Just before the Olympic Games opened in July
1996, for example, BBC 1 screened Michael Waldman's *The Greatest
Show on Earth* about how the events in Atlanta, costing $17 billion,
were organised.

In all these cases part of the scheduler's calculation is that
viewers will have had their interest stimulated by their exposure to
additional media outlets or to other forms of publicity. A somewhat
different form of scheduling strategy employed by broadcasters is to
commission and air contemporary updates of documentaries which
were first screened years, and sometimes decades, previously.
Producers make comparatively regular use of this 'revisitation'
technique, as in those accounts where a documentary team provides

a progress report on an individual, a group or even an institution.[5] Television is the ideal medium for providing these documentary updates, and experience shows that viewers respond positively to the implicit or explicit invitation to reflect on the situation as it once was and to consider the changes that time has brought.

Clustering and zoning

A further strategy that is now increasingly being employed by schedulers is the clustering of programmes that have some thematic affinity one to the other. This results from broadcasters acknowledging that certain sections of the television audience are now accustomed to channels – particularly on cable and satellite – which provide more specialised forms of programming. Some terrestrial broadcasters have responded by introducing what they sometimes refer to as a programming 'zone'. This is a 'roped-off' section of the schedule that is wholly given over to exploring a topic or issue from a number of perspectives and using a variety of programme modes (factual and fictional). Audiences entering these zones know that they are likely to be satiated by the sheer excess of all that is on offer, but this is clearly part of the attraction. Since the mid-1990s Channel 4 has on several occasions adopted this zoning strategy in its scheduling, and each time factual/documentary programmes have been the dominant components. For eight weeks in the spring of 1994, for instance, the channel launched its Red Light Zone, a series of programmes which focused on sex, the sex industries and sexual tourism. This was followed in the spring of 1996 by the Blue Light Zone in which, over a seven-week period, the channel dedicated a substantial part of its late Saturday evening viewing to exploring and investigating 'true crime, television culture and police methods' (Channel 4 programme notes).

All the above strategies reveal just how intense the competition is for viewers in today's heavily commercialised television environment. Broadcasters are always looking to steal a march on their competitors by devising new presentational formats, many involving the blurring of traditional genre boundaries. And if the formula is successful in attracting viewers, one can be sure that it will be acquired or copied by other broadcasters (whether at home or overseas). A good example of this cloning phenomenon is provided by the BBC documentary series *Modern Times*. The series, launched in 1994, aims to provide 'a portrait of the world around us, particularly British society, [that is] modern, moving, witty, thought-provoking and popular' (BBC Press release). To many observers, however, the programmes produced for the *Modern Times* slot have borne more than a passing resemblance – in both subject matter and approach – to the very successful and firmly established Channel 4 series *Cutting Edge* (Kilborn, 1996: 147).

Promoting documentaries

The appropriate scheduling of documentaries is not the only means of ensuring that audiences develop and maintain an appetite for this type of programming; broadcasters also have to be adept at harnessing all available media outlets to their promotional needs, especially now that so many channels are competing for the viewer's attention. Much more time and effort are now spent on programme publicity than they once were, and more funding is made available for specific promotional campaigns, especially when new series are being launched. The promotion of television documentaries takes many forms – from full-page colour advertising in a newspaper or magazine (a tactic sometimes employed by satellite providers such as Sky Television and the Discovery Channel) to placing programme details on the Internet. The most popular, and possibly the most effective promotional tool remains, however, the short (30- or 45-second) trailer, which is played during the continuity or advertising breaks between programmes. Such trailers tend to be reserved for the larger-scale productions in which there has been considerable institutional investment. These appetite-whetting commercials – which are generally repeated at frequent intervals in the days prior to screening – employ the standard rhetorical devices familiar from feature film trailers: short sequences from the work to be screened, together with the promise that the programme will unveil secrets or provide a new slant on received views of an issue or event.

In their promotion of documentaries broadcasters use many of the ploys that are standard across many categories of programming. As with any form of advertising, the principal objective is to create both an awareness of the product on offer and to stimulate desire on the part of the potential consumer. Documentaries – at least those of the more serious variety – differ from certain other types of programming (news, quiz shows and long-running serials) in that they do not have the same 'taken for granted' status. Therefore they may require greater promotional effort to make them stand out from the plethora of other programming on offer. Proportionally more space is devoted to publicising documentaries in listings magazines, such as *Radio Times*, than one might expect given the air time they occupy. Broadcasters may well also have additional forms of promotional gain in mind in giving a relatively high profile to their documentary screenings. The reputation that documentaries have acquired as worthy or serious forms of programming means that broadcasters can legitimately claim that they considerably enhance a channel's identity.

Given the wide range of factual/documentary material that now appears on our screens, it should come as no surprise to learn that broadcasters adopt different promotional strategies for particular documentary styles and subjects. Material that is thought likely to appeal on account of its educational value will be promoted differently from those action-packed drama-documentaries which are likely to be watched as much for their entertainment quotient as for their consciousness-raising potential. As with all forms of advertising, however, one of the major promotional considerations is to create a sense of product awareness. The most tangible way in which this is achieved is by the heavy promotion of particular documentary programmes (see below). A less direct, but nevertheless very significant, form of promotion is through the presentational arrangements which broadcasters have devised for encouraging regular viewing habits. The very act of presenting the majority of documentaries nowadays in a named strand (e.g. *Cutting Edge; Modern Times; Inside Story; Picture This*, etc.) is itself a kind of promotional device which encourages a particular set of expectations on the part of the viewers.

Promotional strategies
Although the nature of this book precludes a detailed examination

of specific promotional campaigns, one can still make a series of general points about how broadcasters seek to engage the interest of their potential audience. As in all other forms of advertising, the promotion of documentaries is a multi-faceted activity. Thus, depending on the budget, a variety of tried and tested techniques will be used in a co-ordinated effort to create in the audience the desired sense of anticipation. Those specifically entrusted with the promotional task will ensure that journalists and reviewers receive appropriate information packs containing details of the channel's forthcoming documentaries. Opportunities for the previewing of material will also be provided and interviews will be arranged with one or more members of the documentary team.

In the relentless quest to gain a competitive advantage over rival channels, publicists leave no stone unturned. Particular attention is paid, for instance, to those publications on which viewers are known to rely quite heavily when deciding what to view. In the UK, listings magazines such as *Radio Times* are assiduously courted to ensure that new documentaries receive the kind of coverage that makes them an attractive viewing proposition. It is instructive to study the way in which documentary material is promoted in such magazines. In many cases more is disclosed than just the information on the time and channel of the programme; some idea is also given of the audience it is targeting. Particular documentaries are also made the subject of extended feature articles which focus either on the issues raised by the documentary or on the making of the programme itself. All in all, such publicity provides numerous clues to how documentaries are often used to enhance a channel's claims to being a provider of 'quality programming'.

The very fact that many documentaries continue to be issue-oriented has also meant that they will often receive a fair amount of press coverage (directly or indirectly) before they are screened, especially if they promise to deliver important new insights on a high-profile topic or, for that matter, to demolish a set of fondly or firmly held beliefs. Whatever form these feature articles take, they can be relied on to have a promotional impact. A good example of this was provided by *Inside Burma: Land of Fear*, a documentary made by John Pilger and David Munro and shown in ITV's *Network First* series in May 1996. Prior to the screening public awareness had been stirred by a number of articles and features in the British quality press. Not only did these articles provide a detailed account of the crisis in which the country in question found itself, they also described how the film itself came to be made – with all the promotional benefits which such coverage bestows.

Sometimes the very making of the documentary becomes a *cause célèbre*, which in itself can be turned to advantage by broadcasting publicists. As far as the latter are concerned, the most exploitable situation occurs when documentary subjects begin to raise major objections about their being victimised by programme makers or where protagonists take exception to allegedly distorted or sensationalised accounts. It is no coincidence that this type of criticism occurs with documentaries which have a serialised format. *Sylvania Waters*, Paul Watson's 1993 fly-on-the-wall documentary made for the BBC, is perhaps the best-known recent example of a work which capitalised on the controversy that it had itself generated. In promotional terms the hue and cry the series caused after the first episode was very much grist to the publicist's mill. And many viewers undoubtedly tuned in to the later episodes to see whether Noeline was indeed the virago she was painted as. A similar, if not so intense, furore surrounded the making and screening of *The Living Soap* (BBC, 1993–94). This documentary also employed a serial format and once again the programme's protagonists – this time a group of students sharing a house in Manchester – became more and more vociferous in the public prints about the pressures on them to deliver dramatic performances (see also Chapter 7).

As with all other types of advertising activity, certain products – in this case particular categories of documentary – are more heavily promoted than others. There are usually sound economic reasons for this, as broadcasters will expect certain types of factual programming to deliver particular audiences at specified times in the schedule. Traditionally, natural history documentaries, in all their many guises, have always been highly prized for their capacity to generate large, appreciative audiences at peak times. Accordingly, much effort goes into their promotion, since viewers always need to be persuaded that what they are being offered is a sufficiently different viewing experience from the hundreds of wildlife programmes to which they have already been exposed. Maintaining audience share for wildlife programming is no easy task in an increasingly crowded market-place, especially when audiences have over the years come to expect the highest standards of photography, and even daring, on the part of wildlife documentarists. Nevertheless, with this type of programming broadcasting publicists have the advantage of usually being able to capitalise on the abundance of visually arresting material captured by wildlife film makers.

Certain aspects of wildlife or natural history programming are worth considering in slightly more detail, since they throw important light on the strategies employed by broadcasting publicists to promote the programmes in question. The first is the heavy concentration on the persona of the presenter. There has always been a tendency in wildlife programming to foreground the figure of the questing scientist/adventurer (Jacques Cousteau, Armand and Michaela Denis, etc.). Nowadays, however, certain types of documentary have become much more closely identified with particular well-known figures, to the extent that it has become almost *de rigueur* for wildlife documentaries shown on the BBC to have some involvement by David Attenborough. The prominence of such a figure allows for an abundance of person-centred promotion. Quite literally, he becomes the programme's major selling-point.

The second noteworthy strategy is the preparation and circulation of material detailing how the programmes were made. These accounts can take the form of feature articles in listings magazines or a fully-fledged behind-the-scenes documentary (*The Making of...*). Though purporting to provide insight into the documentary production process, the primary objective of these 'how we did it' accounts remains promotional. We marvel at what has been achieved by new camera technology and at the patience and tenacity of the documentary hunter-gatherers. On the other hand, we are told remarkably little about other aspects of the production, including the funding arrangements or the editing process.

Third, and possibly most significant, natural history documentaries lend themselves to all manner of tie-ins and spin-offs. It is here that we recognise that television is now part of a huge multi-media, heavily commercialised industry, which always needs to extract the maximum mileage from every product made and circulated in the world's market-places. Thus no opportunity is lost to exploit viewers' continuing fascination with wildlife phenomena (a fascination itself largely stimulated by television programming). The programmes themselves act as a promotional stimulus to alert viewers to a wide range of related goods and services available. The whole spin-off industry is a good illustration of what some commentators have termed 'viewer commodification' (Nichols, 1991: 11). In the case of natural history documentaries the spin-off material takes various forms: lavishly illustrated coffee-table books and attractively pack-aged videos are the major products, but the development of CD-ROM technology has provided new and potentially very productive means of exploiting wildlife (and all other) documentary material.

Finally, brief mention should be made of a further strategy for promoting documentaries. All forms of promotion will attempt to persuade viewers that programmes will excite, stimulate, challenge or involve them in some way. With documentaries – particularly the more 'serious' forms – there has been a recognition that viewers will hope to gain information or elucidation from what they see. For the producers and promoters of such programming considerable store is set on underlining its relevance to viewers' own concerns. One of the techniques for emphasising that relevance is to refer viewers – in a variety of ways – to agencies and organisations from which they can glean more information on a topic or through which they can activate the interest that the programme may have aroused. Some of the factual/documentary programmes that focus on the work of the emergency services, for instance, encourage viewers to join in various types of first-aid and life-saving schemes. Similarly, the many programmes which centre on health issues will arrange for Helplines to be set up to provide advice and support.

Audience/viewer response

So far in this chapter we have concentrated on the broadcaster's attempts to engage the interest of the viewer through a variety of scheduling and promotional strategies. In devising these strategies, however, broadcasters and producers of documentaries have always acted in accordance with perceptions and assumptions about audience behaviour and response: what makes a documentary more accessible; how much knowledge can be presupposed on an audience's part; how material will have to be tailored to the requirements of a mainstream as opposed to a specialist channel (Loizos, 1993: 84, Winston, 1995: 175).

As readers of this book may well be aware, the whole question of audience response has been the subject of a major re-evaluation in the 1980s and 1990s. There was a time – in the early days of terrestrial television – when audiences were regarded as relatively passive and therefore vulnerable to manipulation. This was predicated on the notion that media audiences were locked into an intense, unquestioning relationship with broadcasting institutions and would thus be predisposed to believe in all that they heard and saw. Much attention was accordingly focused on the supposed capacity of large, powerful media institutions to mould public opinion in ways that could prove harmful to the democratic process. There was, in other words, a concern with what media texts could do to the audience rather than what audiences could do with media texts. Members of the television audience were thus likened to empty vessels into which meanings could be poured.

Latterly there has been a recognition that much of this early work was based on less than solid foundations, particularly with regard to the media's presumed effects. As a consequence, there is nowadays greater emphasis on conducting critical ethnographic inquiries into the phenomenon of audience response or viewer activity.

Of particular interest in these debates has been the concern to establish the factors that govern audience response: What are the criteria, for instance, that determine the extent to which viewers accept or contest what are often referred to as the 'preferred readings' of a text (Moores, 1993: 28)? Similarly – and of particular relevance to documentary's claim to have a privileged relation to the 'real' – there are the debates on the production of meaning and on intertextuality: To what extent are the meanings that a reader derives from a particular text significantly determined by that same reader's experience of, or exposure to, a range of kindred texts belonging to the same genre or dealing with the same subject matter (Ang, 1996: 171, O'Sullivan *et al.*, 1994a: 167)?

Changing patterns of response

Any attempt to understand audience behaviour and response, or to define what is involved in 'watching television', must nowadays also take into account the significant transformation that television itself has gone through in the last two decades of the century. Living as we now are in a media-saturated environment, our attitudes to television consumption have also changed significantly. In an age of increasing multi-set ownership, and with access to a rapidly growing number of channels, it can certainly no longer be asserted that television performs the integrative function, once claimed for it, of binding the nation together in a common cause. As channels have proliferated, so audiences have become much more fragmented. Likewise, – in Europe at least – long-established traditions of public-service broadcasting have given way to more commercialised systems with very different ideas on how the perceived needs of the audience should be catered for.

There has at the same time been a major shift in our understanding of audience behaviour – how viewers respond to or make sense of the material they consume. The television audience is no longer conceived as a relatively stable entity, a constituency of viewers with predictable response patterns (see Ang, 1996: 4). In particular, there is nowadays a much greater emphasis on the idea of viewer activity (or the active viewer) and on the importance of the social or domestic context in which viewing takes place. Viewers are thus regarded as active protagonists in the making of meaning. Or, expressed in slightly different terms, each act of viewing takes the form of an encounter between reader and text. Meanings derived from the text are thus the result of a complex process of negotiation rather than a quasi-mechanical decoding operation. As a consequence, any meanings attributed will depend as much on the socially and culturally determined assumptions and beliefs that viewers bring with them to the text as on the text's capacity to 'sway' the reader to its point of view.

The frames of reference which audiences apply when engaging

with documentaries (or any other media text) will differ according to a range of factors, including age, gender, social grouping, political affiliation – and even personal biography. For instance, in one research project conducted by the media scholar John Corner in the late 1980s, groups drawn from different professions and social/educational backgrounds watched a series of documentaries, all of which addressed the issue of nuclear power (Corner *et al.*, 1990). The responses – in terms of the interpretations that the individuals within each group put upon these programmes (which themselves incorporated a cross-section of pro- and anti-nuclear perspectives) – were markedly different according to the particular 'affiliations' of the group. Though they do not suggest that audience interpretation is entirely dependent on respective group membership, Corner and his research team give a persuasive account of how such affiliations contribute to the 'frameworks of understanding' which viewers apply in the decoding process.

This acknowledgement of differential audience response to specified categories of television programming is also reflected in the efforts by the television industry to establish more accurate profiles of their audiences, partly in order to satisfy advertisers that they are getting their messages across to the desired target audience. On the evidence provided by a number of studies, there are some grounds for suggesting that, whereas women will be drawn to certain types of television fiction (especially soap opera), many men claim to have a predilection for the more factual forms of programming, in particular documentaries (Moores, 1993: 23–5). Talking about programme type preference, for instance, Morley has commented:

> My respondents displayed a notable consistency in this area, whereby masculinity was primarily identified with a strong preference for 'factual' programmes (news, current affairs, documentaries) and femininity identified with a preference for fictional programmes (Morley, 1986: 162).

As other commentators have pointed out, however, it would be unwise to privilege just one variable (here gender) above several others in mapping out and explaining audience response to a particular programme category (Ang, 1996: 49–51, 109–29). We must also remind ourselves that an increasing number of variables have to be built in to any explanatory account of viewer behaviour. What consequences does it have, for instance, that we now know that the attentiveness of an audience is something which can by no means be guaranteed? And by the same token: What implications flow from the fact that, for an increasing number of viewers, the experience of television has become synonymous with a persistent and unsettling zapping activity? Snatches of many programmes in a channel-rich environment are rapidly sampled, but not all that many are consumed in their entirety.[6]

Changing technology

The other question which needs to addressed when discussing the experience of viewing documentaries is that, with the rapid advance of CD-ROM technology and the growing availability of learning packages for use in both the domestic and the educational environment, our understanding of what is meant by documentary reception will also change. More and more material culled from documentary archives will make its appearance as part of an interactive CD-ROM programme. CD-ROMs have the particular advantage that they allow for a multiplicity of points of view. Users also have the option of sampling the whole programme to get an overview of the topic under discussion or opting to stop the programme at a particular point of interest and accessing the large multi-media database, thereby considerably enhancing the learning possibilities.[7]

The appeal of documentary

In the first chapter we began to explore the sort of expectations that audiences bring with them to their viewing of documentary. We suggested that much of documentary's appeal was based on the viewers' anticipation that, by tuning into this form of programming, they could enlarge their knowledge of human and social affairs in quite significant ways. In other words, viewers look to documentaries to provide them with an experience which can, among other things, be socially educative or knowledge-enhancing. Documentaries make their appeal by virtue of the fact that they claim to be artefacts with a social function. The pleasure in watching them comes from knowing that what we are witnessing can, potentially at least, spill over into the world which we or others like us inhabit. As Bill Nichols has remarked:

> Documentary realism aligns itself with an epistephilia, so to speak, a pleasure in knowing, that marks out a distinctive form of social engagement ... We are moved to confront a topic, issue, situation or event that bears the mark of the historically real. (Nichols, 1991: 178)

The fact that documentaries appear to have special relevance to the socio-political world can also, it might be argued, help us to gain a better sense of the place which we as individual citizens might occupy within that larger order. (Grierson considered this to be documentary's principal *raison d'être*.) Expressed in slightly different terms, there is what some would regard as a comforting reassurance that we are not entering a universe whose contours have been *principally* defined by an originating author. Seen in this light, the reason why viewers turn to documentaries is that they are interestingly different from much else that is available in television's menu of offerings.

Although documentary has so often claimed the status of work which has social relevance, it is undeniable that – throughout its history – it has also sought to awaken a far more subjective response. Social relevance is far from being the primary source of documentary's appeal, especially where television is concerned. As we have already had occasion to remark (see Chapter 5), documentary deploys many fictional techniques. This – together with other recurrent features of documentary presentation (the skilful marshalling of visual and verbal evidence, the use of various tried and tested story-telling devices, etc.) – has meant that documentaries have been able to stir, perturb or move the viewer in ways that some would claim are no less powerful than those of forms which we would categorise as wholly fictional.

It is through the deployment of such devices and the selection of certain types of subject matter that audiences are manoeuvred into quite strong forms of subjective engagement with what they see and hear in a documentary account (Nichols, 1991: 155–70). Take for instance the many documentary 'portraits' that provide closely observed studies of individuals or groups in their everyday domestic or working environment or confronting problems of the type which audience members may well have encountered. Not all these portraits will be seeking specifically to provoke an affective response, and many may cause us to reflect on wider social issues (e.g. how an individual has been formed by his or her surroundings). In spite of this, the appeal of these 'personal documentaries', which have a long tradition in the history of the genre, lies precisely in that the wider social implications are deliberately downplayed and the human dimensions of the problem or situation emphasised, sometimes by means of particularly poeticised or romanticised treatments (see also remarks on Flaherty's work in Chapters 3 and 6).

The 'personal journey' is a further example of a documentary format which invites a more subjective form of viewer engagement. In the Channel 4 series *Travels with my Camera* (November, 1996), for instance, a number of well-known personalities undertook journeys, most of which involved them in returning to places which had a particular personal significance for them. The mode of presentation, the style of dress and the type of stories told were all calculated to invite an empathic response. Likewise, many *Video Diaries* (see Chapters 3 and 4) contain confessional or self-revealing traits. Viewers are thus actively encouraged to share in what can be intensely moving acts of inner exploration.

From all that we have had to say above about the interpretative activity of audiences, it is clear that viewers are addressed in ways which allow them to gain a number of quite distinct gratifications from what factual/documentary programming offers them.[8] It is certainly not the case – as is implied in some models of viewer behaviour – that audiences lock into a fundamentally different viewing mode when watching documentaries. (The very fact that documentaries are accommodated in schedules which contain such a diversity of programming in itself makes such 'switching' ability highly unlikely.) Documentaries position us in exactly the same way – and using many of the same means (narrative, identification with on-screen characters, inclusion of atmospheric music) – as fictional programming does, and to similar ends. And whilst the commentaries which frequently accompany the documentary image track may sometimes encourage us to believe that we are free to draw our own conclusions from all that we hear and see, there is always a guiding hand which nudges us towards taking a particular view of these events. Like pleasure, knowledge is not always innocent.

Documentary impact and effects

In our discussion of text–audience relations we have chosen to emphasise that the meanings which viewers generate from these programmes are the result of an encounter between reader and text. Meanings are not simply 'read off' but are the outcome of a complex process of negotiation. Thus, whilst it would be going too far to suggest that viewers are entirely free agents in putting their own interpretation on what they see and hear, there is still considerable scope for variation in measuring how programmes are viewed and what readers make of them. In terms of the presumed impact that documentaries – or other forms of programming – have on audiences, this suggests that viewers might be somewhat less vulnerable than has sometimes been supposed to the persuasive rhetoric of programme producers. Certainly there is nowadays a general acceptance that it is overly simplistic to posit a direct, causal relationship between the viewing of a particular television programme and the manifestation of certain types of behaviour, let alone the changing of long- or firmly-held attitudes (O'Sullivan *et al.*, 1994a: 150–85).

Nevertheless, there is still continuing and understandable concern – on the part of broadcasters and other interested parties – to discover more about the impact that programmes have and how it can be measured. A whole series of quantitative and qualitative methods have been developed over the years to track and interpret audience response. As with all such exercises, however, the outcome will always depend on the perspective from which the measuring is being undertaken and the purpose for which it is intended. For the broadcaster, for instance, the primary focus of interest will tend to be on how well the documentary has performed: how many viewers tuned in to it and whether it attracted favourable reviews. Others (media critics or social observers) will be more concerned to assess its cultural impact: in what ways it has contributed to some ongoing debate or how it relates to other accounts tackling the same issue.

In spite of the caution with which the issue of media effects is now approached, it is perhaps inevitable, given the highly public character of television and some of the defining features of documentary (its engagement with the historical world), that some of the fiercest battles have been fought over the effects which documentaries are presumed or feared to have had. In what follows we reflect on some of the issues surrounding documentary's reception and consider in what ways, if at all, documentaries might be said to have had a discernible effect in swaying opinion or moulding attitudes. Readers will be well aware that, in considering such issues, we are entering a debate which has been characterised rather by heat generated than light provided.

Any conjecture about the purported effect of documentaries in general or one programme in particular will always need to be set in the context of wider considerations, including the role played by other forces or influences at work in society and by the public's changing attitude to the medium of television itself. For instance, it may well have been the case that in the early days of television, in a single-channel environment, certain documentaries made more of an impact simply because a larger proportion of the available television audience attended to them. Nowadays the impact of individual programmes is likely to be less because they have to compete for attention in an increasingly crowded market-place.

We also have to bear in mind that many claims about documentaries are made by programme makers and broadcasters who are anxious to secure an audience for their work (see above). It is understandable that producers will wish to talk up the importance of their work ('a major contribution to the debate on...'; 'an influential new study of...') when they attempt to maintain the support of a sponsoring agent or to persuade a commissioning editor to provide funds for a new project. It is on the other hand much more difficult to show that the work has been instrumental in creating a new climate of opinion or initiating social reform. For instance, for many years the received wisdom was that the social documentaries made by John Grierson in the 1930s had so moulded public opinion as to pave the way for social reforms in the years that followed. As Brian Winston has convincingly argued, however, these claims do not really stand up to close historical scrutiny (Winston, 1995: 67–8).

Given the large number of documentaries that claim over the years to have exposed all manner of malpractices, deficiencies and even crimes, one is rather surprised to discover that only in remarkably few has the act of exposure led *directly* to corrective action being taken. And even where a causal link appears to have been established, subsequent investigation often throws doubt on just how strong the connection may be. Take for example the case of *Cathy Come Home* (BBC, 1966), a moving documentary-drama chronicling a young woman's fruitless attempts to find accommodation for herself and her two children. The work, which drew attention to the plight of homeless young families, is often credited with having led directly to the setting up of Shelter, the organisation for the homeless. Although *Cathy Come Home* undeniably helped the cause of those who were already advocating more enlightened policies and more caring attitudes in meeting the needs of the disadvantaged (see Goodwin *et al.*, 1983: 19), the programme was certainly not alone in creating the climate of opinion which ushered Shelter into existence.

We are thus inclined to take the view of those who say that documentaries, as other forms of media output, cannot be isolated from those other forces at work in society (political, social and cultural), which, over the longer or shorter term, result in change occurring. In Brian Winston's words:

> The record suggests that the media in general and the documentary in particular are actually not powerful *instigators*. Their power resides in their ability to amplify. Thus issues already under consideration within the body politic, situations upon which the whistle is being blown, are more likely to produce films which have an after-effect than those dreamed up by the flyblown-eyed documentarists themselves (Winston, 1995: 237).

This view tends to be reinforced by research conducted by the broadcasting institutions themselves. Thus, in a series of investigations conducted by the research department of the IBA (now the ITC) into the impact of drama-documentaries broadcast on the ITV network, researchers found that the programmes in question – even though they often unleashed a lively and at times furious debate – did not in themselves radically alter the opinions of viewers on, or change their attitudes to, the issue or subject under discussion.

The picture that emerges from all these surveys is of a relatively sophisticated audience. Viewers are very far from taking what they see and hear at face value. They will wish to test the account given in this particular programme against other available sources of information before forming a view or amending an opinion they may hold. Thus, viewers of *Who Bombed Birmingham?* – a 1990 drama-documentary produced by Granada television for the ITV network – were asked what impact the programme had had on their views on the case of the Birmingham Six (the six Irishmen imprisoned on terrorist charges and subsequently released). The programme itself made a powerful case that others had been responsible for the Birmingham pub bombing and even went so far as to identify four other suspects. What is significant for our present concern with documentary effects, however, is that when viewers were questioned about the impact of the programme on their own views, their responses indicated that they were very far from being won over to the arguments advanced by the programme makers. The majority of viewers, whilst recognising how the programme was seeking to persuade them, were quite reluctant to accept its basic proposition (at least until they had access to more evidence). Consequently, although seventy-six per cent of viewers questioned acknowledged that *Who Bombed Birmingham?* gave them new information on the possible circumstances of the bombings, a much lower percentage (fifty-nine per cent) was willing to accept that 'the great majority of information given in the programme was true' (Wober, 1990).

The above discussion suggests that caution is advised in any speculation about documentary effects. This leads us to make a further point concerning effectivity – namely, that problems and controversy frequently arise when the programme in question proves to have a very different impact than the one imagined by those who have co-operated in the film's making. The history of documentary is full of examples of individuals and groups who have sought the oxygen of publicity that an appearance on television brings, only to be appalled at the results of this media exposure. Indeed, one might even go so far as to say that some of the most demonstrable effects of screening documentaries occur where the cameras have revealed a very different reality from that which the participating subjects clearly thought would be unveiled. In Roger Graef's landmark documentary series *Police* (BBC, 1982), for instance, police officials clearly thought that allowing Graef and his team in to produce a fly-on-the-wall account of police practices could have a positive public-relations pay-off (see also Chapter 3). When, however, in one episode (*Complaint of Rape*) police officers were seen dealing with a female rape victim in a highly insensitive fashion, the result was a public outcry which did actually lead to a revision of police interviewing procedures. In similar vein, as we have seen with *The Club*, the members of Northwood Golf Club who naively believed that letting the cameras in could bring some welcome publicity were cruelly disillusioned when the documentary proved to have the opposite effect (see Chapter 8).

Caution advised

Complaint of Rape and *The Club*, where it is possible to draw a causal link between the screening of a documentary and a subsequent event, are very much isolated examples. It is also true that documentarists, when not actively seeking to promote their work by talking up its potential impact, are almost self-deprecating in their assessment of their capacity to move minds or bring about policy reforms. For example, the investigative documentary series *Trial and Error* (Channel 4) and *Rough Justice* (BBC) have both been credited with drawing public attention to legal cases where there appear to have been miscarriages of justice. Those involved in making the programmes, however, have been surprisingly candid about what they see as the limitations of having to work in a medium which normally requires considerable simplification of often complex processes and where some measure of the programmes' success is whether they result in a retrial or some form of judicial review (see Young and Hill, 1985: 140).

In assessing the actual impact – measured in terms of their social utility – of documentaries on their audiences, we have therefore every reason to be circumspect. Producers of documentary will, understandably enough, continue to indulge in all manner of special pleading, arguing that their work has considerable consciousness-raising potential. The historical evidence and consensus of opinion amongst critical commentators, however, suggests that these claims are often exaggerated. And even some documentarists, when called on to reflect self-critically on their work, are not beyond taking a much more muted view of its likely efficacy. Consider for instance the following chastening observations made by the well-known American film maker Frederick Wiseman:

> Documentary film-makers are supposed to make films that educate, expose, inform, reform, and effect change in a resistant and otherwise unenlightened world. Documentaries are thought to have the same relation to social change as penicillin to syphilis. The importance of documentaries as political instruments for change is stubbornly clung to despite the total absence of any supporting evidence ... The basic assumption [of film-makers] is that the film is going to be such an important event in the life of the audience that all else will be dropped. The obvious fact that other sources of information exist – newspapers, books, personal experience and judgement – is often lost sight of in the passionate rush to present and impose what is inevitably a limited view. (Wiseman, 1986: 40–2)

Concluding remarks

Finally, in this brief assessment of the impacts and effects of documentary, we would like to return to a question we have already broached several times in the course of this study: How will documentary fare in the broadcasting climate of the late twentieth and early twenty-first centuries? The more pessimistically inclined take the view that – given the pressures on broadcasters to produce or acquire programming which will result in respectable ratings – we will see an increase in those softer, more easily accessible documentaries which can be relied on to generate those ratings. As far as British television is concerned, there are – in spite of some honourable exceptions – signs that documentaries are increasingly regarded as a vehicle for delivering audiences rather than one which allows scope for creativity, formal experimentation and the contestation of received views. Documentaries which peer voyeuristically into people's private lives or which are politically uncontroversial are being given preferment.

There are, however, still some grounds for optimism. As we have seen, some of the new factual/documentary formats have significantly extended the communicative and expressive range of documentary. Many of these developments are to be welcomed, in so far as they have supplanted the often earnest and sometimes turgid character of the traditional documentary and opened up new ways for the audience to interact with these works (see Williams, 1993: 12). In short, there are welcome signs that producers of television documentaries are now treating their audience far more as equal partners than they once did.

The new relationship which programme makers cultivate with their audience is partly born of the acknowledgement that viewers have become much more knowing and sophisticated in their relations to the television medium. At the same time there is clearly less of a wish to be patronising and concerned with educational enlightenment than to speak to audiences in a language they will readily understand. This is nowhere better illustrated than in the increasing use of irony in the commentaries or voice-overs that accompany contemporary accounts. (Irony presupposes a knowing relationship between communicator and addressee and can be a source of considerable pleasure on the part of those thus addressed.) Not a few contemporary programme makers acknowledge that the viewer will be taking up a possibly sceptical position with regard to the documentary's foregrounded messages. Thus, in anticipation of such responses, they will acknowledge that, in the accompanying commentary or through a self-reflexive style of editing, much may be different from what it appears to be. As with any piece of creative or critical work, the final arbiters are always going to be the audience or readers at whom the work is directed!

Notes

Chapter 1

1 Documentary's 'persuasiveness' can take several forms and can range from viewers feeling they are being gently nudged towards a particular interpretation to their sensing that they are being exposed to blatant propaganda.

2 It is worth noting that when John Grierson first espoused the documentary cause in the 1920s he used a similar tactic to talk up the significance of documentary by drawing attention to what he saw as the trivialising, escapist tendencies of Hollywood fiction film.

3 This may partly explain why those responsible for producing television listings will often refrain from using the label 'documentary' in advance publicity.

4 The German documentary *Crash 2030: Investigating a Catastrophe* (1994, directed by Joachim Friedrich) is a work which makes extensive use of digital techniques. The film projects a nightmare vision of the catastrophe waiting to happen if global warming is allowed to continue unabated. Digitally generated images of ever higher water levels and flooded landscapes are integrated with traditionally filmed sequences to produce a disturbing and highly credible account.

5 Of those channels which still include documentaries amongst their offerings the majority concentrate on recently produced, often specially commissioned, work dealing with contemporary subjects. However, certain channels (in Britain, BBC 2 and Channel 4) will sometimes showcase much earlier documentary work, thus giving viewers the chance to savour material belonging to the classic documentary canon.

6 A number of satellite channels (e.g. the Discovery Channel and the History Channel) have been set up in recent years that concentrate largely or exclusively on documentary programming.

7 This is again well illustrated if one considers documentary work produced in the Cold War period by film makers in eastern and central Europe. Although the state exercised strict control over all media operations and output, those working for the state-owned film units (including documentarists) still had, relatively speaking, greater freedom than those working in television.

8 Mindful that the viewing conditions in a cinema were not conducive to encouraging debate, many documentary film makers explored the possibilities offered by alternative venues. Screenings that were often followed by

discussion and debate were thus arranged in working men's clubs, film societies, factories and other places where a keen interest in the subject or subjects covered could be presumed.

9 Documentarists have come under careful scrutiny from external and internal bodies entrusted with the task of ensuring that broadcasters maintain due standards and do not overstep certain marks.

10 Documentarists, like all producers of work for television, have always had to pay particular attention to the sound-track. Even if viewers' 'visual' attention temporarily wavers, a strong verbal component can ensure that their interest in the programme is sustained!

11 Currently, an increasing number of documentarists are turning to the satellite channels (especially Discovery) as their best hope for getting work commissioned.

Chapter 2

1 Since the introduction of digital technology, computer-generated images can be virtually indistinguishable from lens-based ones. The technology is frequently used in matting together images in natural history documentaries, where it permits the film maker to take flights of fancy (literally allowing us to cruise alongside birds) while remaining true to the life-cycles that it represents.

Chapter 4

1 A detailed explanation of the way film can be read can be found in Bordwell and Thompson, 1996, and Izod, 1984.

2 Documentarists' own accounts of the editing process are found in Vaughan, 1993: 99–115; Craig Gilbert's reflections on the editing of *An American Family* in Rosenthal, 1988: 203–7; and Jacobs, 1979: 409–11. Occasionally, in more reflexive documentaries, the issue of how to edit material becomes part of the film itself, see Loizos, 1993: 56–64.

3 Documentarists sometimes prefer to use some form of titling to give important additional information.

4 This is a standard dramatic convention, borrowed from the world of soap opera, to generate interest and variety and keep the pace brisk.

Chapter 5

1 There is an analogy here with the moral that can be deduced from fictional stories like *Aesop's Fables*. They are attended to because the audience delights in the telling while being simultaneously aware that the tellers are communicating something more than a diversion.

2 Indeed, the documentary itself sometimes imitates these forms (Breitrose, 1986: 48–51).

Chapter 6

1 In general parlance the terms 'reconstruction' and 'dramatisation' are often used interchangeably. More accurately, however, 'reconstruction' suggests the production of a reasonably accurate account of a past event on the basis of the available evidence. 'Dramatisation' has an altogether wider range of association and suggests the process of presenting material in such a way as to enhance the impact on an audience.

2 Sometimes producers preferred a faked re-enactment to available recorded footage if they felt it made for a more dramatic story (Jacobs, 1979: 108).

3 The drama-documentary unit at Granada Television was responsible for the following 'behind the Iron Curtain' works: *The Man who Wouldn't Keep Quiet* (1972), *Subject of Struggle* (1972), *Full Circle* (1974), *Three Days in Szczecin* (1976), *Collision Course* (1979) and *Invasion* (1980).

4 *The War Game* was one of the first of the works produced during the Cold War decades that explored in dramatic form, but with documentary underpinning, the nightmarish consequences of a nuclear attack. The American programme *The Day After* (ABC, 1983) and the British documentary drama *Threads* (BBC, 1984) are perhaps the other best-known examples.

5 Dramatisations such as *The Trial of Lord Lucan* have much in common with programmes which appear under the rubric 'unsolved mysteries'. They also have common features with the category of programming known as 'hypotheticals', in which experts in a particular field are required to conjecture how they might have acted when placed in a particular situation or confronted with a certain dilemma.

6 The programme did not wholly succeed in realising this aim, partly because viewers had difficulties in coming to terms with the fact that actors were playing the parts of well-known living politicians.

7 In their enthusiasm for drama-documentaries some commentators (e.g. Kuehl, 1981) give what we consider to be a mistaken impression that traditional documentarists are so heavily constrained that any psychological or emotional probing is off-limits for them. Such views are clearly exaggerated. That kind of probing can take place in any documentary. It is just that in drama-documentaries it is achieved by different means.

8 Needless to say, the basic *Crimewatch* formula has been much emulated and in Britain alone has given rise to several clones, such as *Crimestoppers* and *Crime Monthly*. *Crimewatch* was itself based on the West German *Aktenzeichen XY ... ungelöst* (Case XY ... unsolved).

9 Not surprisingly, there has been some criticism of the more populist reality shows, such as the American *Cops*, which seem to exploit the sensational aspects of drugs raids or violent arrests. (See Kilborn, 1994b.)

10 Some commentators have drawn an analogy between the narrative structuring devices of 'rescue' scenes with those employed in disaster movies (Bondebjerg, 1996: 40).

Chapter 7

1   One should note in this respect, however, that some critics are of the belief that private sponsorship can on occasions enable documentarists to conduct probing investigations which other funding arrangements would not permit. (See Winston, 1995: 83–5.)

2   For further discussion of *The War Game*, see Corner, 1996: 39–41.

3   It is interesting to note that *The War Game*, despite being banned by the BBC, was still seen by an estimated six million viewers. Between 1965 and 1985 (the year when it received its first television screening) it was circulated in 16-mm format around film societies, anti-nuclear pressure groups and other interested bodies. In this case the act of censorship enhanced rather than detracted from the film's reputation.

4   Two of the most notable controversies involving documentaries screened in recent years were those surrounding *Real Lives: At the Edge of the Union*, (BBC, 1985) and *Death on the Rock* (Thames Television, 1988). The former was a study of two Derry politicians, whilst the latter was a dramatic reconstruction of the shooting of suspected IRA terrorists by members of the British SAS. Some commentators have seen a connection between the Government's displeasure at the programme being screened and the non-renewal of Thames Television's licence in the 1991 franchising round. For more on this, see Rolston and Miller, 1996: 96–141.

5   In Britain this community spirit is exemplified by the high turn-out of practising documentarists at the annual Sheffield International Documentary Film Festival.

6   Some documentarists, including the American film maker Jayne Loader, have begun to specialise in the production of 'digital documentaries' on CD-ROMs. Such artefacts use the full scope of computer technology to allow users to move through a vast range of photographic, video and printed material, thereby creating in one sense their own documentary account.

7   In the UK it has been quite noticeable in recent years that the most successful documentary strands have all tended to favour British stories and subjects.

8   Peter Wintonick's and Mark Achbar's 1992 documentary *Manufacturing Consent: Noam Chomsky and the Media* originally ran for three hours, but subsequently five different versions of the film were produced, each designed to fit a different broadcasting slot.

9   Some have linked this reluctance with the fact that the BBC charter was up for review in 1996 and that the BBC did not wish to incur the Government's displeasure by becoming involved in too many controversies.

10 Many of those involved in the commissioning of documentary work for television have personal experience of making documentaries. They are well aware of the conflicts that arise between the desire of programme makers to produce stylistically innovative work which may challenge the

status quo and the channel's need to screen material which will appeal to the audience being targeted.

Chapter 8

1 The most useful book of this type currently available is Michael Rabiger's *Directing the Documentary* (1987).
2 There have been a number of individual studies which have chronicled the making of particular documentaries or have examined particular phases of documentary production (Rosenthal (1971), Jacobs (1979), Silverstone (1985), Rosenthal (1990)). Programme makers themselves are also sometimes asked to come up with 'how-we-did-it' accounts giving some indication of how the programme or series was produced. It is very seldom, however, that such behind-the-scenes accounts address important issues such as how the series came to be commissioned or who came up with the funding for the production.
3 In Dineen's work one never has the impression, however, that she is intent on exploiting her subjects' vulnerability. Her major concern is, in her own words, to 'tell stories through characters' (Sheffield Documentary Festival, 1996). In almost all her documentaries to date the story centres on a 'quirky view of collapsing British institutions'.
4 Preparing the ground in this way has a good deal in common with many other types of inquiry which precede the production of both factual and fictional accounts. There are, for instance, interesting analogies to be drawn between the work of the social anthropologist and that of ethnographic film makers. In both cases the cultural knowledge acquired as a result of living amongst a particular group can be translated into a sensitively nuanced account (Loizos, 1993: 91–114).
5 There have of course been many occasions when documentarists have been prevented from filming in certain locations or from recording interviews with particular individuals. Even when cameras have been allowed in, there has often been subsequent bitter criticism that the terms of the access agreement have not been honoured.
6 It is here that documentarists have to resort to the various forms of reconstruction described at greater length in Chapter 6.
7 Readers might find it instructive to compare this section with some of the points made about the editing process in earlier chapters. See especially the observations made on editing in the different documentary modes (in Chapter 3) and remarks on how editing contributes to the impact of individual works (in Chapter 4).
8 When film makers resort to secret filming, they still have to seek the consent of the company or organisation for whom they are producing the account.

Chapter 9

1 In Britain the major terrestrial channels all have core strands into which documentary work has to be slotted. Each strand has its own thematic and stylistic requirements, details of which are contained in special booklets obtainable by independent producers from the broadcasters.

2 This situation is further exacerbated by the fact that those channels which have had to adopt a more populist, commercially-driven approach to programme scheduling (e.g. ITV) have always traditionally looked to the BBC and to Channel 4, with their protected funding and distinct remit to maintain the cause of 'serious' documentary.

3 In January 1996 the natural history documentary *Gorillas* (BBC) was followed the next day by a two-hour biopic *Gorillas in the Mist* (made in 1988, starring Sigourney Weaver and directed by Michael Apted).

4 Producers of drama-documentaries have been particularly adept at piggybacking on recent newsworthy events – e.g. *Death on the Rock* (Thames Television, 1988) and *Why Lockerbie?* (Granada Television, 1990).

5 A good example of revisitation is provided by the *Network First* programme *Bhopal: The Second Tragedy* (ITV, January 1995), when Mark Tully and a documentary team returned to the Indian city of Bhopal ten years after a lethal chemical leak there.

6 At the 1996 Sheffield International Documentary Festival Chris Haws, commissioning editor and head of production at Discovery Channel Europe, produced the remarkable statistics that, according to some in-house (Discovery) research, a mere six per cent of documentary viewers watched programmes right through from the opening to the closing credits.

7 The American documentary film maker Jayne Loader recently produced *Public Shelter* (1996), the CD-ROM sequel to her 1980s classic film *The Atomic Café*.

8 Here we would refer readers to the discussion in the debate on text–reader relations which focuses on the idea of 'preferred', 'alternative' or 'oppositional' readings (see Moores, 1993: 16–31).

Bibliography

Allen, Robert C. and Gomery, Douglas (1985). *Film History: Theory and Practice*, New York: Alfred A. Knopf.

Andrew, J. Dudley (1984). *Concepts in Film Theory*, Oxford: Oxford University Press.

Ang, Ien (1996). *Living Room Wars: Rethinking Media Audiences for a Postmodern World*, London: Routledge.

Armstrong, Dan (1990). 'Wiseman and the politics of feeling', *Quarterly Review of Film and Video*, 11: 4, 35–50.

Arthur, Paul (1993). 'Jargons of authenticity (three American moments)', in Renov, 108–34.

Aubrey, Crispin (ed.) (1982). *Nukespeak: The Media and the Bomb*, London: Comedia.

Barnouw, Erik (1974). *Documentary: A History of the Non-Fiction Film*, New York: Oxford University Press.

Bazin, André (1967). *What is Cinema?*, vol. 2, London: University of California Press.

BBC (1994). *Documentaries: The Independents' Guide*, London: BBC.

Bell, Elaine (1986). 'The origins of British television documentary: The BBC 1946–1955', in Corner, 65–80.

Belsey, Catherine (1980). *Critical Practice*, London: Methuen.

Bolton, Roger (1992). 'Disturbing wishes', *Sight and Sound*, 1:10 (NS), February, 29.

Bondebjerg, Ib (1994). 'Narratives of reality: documentary film and television in a cognitive and pragmatic perspective', *Nordicom Review*, 1, 65–85.

—— (1996). 'Public discourse/private fascination: hybridization in "true-life-story" genres', *Media, Culture and Society*, 18:1, January, 27–45.

Bordwell, David and Thompson, Karen (1996). *Film Art: An Introduction*, 5th edn, London: McGraw-Hill.

Bourelly, Robert (1993). 'Forum for international co-financing of documentaries', Interview with Thomas Stenderup, *DOX*, 0, Winter, 48–52.

Branigan, Edward (1992). *Narrative Comprehension and Film*, London: Routledge.

Brecht, Bertolt (1938). 'Against Georg Lukács', in Ernst Bloch, Georg Lukács, Bertolt Brecht, Walter Benjamin, Theodor Adorno, *Aesthetics and Politics*, London: Verso, 1980.

Breitrose, Henry (1986). 'The structures and function of documentary film', *CILECT Review*, 2:1, November, 43–56.

Britton, Andrew (1992). 'Invisible eye', *Sight and Sound*, 1:10 (NS), February, 26–9.

Buruma, Ian (1996). 'Marcel Ophüls', in Macdonald and Cousins, 224–33.

Carr, Edward (1961). *What is History?*, Harmondsworth: Penguin, 2nd edn 1987.

Chanan, Michael (1993). 'Coping with co-production', *DOX*, 0, Winter, 37–42.

—— (1995), 'Europe at work', *DOX*, 5, Spring, 39–41.

Christie, Ian (1994). *The Last Machine: Early Cinema and the Birth of the Modern World*, London: British Film Institute.

Collins, Richard (1986). 'Seeing is believing: the ideology of naturalism', in Corner, 125–38.

Cormack, Mike (1992). *Ideology*, London: Batsford.

Corner, John (ed.) (1986). *Documentary and the Mass Media*, London: Edward Arnold.

—— (1995). *Television Form and Public Address*, London: Edward Arnold.

—— (1996). *The Art of Record: A Critical Introduction to Documentary*, Manchester: Manchester University Press.

——, Richardson, Kay and Fenton, Natalie (1990). *Nuclear Reactions: Form and Response in 'Public Issue' Television*, London: John Libbey.

Cosgrove, Stuart (1995). 'War Cries', *DOX*, 6, Summer, 20–3.

Crawford, Peter Ian and Turton, David (eds) (1993). *Film as Ethnography*, Manchester: Manchester University Press.

Curran, James, Smith, Anthony and Wingate, Pauline (eds) (1987). *Impacts and Influences: Essays on Media Power in the Twentieth Century*, London: Methuen.

Dunn, Elizabeth (1993). 'Documentary the Dineen way', *Daily Telegraph*, 30 January, 18.

Edgar, David (1982). 'On drama documentary', in Pike, Frank (ed.). *Ah! Mischief: The Writer and Television*, London: Faber and Faber.

Ellis, Jack C. (1989). *The Documentary Idea*, Englewood Cliffs, NJ: Prentice Hall.

Ellis, John (1982). *Visible Fictions: Cinema: Television: Radio*, London: Routledge and Kegan Paul.

Feldman, Seth (1986). 'Footnote to fact: the docudrama', in Grant, Barry (ed.). *Film Genre Reader*, Austin: University of Texas Press.

Fiske, John (1982). *Introduction to Communication Studies*, London: Methuen.

Goodwin, Andrew (1986). *Teaching TV Drama-documentary*, London: British Film Institute.

—— (1993). 'Riding with ambulances: television and its uses', *Sight and Sound*, 3:1, January, 26–8.

—— and Whannel, Garry (1990). *Understanding Television*, London: Routledge.

——, Kerr, Paul and MacDonald, Ian (1983). *Drama-documentary* (BFI Dossier No. 19), London: British Film Institute.

Grierson, John (1966). *Grierson on Documentary*, London: Faber. (First published in 1946.)

Grigsby, Michael and McClintock, Nicholas (1995). 'The state we're in', *DOX*, 6, Summer, 6–10.

Haws, Chris (1995). 'The discovering of cable', *DOX*, 6, Summer, 14–17.

Holt, Hazel (1978). 'The BBC a prime offender in the area of half-truths', *The*

Stage and TV Today, 27 April, 12.

Hutcheon, Linda (1989). *The Politics of Postmodernism*, London: Routledge.

Izod, John (1984). *Reading the Screen*, Harlow: Longman.

Jacobs, Lewis (ed.) (1979). *The Documentary Tradition: From Nanook to Woodstock*, 2nd edn, New York: W. W. Norton.

Johnson, Lawrence (1992). 'How to avoid a knife job', *Times Educational Supplement*, 15 May, 8.

Johnson, Paul (1981). 'Truth is a precious and vulnerable commodity not to be adulterated', *Listener*, 19 March, 363.

Keighron, Peter (1993). 'Video Diaries: what's up Doc?' *Sight and Sound*, 3:10, October, 24–5.

Kent, Raymond (1994). *Measuring Media Audiences*, London: Routledge.

Kilborn, Richard (1992). *Television Soaps*, London: Batsford.

—— (1994a). 'Drama over Lockerbie: a new look at television drama-documentaries', *Historical Journal of Film, Radio and Television*, 14:1, 59–76.

—— (1994b). 'How real can you get?: recent developments in "reality" television', *European Journal of Communication*, 9, 421–39.

—— (1995). 'Being there: a long, hard look at the future of the fly-on-the-wall documentary', *DOX*, 6, 24–7.

—— (1996). 'New contexts for documentary production in Britain', *Media, Culture and Society*, 18:1, January, 141–50.

Kuehl, Jerry (1981). 'Truth claims', *Sight and Sound*, 50:4, Autumn, 272–4.

Lier, Miryam van (1994). 'Editorial: the art of documentary film', *DOX*, 3, Autumn, 3.

Lockerbie, Ian (1991). 'The self-conscious documentary in Quebec: *L'Emotion dissonante* and *Passiflora*', in Peter Easingwood *et al.* (eds), *Probing Canadian Culture*, Augsburg: AV-Verlag, 225–34.

Loizos, Peter (1993). *Innovation in Ethnographic Film: From Innocence to Self-consciousness, 1955–85*, Manchester: Manchester University Press.

Lovell, Alan and Hillier, Jim (1972). *Studies in Documentary*, London: Secker and Warburg.

Lyotard, Jean-François (1984). *The Postmodern Condition: A Report on Knowledge*, Minneapolis: University of Minnesota Press.

McArthur, Colin (1980). *Television and History*, London: British Film Institute.

Macdonald, Kevin and Cousins, Mark (1996). *Imagining Reality: The Faber Book of the Documentary*, London: Faber and Faber.

Macpherson, Don (1980). *Traditions of Independence*, London: British Film Institute.

Marshall, John (1994). 'The right pitch', *DOX*, 4, Winter, 49–50.

—— (1995). 'Europe's documentary New Wave', *DOX*, 6, Summer, 12–13.

Moores, Shaun (1993). *Interpreting Audiences: The Ethnography of Media Consumption*, London: Sage.

Morley, David (1986). *Family Television: Cultural Power and Domestic Leisure*, London: Comedia.

Musburger, Robert (1985). 'Setting the stage for the television docudrama', *Journal of Popular Film and Television*, 13:2, 92–101.

Nichols, Bill (1981). *Ideology and the Image: Social Representation in the Cinema and Other Media*, Bloomington: Indiana University Press.

—— (1991). *Representing Reality: Issues and Concepts in Documentary*, Bloomington: Indiana University Press.

—— (1993). '"Getting to know you...": knowledge, power, and the body', in Renov, 174–91.

—— (1994), *Blurred Boundaries: Questions of Meaning in Contemporary Culture*, Bloomington: Indiana University Press.

Nimmo, Dan and Combs, James (1983). *Mediated Political Realities*, London: Longman.

Niney, François (1994). 'One image always conceals another', *DOX*, 3, Autumn, 18–23.

O'Sullivan, Tim, Dutton, Brian and Rayner, Philip (1994a). *Studying the Media*, London: Edward Arnold.

——, Hartley, John, Saunders, Danny and Fiske, John (1994b). *Key Concepts in Communication and Cultural Studies*, London: Routledge.

Paget, Derek (1990). *True Stories? Documentary Drama on Radio, Screen and Stage*, Manchester: Manchester University Press.

Petley, Julian (1996). 'Fact plus fiction equals friction', *Media, Culture and Society*, 18:1, January, 11–25.

Powell, Rod (1992). 'Real to reel', *Broadcast*, 9 April, 32.

Prebble, Stuart (1993). 'Compete to survive', *Daily Telegraph*, 29 May, 6.

Rabiger, Michael (1987). *Directing the Documentary*, London: Focal Press.

Rayner, Joy (1993). 'An audience of one', *Guardian*, 16 February, 5.

Renov, Michael (ed.) (1993). *Theorizing Documentary*, London: Routledge.

Rolston, Bill and Miller, David (1996). *War and Words: The Northern Ireland Media Reader*, Belfast: Beyond the Pale.

Rosen, Philip (1993). 'Document and documentary: on the persistence of historical concepts', in Renov, 58–89.

Rosenthal, Alan (1971). *The New Documentary in Action*, Berkeley: University of California Press.

—— (1980). *The Documentary Conscience*, Berkeley: University of California Press.

—— (1988). *New Challenges for Documentary*, Berkeley: University of California Press.

—— (1990). *Writing, Directing and Producing Documentary*, Carbondale: Southern Illinois Press.

Ross, Nick and Cook, Sue (1987). *Crimewatch UK*, London: Hodder and Stoughton.

Rotha, Paul (1966). *Documentary Film*, 3rd edn, London: Faber: 1935.

—— (1973). *Documentary Diary: An Informal History of the British Documentary Film, 1928–1939*, New York: Hill and Wang.

Roud, Richard (ed.) (1980). *Cinema: A Critical History*, New York: Viking Press.

Saynor, James (1990). 'A grand inquisitor', *Listener*, 15 November, 46–7.

Scannell, Paddy (1979). 'The social eye of television, 1946–1955', *Media, Culture and Society*, 1, 97–106.

Schlesinger, Philip and Tumber, Howard (1993). 'Fighting the war against crime', *British Journal of Criminology*, 33:1, Winter, 19–32.

Searle, John R. (1975). 'The logical status of fictional discourse', *New Literary History*, 6, 2.

Selway, Jennifer (1993). 'Clichés come alive in Oz', *Observer*, 18 April, 67.

Silverstone, Roger (1985). *Framing Science: The Making of a BBC Documentary*, London: British Film Institute.

—— (1987). 'Narrative strategies in television science', in Curran *et al.*, 291–330.

Stenderup, Thomas (ed.) (1995). *The European Documentary Sector*, Copenhagen: MEDIA.

Triffitt, John (1996) 'How will the medium of documentary change in the future?', Internal BBC discussion paper, Unpublished.

Vaughan, Dai (1983). *Portrait of an Invisible Man: The Working Life of Stewart McAllister, Film Editor*, London: British Film Institute.

—— (1988). 'Television documentary usage', in Rosenthal, 34–47.

—— (1993). 'The aesthetics of ambiguity', in Crawford and Turton, 99–115.

Waldman, Simon (1994). 'Tearing down the bamboo curtain', *Evening Standard*, 9 March, 48.

Waugh, Thomas (ed.) (1984). *'Show Us Life': Towards a History and Aesthetics of Committed Documentary*, London: Scarecrow.

Whitby, Max (1994). 'The new media landscape', *DOX*, 3, 44–6.

Williams, Christopher (1980). *Realism and the Cinema*, London: Routledge and Kegan Paul/British Film Institute.

Williams, Linda (1993). 'Mirrors without memories: truth, history and the new documentary', *Film Quarterly*, 46:3, Spring, 9–21.

Williams, Raymond (1974). *Television: Technology and Cultural Form*, Glasgow: Fontana.

Winston, Brian (1995). *Claiming the Real: The Documentary Film Revisited*, London: British Film Institute.

Wiseman, Frederick (1986). 'Pride, patience and prejudice', *CILECT Review*, 2:1, November, 40–2.

Wober, J. Mallory (1990). *Effects on Perception from Seeing a Drama Documentary. The Case of 'Who Bombed Birmingham?'*, London: IBA.

Wollen, Peter (1972). *Signs and Meaning in the Cinema*, 3rd edn, London: Secker and Warburg/British Film Institute.

—— (1982). *Readings and Writings: Semiotic Counter-strategies*, London: Verso.

Wood, David (1996). 'All telling the same tales', *Broadcast*, 25 October, 18–19.

Woodhead, Leslie (1990). 'Leads to disaster', *Listener*, 22 November, 12–13.

Young, Martin and Hill, Peter (1985). 'If we weren't there, four innocent people would still be in jail', *Listener*, 12 September, 10.

Index

access
   to locations 140
   to people 196–9, 245
   to television 21, 214
aesthetics 40–2, 76–8, 81–2,
   107–8, 189; *see also* style
American Family, An 205, 242
America's Most Wanted 86
Animal Hospital 187
Anne Frank Remembered 146–7
argument 6, 119–21, 126–9
   point of view 127–8
Attenborough, David 64, 225
audience 215–39
   accommodating interests of 39
   active 228–30, 232–3, 246
   awareness 7, 19
   broadcaster–audience interface x,
      215–26
   expectations of 3–4, 15–16, 79,
      133–4, 156, 230–3
   perspective 38–40, 44, 59
   response 9–11, 48, 51, 112,
      122–4, 226–30, 246
   sophistication 76, 149, 236
authorship 4–5, 78–9, 101–12,
   191–2

Battleship Potemkin, The 139
BBC 184, 186–8, 217, 241, 244
Berlin: Symphony of a City 17
Beyond the Clouds 197
Bill, The 34
Blair, Jon 146–7
Blakstad, Lucy 84, 109–12
Blue Light Zone 220
Brecht, Bertolt 50–2, 77, 79, 102,
   173–4

British Documentary Movement 19,
   41, 46, 64, 80
Broomfield, Nick 78–9, 101, 202
Buerk, Michael 160

cable and satellite 178–9
Cathy Come Home 87, 150, 235
censorship 142, 149, 166–9
Channel 3 184–5
Channel 4 185–6, 220, 221, 241
characters 29, 38, 117, 118–19,
   123–4, 129–32; *see also*
   subjects
Children at School 84, 121
Children's Hospital 187
Chronique d'un été 71, 75–6
cinéma vérité 65, 70–2
cloning 175, 187, 221
Club, The 211, 237
Coalface 41
co-financing 182–4
commentary 49, 58–9, 69, 91, 117,
   130; *see also* narration
commercialism 21–3, 26, 165, 170,
   172–3, 175, 177, 185, 225–6
Complaint of Rape 237; *see also Police*
co-production 180–2, 187–8
Cops 86, 243
*Crash 2030: Investigating a
   Catastrophe* 241
creative treatment of actuality
   12–13, 46, 115–17
Crimestoppers 87, 243
Crimewatch UK 77, 86, 87, 136,
   155–7, 159, 243
Crumb 188
Culloden 141–2
Cutting Edge 94–8, 186, 187, 204,

211, 221, 222

Day After, The 146, 243
'day in the life' format 117
Death on the Rock 244, 246
Decisions 73
deregulation *see* commercialism;
    institutional control;
    regulation
Diary for Timothy, A 129
digitalisation 10, 11, 26, 205, 207,
    241, 242, 244, 246
Dineen, Molly 194, 245
direct cinema 66–70, 130–1
Disappearing World 184
Discovery Channel 179, 241, 242
Dixon of Dock Green 34
documentary
    actuality entertainments 18
    address, modes of 23–6, 56–87
    definitions 3–4, 8, 11–16
    discourse 4, 30–2, 97, 107
    and drama 9
    and fiction 125, 126, 127
    forms and functions 3, 6–7,
        230–1
    history of 7, 16–19, 57
    impact and effects 233–8
    imperative 38
    impulse 29
    media formats 8
    modes of 56–87
    origins 17
    pioneers 16–17
    portraits 232
    production ix, 165–214
    radio 8
    serious pursuit 7–8, 21, 125,
        184–5, 217
    subjects and characters 9,
        129–32
    tradition ix, 170–1
drama-documentary 21, 60–1, 88,
    131, 135–57, 204, 235–6

Drew, Robert 65–8
Drifters 58
Dying Rooms, The 212

economics of production 165–89
editing 36–7, 62–3, 69, 72, 89–90,
    95–6, 99–100, 103, 105, 106,
    107, 203–7
Edward on Edward 145
Eisenstein, Sergei 46, 139
ethical issues 29, 73, 86, 138,
    153–4, 197–9, 201, 207–11
ethnography 47, 118, 195, 202,
    213, 245
European documentary 177–84
expert observers 30–1, 129, 201
expository documentary 58–64,
    94–8, 130, 161, 209

faction 145–6
factual entertainment x, 74, 85–6,
    100, 136–7, 154–61, 177,
    185, 217
Family, The 73, 74, 194, 213
fiction 5, 9, 14–15, 28–9, 37, 38,
    86, 90, 92–3, 118, 119,
    121–5, 129–30, 205; *see also*
    characters; narrative
filmic conventions and practices
    36–7, 44, 199
first-person documentary 81–3, 90,
    104–9
First Tuesday 184
Flaherty, Robert 12, 17, 140, 195
fly-on-the-wall documentary 73–4,
    158, 204, 210
For Richer, For Poorer 98–101
framing 32–3, 52–4

genre ix, x, 13, 15–16, 34–5, 57
Godard, Jean-Luc 132–3
Graef, Roger 68, 69, 73, 74, 193,
    197, 237
Greatest Show on Earth, The 219

Grierson, John 6, 12, 17, 19, 24, 41–2, 46, 64, 80, 84, 116, 139, 169, 231, 234–5, 241
Grigsby, Michael 6–7, 192–3

Herzog, Werner 92
Hidden Voices 192–3
High School 69
Hillsborough 87, 144
Hitchcock, Alfred 91
Holocaust 147
home movies 81, 106, 107, 195
Hoop Dreams 13, 188
Horizon 127–8
Housing Problems 66, 121
How Yukong Moved the Mountains 195
hybridisation ix–x, 7–8, 21, 57–8, 74–5, 85–7, 136, 138, 148–9, 152, 157–8, 160–1, 177

ideology 35, 39, 42–3, 46–7, 54, 70, 72–3, 189
indexical bond 10, 27–8, 29–30, 37
Industrial Britain 43
Inside Burma: Land of Fear 223–4
institutional control 7–8, 20, 30, 142, 165–74, 179–80, 215–16, 241
interactive documentary 65, 70–3, 130, 209
intertextuality 33–5, 125, 132–3, 227–8
intervention 18, 199
interviewing 71–2, 95, 99, 102–4, 111, 199–203
ITV *see* Channel 3
Ivens, Joris 195

Jennings, Humphrey 129
journalism 7, 13, 24–5, 64, 71, 125, 126, 137, 139, 150–2, 172, 191

King, Rodney 60
knowledge 38, 115–16, 230–1

Last Machine, The 189, 219
Leacock, Richard 68
Leader, his Driver, and the Driver's Wife, The 78, 202
lecture film 115–16
Lessons of Darkness 92
Lido 84, 85, 91, 109–12
Living Islam 182
Living Soap, The 187, 210, 224
London Can Take It 129
Loridan, Marceline 195
Lumière brothers 18, 115

Manufacturing Consent 244
Man with the Movie Camera, The 17, 19, 75
March of Time, The 139
Maysles brothers 69
Méliès, Georges 138–9
metonymy 37–8, 134
Moana 12
Modern Times 187, 221, 222
modes x, 16, 57–89, 93–112, 173
   cinéma vérité 65, 70–2
(modes)
   direct cinema 66–70, 130–1
   drama-documentary 21, 60–1, 88, 131, 135–57, 204, 235–6
   expository 58–64, 94–8, 130, 161, 209
   first-person 81–3, 90, 104–9
   fly-on-the-wall 73–4, 158, 204, 210
   hybrid 74–5
   interactive 65, 70–3, 130, 209
   observational 64–75, 98–101, 110–11, 209
   poetic 84–5, 109–112
   reality programming 85–6, 157–61
   reflexive 75–80, 101–4, 131,

133
Moore, Michael 78–9, 101, 120,
    131
Morin, Edgar 65, 75–6
Morris, Errol 77–8
Munro, David 189, 223
music 92, 100, 103, 111
My Demons: The Legacy 83, 104–9

999 86, 87, 136, 159–60
Nanook of the North 17, 58, 84, 116,
    139–40, 195
narration 45, 58–60, 67–8, 69, 82,
    91, 93, 95, 105, 160; *see also*
    commentary
narrative 9, 12, 115–21, 127
natural history 39, 64, 118, 224–6
naturalism 44–5, 63, 70; *see also*
    realism, empiricist
Network First 184
news and current affairs *see*
    journalism
niche providers 174, 178–80
Night Mail 41, 84
November Days 90, 91, 101–4, 129,
    201

objectivity 31
observational documentary 64–75,
    90, 98–101, 110–11, 209
Ophuls, Marcel 90, 91, 101–4, 129,
    201

People's Century 93, 187–8, 190,
    202–3, 204, 218
perception 48, 52–4
photography 17, 27, 50
Pilger, John 189, 223
place 89, 91–2, 99, 109, 117
poetic documentary 84–5, 109–12
Police 69, 73, 193, 237; *see also*
    Complaint of Rape
political control 165–9
political sensitivity 137–8, 142,

148–9, 165–9
postmodernism 10–11
Primary 68
problem–solution structure 5–6,
    119; *see also* argument
pro-filmic conventions 28, 35–6
promoting documentaries 97,
    221–6
public service broadcasting 21, 173,
    216

realism 4–5, 27–53, 63
    aesthetics 40–2
    construction of 30, 38–9
    conventions of 30–1, 35–40
    deconstructing 49–52
    denial of 78–9
    and documentary discourse 32–4
    empiricist 44–5, 63, 70, 97
    forms 43–52
    and ideology 42–3
    psychological 47–9
    social and historical 45–7
    style 37
    see also reality programming
reality programming 77, 85–6,
    157–61, 217
Real Life 210
Real Lives: At the Edge of the Union
    244
Red Light Zone 220
referentiality 9, 11, 12–13, 28–9
reflexive documentary 42, 52,
    75–80, 101–4, 131, 133
    political 79–80
regulation 24, 152–4, 156
    deregulation 164, 170
repetition 39–40
representation 4–5, 12–13, 53–4,
    123
Rescue 911 86, 87, 159
research 141, 144, 191, 192–3,
    194–6
restaging and reconstruction 60–1,

67, 76–8, 86–7, 135–61, 243
reversioning 180, 244
Riefensthal, Leni 168–9
Road Racers 61
Roger and Me 78, 79, 120
Rouch, Jean 65, 70–1, 75–6
Rough Justice 237
Ruttman, Walther 17

Sad, Bad and Mad 58, 61, 94–8, 100,
     128; *see also Trial, The*
Salesman 69
satellite and cable services 178–80,
     241, 242
scheduling x–xi, 73, 137, 150,
     172–3, 174, 215–21, 246
Selling of a Serial Killer, The 78
series 73, 176
Shoah 201
Soho Stories 187
Song of Ceylon, The 84, 85
stereotyping 39, 47, 61–2, 97, 118,
     211–13
style 37–8, 39, 94–5, 107–8,
     110–12, 132, 207
     deconstruction of 50–1, 79
     as organising principle 85
     as perspective 127–8
     see also aesthetics
subjectivity
     of documentarist 31–2
     of interviewee 48, 82–3
     of viewer 38–40, 231–2
subjects 129–32; *see also* characters
Summerhill at 70 212
Sylvania Waters 73, 194, 197, 209,
     213, 224

tabloid television 160–1, 171–2,
     181
targeting 76, 149–50, 215–16
technology 17–18, 25, 34–5, 41,
     64, 65–6, 67, 81, 106–7, 140,
     174, 177, 183–4, 190–1, 198,

     205, 230, 242
television
     history of 7–8
     impact on documentary ix, x,
          7–8, 20–6, 64, 65
     institutions ix, 165–89
     tabloid 160–1, 171–2, 181
     see also institutional control
Thatcher – The Final Days 143, 243
Thin Blue Line, The 72, 77–8, 84,
     133
time 89, 91, 92–3, 95, 98–9, 110,
     117
Tout va bien 132–3
Tracking Down Maggie 78, 79, 202
Travels with my Camera 232
Trial, The 42, 58, 94–8; *see also Sad,
     Bad and Mad*
Trial and Error 237
Trial of Lord Lucan, The 143, 243
Triumph of the Will 168–9
True Crimes 156
typicality 37–8, 60–1, 70, 97,
     98–101, 155–6, 211–14

Undercover 186

Vertov, Dziga 4, 17, 19, 46, 75, 206
Video Diaries 21, 82–3, 90, 104–9,
     187, 214, 232
Video Nation 131
Viewpoint 184

War Game, The 142, 146, 166–7,
     243, 244
Watkins, Peter 141–2
Watson, Paul 15, 73–4, 183–4,
     194, 197–8, 210
Who Bombed Birmingham? 87, 236
Why Lockerbie? 151–2, 246
Wiseman, Fred 48, 68, 130–1, 238
Woolston, Willa 83, 104–9
World at War, The 218
Wright, Basil 84; *see also Children at*

School; Night Mail; The Song of Ceylon

You've Been Framed 85

Z Cars 34